THE LIFE AND EXPLOITS

OF

A MALTESE SAILOR

BY DANNY MARKS

Acknowledgments

I thank my wife, Margaret and my children Paul, Ruth and Simon for their help and encouragement. I wish to express my sincere gratitude to my friends Philip Barnett, for his invaluable assistance, particularly in reproducing the photographs and maps as well as transactions with the publisher, Henry Frendo, Professor of History at the University of Malta for scrutinising the historical contents of the book, Barrie Bradburn for his expert editorial advice, and the many ex-shipmates who have jogged my memory.

I also wish to thank the Imperial War Museum and Bernard Akerman for providing some photographs, my brother Bob Marks for his help and advice and Lt Cdr T C Wright RN (Rtd), the author of *HMS Gambia 1957-58 Commission Magazine* for allowing me to rearrange and include some of the articles in that publication.

Every effort has been made by the author to obtain copyright permission to reproduce photographs and extracts included in this book. In the event of any omissions please contact the author by E-Mail: mmb.marks@ntlworld.com

First Published 2010 by Appin Press, an imprint of Countyvise Ltd
14 Appin Road, Birkenhead, CH41 9HH

British Library Cataloguing in Publication Data.
A catalogue record for this book is available from the British Library.

ISBN 978 1 906205 70 6

For Margaret

PREFACE

Since I joined the Rotary Club of Bebington in the Wirral in 1994, in keeping with Rotary tradition, I have been talking to the club at approximately eight-monthly intervals. I chose as my subject a description of my twenty nine years in the Royal Navy, 'Life on The Ocean Wave'. Many of my colleagues, listening to my story with some amusement have, from time to time, urged me to write a book about my exploits. At eighty two years of age I thought this was too big a task to undertake. But after some encouragement from my family I decided to have a go. Another reason for writing the book was that, after thirteen years, I have only covered six of my twenty nine years in the Service, concluding that I will not be finishing my story until 2067! I want my fellow Rotarians to read what was to follow before they and I depart into eternity. I decided to augment my story with my childhood, some important events in the history of Malta, my experiences during The Second World War and the transition to civilian life.

Unfortunately, never having kept a diary, I have had to rely largely on my memory. I had extensive consultations with ex-shipmates, friends and relations and referred to the commissioning books and maps issued at the end of each commission, showing the countries visited during each ship's tour of duty. I have tried my best to describe events in chronological order but, in some cases, I may have strayed beyond those bounds and some of my exploits may not be totally accurate. I have also searched for information from ships' log books kept at the National Archives at Kew in London. Sadly, the logbooks of one of the ships in which I served, HMS Chaplet, between 1946 and 1948, were destroyed in a fire at Deptford in 1950.

Ships and personnel, whether at sea or in harbour, are subject to a continuous programme of training and drills at all times of the day and in various sea conditions. Conscious that I may bore the reader, I have done my best to avoid repeating references to such training which is almost identical in every ship. On the other hand I do not want the reader to think that serving in a warship is one long holiday. While writing, I couldn't help feeling how lucky I was to have witnessed or taken part in so many events and visited so many countries. Without these experiences, and the excitement of it all, it would seem that my life would have been very dull. Throughout the book I was very careful not to name anyone with whom I formed an acquaintance of any sort. Every effort has been made to preserve their anonymity.

LIST OF CONTENTS

VII

VIII

CHAPTER 1

MALTA

The Island's Rich History and its Connection with the Royal Navy
Early Days and Family Background

I was born on the 10th July, 1925 on the island of Malta, situated in the middle of the Mediterranean almost equidistant from Gibraltar to the West and Port Said at the entrance of the Suez Canal to the East. Throughout history, because of its strategic position, commanding the main channel through which all shipping between the East and the West must pass, and because of its deep and sheltered harbours, without a tide, Malta was, since about 700 BC, occupied by the most powerful nations who commanded the Mediterranean. The Phoenicians, who were the first to occupy the island, were followed by the Carthaginians, the Romans, the Aglabite Arabs who introduced the Maltese Language, the Normans and the Aragonese who gave the island to the Order of St John of Jerusalem in 1530. The island endured two historic sieges, the first at the height of the Ottoman Empire and the second, during the Second World War, between 1940 and 1942, when I was in my mid-teens.

Historians have written numerous accounts of the first siege by the Turks in 1565 when Suleiman the Magnificent ordered a fleet of about 200 ships and 40,000 men to capture the island, one of the main Christian bastions under the control of the Knights of St John who he had earlier driven out of Rhodes. The island was kept under siege for almost five months when a few hundred Knights and a few thousand Maltese, under the leadership of Grand Master La Vallette, set several of the enemy's ships on fire and, with their fierce resistance and, starving them out of water and provisions, forced the Turkish forces to retreat. The defeat was one of the heaviest inflicted on the Ottoman Empire at a time when the Turks were masters of most of Eastern Europe. The Sultan failed to achieve mastery of the Mediterranean. Considering that the island was a British protectorate from 1814, British historians have written little about the siege especially since, at the time, Grand Master La Vallette's secretary was an Englishman, Sir Oliver Starkey. The famous French writer, Voltaire, remarked 'Nothing is better known than the Siege of Malta', one of the most decisive actions in the history of the Mediterranean and the Western World. One of the reasons for the lack of interest on the part of British historians is that the English Langue (the House of England of the Order of St John) was dissolved several years before the siege took place.

Unfortunately, the Order of St John became complacent and corrupt and Malta fell prey to the strongest power which ruled the Mediterranean. The French Fleet under the command of Napoleon Bonaparte occupied the island. While at Naples, in July 1799, Nelson was asked by the Maltese to place the island under the protection of the King of Great Britain. Nelson drove the French out and the British occupied Malta until 1964. They lost no time in turning the island into a naval base. At the end of the nineteenth century, a formidable fleet including battleships, aircraft carriers, destroyers, submarines, and other forms of warship were stationed there dominating the sea routes of the Mediterranean. British sailors could be seen on the streets everywhere. Malta's economy became largely dependent on the Mediterranean Fleet.

I was brought up in Senglea, one of the three cities that form a large part of the famous and historic Grand Harbour. Sailors, drunk or sober, strolled every street. The sea front, known as the 'Barbary Coast', was dominated by a string of bars named after ships in the creek, 'The Despatch Bar', 'The Cairo Bar', 'The Royal Sovereign', and so on. In the creek there were so many destroyers that they had to be tied three at a time to the same buoys. A steady flow of liberty boats and Maltese 'dghajsas', (resembling gondolas), ferried sailors ashore and back to their ships. Every Sunday, ships companies, led by bands of the Royal Marines and officers with drawn swords were paraded to church, Catholics to a Catholic Church and the majority to a Protestant Church. Thousands of local inhabitants turned out to watch this weekly ritual. The sight of ships leaving and entering harbour and the daily routine of hoisting and lowering the flag, with every ship acting in unison with the sounding of bugles and bands playing, fascinated me from a very early age. From the breakwater, at the entrance to Grand Harbour, I watched the Fleet sailing for exercises. From about nine in the morning until late in the afternoon, ship after ship sailed out of the harbour. Other flotillas of destroyers, submarines and aircraft carriers came out of the adjoining creeks and harbours to form a formidable armada outside the Grand Harbour as far as the eye could see. As the signal flags were hoisted, to the sound of bugles, the ships moved together as one mass to form themselves into task forces to begin their manoeuvres.

My English grandfather, Daniel, was the son of a German Jew born in Varsavja in Poland in 1849. His father, Harries, was a merchant tailor who emigrated to Manchester with all his family. Daddy Dan, as we called him, joined the navy at a time when ships were rigged with sails and there was a demand for tailors. Although he married into a strict Roman Catholic family he remained a Jew, registering in the Navy as an Anglo-Catholic, but he never practised any religion. A few days before he died, his daughters arranged for him to be baptised a Catholic fearing that he may go to hell. He served in HMS Superb and took part in the bombardment of Alexandria on the 11th June 1882, after an Egyptian uprising, and on HMS Iron Duke, one of the biggest battleships which could be driven by sail as well as steam generated by coal-fired boilers, as 'Captain of the Sails Forward.' While serving in Malta he met a Maltese girl and decided he wanted to marry her. In those days the Services frowned on any serviceman who wished to marry a 'native'. But he was determined, and eventually the Navy relented and 'invalided him'. He couldn't speak a word of Maltese, and she could hardly speak English. Predictably there was a breakdown in communications, and it was not surprising that they produced twelve children. Three of them died in infancy of Malta fever, a common disease in those days. Two of the boys joined the Royal Navy.

On failing the naval medical, my father joined the Admiralty Service at the Royal Dockyard. He spent most of his life in Maltese politics and was at one time, Deputy Leader of the Labour Party, at a time when the Catholic Church had a strong hold over the Maltese population, influencing the way they voted by preaching from the pulpits that a vote for Labour was a sin which could lead to excommunication. He was subjected to many threats to his life and his family was put in danger of physical assault by hysterical partisan behaviour. He was given police protection and issued with a gun for self-defence. He worked tirelessly to help the poor and deprived and organised charity meetings to distribute food to the needy.

He drafted several Acts of Parliament related to social reforms which, although not presented to Parliament at a time when the Labour Party was being hounded by the church, were used after the Second World War, when the church's influence was waning and a Labour Government came to power. He introduced Trade Unionism to Malta and guided Mr. Dominic Mintoff, a future Prime Minister, into politics. Mintoff paid several visits to our house before he went to Oxford University as a Rhodes Scholar in 1939. On his return to Malta, he became Secretary of the Labour Party until he broke ranks with the main stream, splitting the party, and eventually becoming the party leader. During the persecution of the Labour Party by the church, books written by H.G. Wells and Bernard Shaw were considered seditious and my father had to destroy his copies. He was often threatened with excommunication and, disillusioned by the church, stopped practising his religion. It was the interference in matters of state by the Church which most annoyed him. He did, however, receive the Last Rites just before he died in 1954. He fought vigorously against those, particularly the judiciary, who wanted Italian to become the official language in the law courts. With other non-political, literary men, he used his intellectual abilities to encourage and develop the Maltese language with a new alphabet, largely in use today. Maltese and English are now the two official languages of the State.

As well as being a politician and author of several short stories and a novel, he wrote extensively in the local newspapers in both English and Maltese. He was also gifted at chess and draughts and became the Maltese Champion at both games having played against many famous British champions. His games were published in the London editions of the weekly newspaper *Reynolds News*. The biography *John F. Marks*, by Edwin Camilleri, was published in 2000 in the Maltese language so close to my father's heart. Many of his articles and letters were included in the biography. The irony remains that he became more famous after his death, when just how much he had contributed to Maltese politics became apparent, and a street was named after him. For his services to the Admiralty, he was awarded the Imperial Service Medal.

My Maltese grandfather used to take me in his small rowing boat to view the fleet at anchor at close quarters. I would watch the sailors painting their ships, loading equipment, taking water and provisions from water boats and barges which he owned. It was during one of these trips, when I was only six years of age, that a pinnace* from the battleship H.M.S Revenge, manned

*A large motor cutter used for ferrying stores and personnel, carried by large warships, now no longer used.

by a crew of Royal Marines, hit us and cut the boat in half. I started sinking when 'Nannu', as we called my grandfather, dived in to rescue me. Another young lad and friend of the family, about sixteen years of age, dived into the water and swam ashore as the pinnace was about to hit us. Numerous boats came over to help with the rescue and we were taken ashore to the Customs House on the Custom Patrol boat manned by my uncle who happened to be the Customs Duty Officer. My main recollection of the incident is when, wearing my uncle's oversize jacket, I saw hundreds of neighbours lining the streets before I reached home into my mother's arms. With my family connections with the Royal Navy, it was inevitable that I would develop a love for the Senior Service leading to a naval career. Seeing my two uncles resplendent in their naval uniforms added a further incentive. One of them, Uncle Ted, was decorated with the DSM during the Second World War.

At my christening, in 100% Catholic Malta, my mother and father, my godparents and Parish Priest, each gave me a name. I was christened, Daniel Francis Xavier Henry George Salvatore Marks. Educated at the local Elementary School I graduated to the Lyceum, a Government Controlled Secondary School. I found most of my three years hard-going and was interested only in the subjects I liked best, Italian, English and Mathematics, made interesting by inspired teachers. I lost interest in the other subjects which were poorly taught.

My only hope of joining the Navy was to qualify as a Dockyard apprentice and follow the route taken by Uncle Ted, who started his naval career as an Engine Room Artificer (ERA) and was eventually granted officer status. At the age of fourteen, my father gave me the option either to continue in full time education or to sit the Dockyard Entrance Examination to become an apprentice. This is the path I chose. Competition for the exam was fierce. Thousands of boys applied with only one hundred and fifty qualifying. I came fourth in order of merit and began a five-year apprenticeship while, at the same time, attending the Dockyard Technical College. Here again, competition was demanding. Every year half the students were weeded out of the college. After four years, only twelve qualified for the final certificate.

Just as the defeat of the Turks by the Knights of St John signalled the beginning of the end of the Ottoman Empire, so the successful outcome of the second siege, between 1940 and 1942, triggered the defeat of Rommel in the African Desert and the beginning of the Allied assault on mainland Europe. When war was declared on the 3rd September 1939, Malta was happily positioned far from the area of likely intense hostilities, and almost dead centre in the friendly Mediterranean. The entire coastline was either neutral or under Allied influence. The British and French were joint guardians of the sea. The job of the French was to look after the west side, with a heavy naval concentration at Toulon, and the British, the east with a concentration of heavy naval units at Alexandria, with Malta as the attacking base for submarines and fast surface units. The entry of Italy into the war on 10th June, 1940, and the totally unforeseen capitulation of France, 15 days later, entirely changed the situation. The whole Mediterranean strategy collapsed and Malta was immediately placed in a precarious position. A few hours before declaring war, Mussolini ordered his air force to attack Malta. We were completely unprepared, especially as he had declared that Italy would remain neutral. To defend the island there were only 16 Bofor Anti Aircraft Guns and three Gloster Gladiator aircraft, known as Faith, Hope and Charity. During the first attacks, the Italians caused a great deal of damage and casualties, but the few guns and the 3 Gladiators were enough to terrify the ineffective Italian Air Force.

When the bombs started falling, living close to the dockyard, we were evacuated to Balzan, a village in the middle of the island. We stayed with a local family where we were allocated just one large room for all six of us with restrictions to our movements. We soon got tired of the discomfort and, as the Italians proved ineffective and the island's defences were strengthened, father decided to move to Sliema, a seaside town much closer to the danger area. Later, when the Germans took over, a bomb fell close to our house causing severe damage during the middle of the night. All the family, except my father, were in the shelter. He insisted on sleeping through the air raids. We eventually found him a few yards away from the house holding a pillow over his head. He was obviously shaken and was covered in dust from head to foot.

In November, 1940, when aircraft from HMS Illustrious attacked and destroyed a large part of the Italian navy at Taranto, the Germans decided they could no longer trust the Italians to take command of the Mediterranean. Hundreds of bombers and fighter aircraft were sent to Southern Italy to start an offensive against British shipping. On 10th January, 1941, Illustrious and her supporting task force, while escorting a convoy east of Sicily, was attacked by wave after wave of Stuka dive bombers. She came into Malta badly damaged with 165 of her crew dead and many others wounded. The Luftwaffe, using about 200 aircraft, came to sink her in harbour and to launch their first attack on the island as dockyard workmen were patching her up while she was afloat. On that day, the 16th January, 1941, I joined as an apprentice in the Royal Naval Dockyard and was given a tool box which I proudly placed on a designated workbench. At about 3pm, the air raid sirens sounded and we retreated to the shelters. Hundreds of bombs were dropped, devastating a large part of the Dockyard and surrounding cities. I emerged from the shelter to find the workshop demolished, my tool box gone and where the work benches had stood, a large crater and a heap of twisted metal.

With the devastation of the dockyard, the authorities decided to send all new entry apprentices home. Some of us volunteered for the job of spotting mines released by the German planes by parachute at night. When we were recalled, we took part in transferring repair work to the underground workshops. That was the beginning of two years of relentless bombing. There was destruction everywhere. The Grand Harbour became littered with wrecks, but Illustrious, after temporary patching of her ship's side, miraculously escaped to America, via Suez, for permanent repairs. By this time petrol was getting scarce and bus services were curtailed. I often had to walk to the dockyard, a distance of five miles. As food became scarce, the lack of nourishment sapped much of my energy. We were not allowed to cook or buy food but queued up at Victory Kitchens, where all available food was pooled, prepared and issued against coupons. My parents shared most of their ration between their four children.

As the Germans occupied Crete and controlled the Eastern Mediterranean, the Fleet at Alexandria was withdrawn. Malta was isolated and became the only base for attacking the supply lines to Rommel in North Africa and for attacks on Southern Europe. Efforts to bring supplies to the island failed time and time again. Food, fuel and ammunition were running out. A message sent by Churchill to the Admiralty from Moscow, during a meeting with Stalin read, 'Malta must be saved at all costs.' Submarines broke the siege from time to time, bringing just enough supplies to keep us ticking over. Aircraft Carriers flew Hurricanes and Spitfires specially fitted with spare fuel tanks only to be destroyed on landing. Many young pilots were killed but many survived to find that there were no aircraft to fly. At one time there were only five Hurricanes and about 140 pilots. They took it in turn to fly the five planes on a twenty four hour schedule. From time to time the fast minelayers Manxman and Welshman broke the siege, arriving at dusk, unloading and departing at dawn. Sadly Welshman was sunk on her last attempt at leaving Malta.

After two years, when it was clear that Rommel could only be defeated if Malta was saved, and with only 14 days to go before Malta would be forced to surrender, a convoy set sail from Gibraltar. Fourteen of the fastest merchant ships and tankers available to America and Britain, protected by the strongest naval escort formed during the war, consisting of 2 battleships, 4 aircraft carriers, 7 cruisers and 40 destroyers set out to relieve the island. It was named *Operation Pedestal*. When the convoy was within two hundred miles of Malta, the Germans and Italians, using eight hundred aircraft, began their assault. The aircraft carrier, Eagle and the cruisers Nigeria and Manchester were sunk. Another aircraft carrier, HMS Indomitable, was incapacitated and had to withdraw. One after another, the merchant ships were hit. As the convoy approached Malta, three of the merchant ships having already been sunk, the remaining carriers and the battleships were withdrawn. The aircraft carrier Furious, managed to fly 37 Spitfires to the island to be used to protect the surviving ships on entering Grand Harbour. One merchant ship, the Brisbane Star, was crippled and, breaking all international rules, it detached from the convoy to find its own way to Malta via the Tunisian coast. Its whereabouts were unknown until, to everyone's astonishment, it reached the island with its bows blown off.

During the last hundred miles, another six merchant ships were sunk. Of the five ships which reached the island, only three arrived unscathed. After having been hit several times, and after two dive-bombers which had crashed on its decks were ditched over the side, with her engines out of action and her rudder stuck in one position, the famous American tanker Ohio manned by a British crew, entered Grand Harbour. Two destroyers, one on each side, to prevent her veering away in one direction, towed her to a designated berth. As soon as she berthed alongside I, with my instructor, was one of the many dockyard staff who boarded her to start connecting emergency pumps, to discharge her oil cargo to the shore storages before the Germans came to attack her in harbour. When the German aircraft came to sink her and the other four ships, the Spitfires, flown from Furious, pounced, inflicting heavy losses on them. The Germans gave up and Hitler recalled the Luftwaffe from Southern Italy to the Russian Front where they were badly needed. Ohio never sailed again, but her badly damaged hulk was used for accommodating light forces in Malta, and later towed outside the harbour and sunk. The story of the miraculous survival of this famous ship has been well chronicled and is vividly described in the book *Pedestal* an account of the convoy operation that saved Malta, by Peter C Smith.

The memory of those two years will never be forgotten, nor will the excitement and jubilation which followed the siege and the build up to the invasion of Southern Italy and Sicily. Several thousand American and British servicemen arrived on the island and visits were made by King George VI as well as Churchill and Roosevelt when every inhabitant turned out to cheer them. Combined Service Chiefs, including Eisenhower, Montgomery and other famous Generals were to be seen daily, travelling on their jeeps as they inspected their troops. Every inch of coastline was occupied by warships and landing craft, and hundreds of ships anchored outside the harbour for as far as the eye could see. Hourly, by day and by night, the continuous drone of aircraft engines could be heard as flyers left and returned on missions over Southern Italy.

On April 17, 1942, the Times of Malta printed the news that King George VI had taken the unprecedented step of awarding the entire island the George Cross, with the citation 'To honour her brave people I award the George Cross to the Island of Malta to bear witness to a heroism and devotion that will long be famous in history'. Malta, a mere smudge in the Mediterranean, just 17 miles by 9 had been the target of a furious air assault by Axis forces. In one 12 hour period, from March 20 to 21, more than 1,000 bombs, weighing nearly 300 tons, were dropped on the tiny airfield at Ta'Qali. In April, 6,728 tons of bombs fell on Malta. To put this into perspective, the city of Coventry was destroyed by 260 tons of bombs and London received 18,000 tons in the whole of the Blitz. During the first three months of 1942, according to RAF official historians, 151 daylight enemy sorties were carried out over Britain. By contrast, during the same period the Luftwaffe made 1700 raids on the island. In March and April alone, Malta withstood twice the tonnage of bombs that fell on London during the whole of the worst 12 months of the Blitz. It was 'a siege of annihilation', wrote war correspondent Alan Moorhead. One after another all the great sieges were eclipsed. Malta became the most bombed place on earth, a desolation of craters and rubble. The citation left by President Roosevelt when he visited Malta in December 1943 read:

'In the name of the USA I salute the Island of Malta, its people and its defenders, who in the cause of freedom and justice and decency throughout the world, have rendered valorous service far beyond the call of duty. Under repeated fire from the skies Malta stood alone and unafraid in the centre of the sea, one tiny, bright flame in the darkness, a beacon of hope in the clearer days which have come. Malta's bright story of human fortitude and courage will be read by posterity with wonder and gratitude through all ages. What was done in this island maintains all the highest traditions of gallant men and women who from the beginning of time have lived and died to preserve the civilisation for all mankind.'(sgd) Franklin D. Roosevelt, 7 December 1943.

Although the medal boosted morale, the island was still under siege and the population still starving. One soldier recalled a daily diet of 3 boiled sweets, half a tin of sardines and a spoonful of jam. Virtually every edible animal on the island had been eaten, water supplies were erratic, disease was rife and a large portion of the population homeless. But the island not only survived, it became the base for the Allies forces to cut supplies to the Axis troops in North Africa, then later for those that invaded Sicily. When the sound of guns and aircraft eventually receded, we began the task of rebuilding the island. It took a long time to return to some sort of normality. At the end of it all, we found it hard to comprehend what we had lived through, and how much the little island of Malta had contributed to a crucial period of the Second World War.

The part played by the Royal Navy during the siege strengthened my resolve to join the Service. After it had ended, I settled down as an apprentice Engine Fitter and Turner, working in underground workshops and attending the Technical College where I was taught by Naval Instructor Officers. The bombing had ceased and we no longer had to queue outside Victory Kitchens for our food. As petrol became available, I was able to travel all the way to work by bus. Mother's cooking resumed and proved a blessing as I regained the weight I had lost as a result of the near-starvation diet during the siege. Unfortunately, I had to wait until I was of age and finished my apprenticeship before I could apply to join the Navy. After a 5-year apprenticeship and successful completion of my 4-year Technical College Course I applied to join as an Engine Room Artificer and was successful in my trade test in November 1945, after which I awaited further instructions from their Lordships.

CHAPTER 2

THE NAVY

Starting Out
The Wrong Track

My naval career, lasting 29 years, began after the Second World War and was to become a most exciting, happy and rewarding period of my life. The size of the Navy had been drastically reduced with hundreds of ships being mothballed or sent for scrap. Battleships, which proved to be ineffective in the latter stages of the war, were paid off. Although the size of the Mediterranean Fleet was depleted, we retained enough ships to present an impressive spectacle as they entered and left Malta's Grand Harbour and the adjoining creeks. Showing the flag was resumed after the war and the opportunity to see the world was still a good reason for joining up. Having spent a large part of my life in the Royal Navy, serving in destroyers, frigates, a cruiser, an aircraft carrier, a submarine base and in shore establishments throughout the world, and having travelled to all five continents, I can recall experiences without number.

Each ship in which I served has a story all of its own. Living in a small ship you get to know all members of the ship's company. When my time on the ship ended after two years it felt like leaving a family. On the other hand, while serving in an aircraft carrier most of the crew of some 3500 remained remote. I had become, in that case, just a member of the Engine Room Department. But all ships are subject to excitement and sometimes danger as well as events unheard of elsewhere. On an aircraft carrier, one has to admire the skill and courage of the pilots who take off and land while the ship is steaming at high speeds, sometimes in force 4 or 5 conditions. Despite regular accidents and the loss of aircraft and pilots, men continue to volunteer to fly in the Fleet Air Arm. A submarine was lost with seventy five men on board. Losing a man overboard and narrowly avoiding a collision, are incidents all in a day's work for the man at sea which will be described as my story unfolds.

But there is another more pleasant aspect to the Navy. In between exercises, as near as possible to wartime conditions, ships would cruise the world,

'Showing the Flag'. I sailed to practically every major port and resort in the Mediterranean, to Norway, Denmark, Germany, France, Portugal, Greece, Turkey, Sevastopol in the Black Sea and other countries in Europe, to North and South America, all the major ports of the Indian Subcontinent, to Ceylon as it was called, the Maldives, Fiji, Singapore, Hong Kong, Australia, New Zealand as well as faraway places in the South West Pacific, including the beautiful islands of French Noumea and Tonga, for the coronation of its king. I have been to Africa, to Mombasa, Durban, Cape Town, Simon's Town and the West Coast and to Mauritius. I often lose count of the places I visited.

Soon after my application to join the Navy as an Engine Room Artificer (ERA) was accepted I was ordered by their Lordships to report to HMS St.Angelo on 12th February, 1946, an old fortification in the Grand Harbour in Malta, built by the Knights of St. John used as a Naval Base, to be kitted out with a provisional uniform to enable me to travel to the United Kingdom for training during one of the worst winters in history in 1946. I was at that time a completely innocent young man brought up under the discipline of very strict parents. I didn't drink, smoke or swear. I was shy and reserved and had not yet had the pleasure of any encounters with the opposite sex. I certainly didn't know 'How to state a Complaint'. So when the uniform and kit, including shirts, shoes, socks, boots and gaiters, shoe cleaning gear and a housewife (a sewing kit), were thrown at me, I accepted everything without a murmur. I was directed to the New Entry Mess where I donned my oversize uniform for the first time, but I didn't complain. After about three hours I proudly set off for home to my mum in Sliema, about five miles away, wearing oversize trousers and jacket and a peak cap which I had trouble keeping from slipping over my nose. I crossed the waters of the Grand Harbour on a navel picket boat and landed at the Customs Steps where liberty men proceeding ashore, as well as Admirals and Senior Officers landed. The beautiful harbour, surrounded by high stone wall fortifications built by the Knights of St John, was buzzing with activity. Several warships were at anchor, boats moved from ship to ship and 'dgħajsas', beautifully painted with bright colours and gold paint, rowed sailors to and from their ships. Admirals and Generals were saluted with pomp and ceremony as they embarked or disembarked.

As I landed amongst all ranks, heading towards Valletta to catch the bus home, I heard a loud voice and saw a six foot plus smartly dressed Royal Marines Colonel beckoning me,

'Hey you' he said 'how long have you been in the Navy?'

I looked at my watch, 'About three hours' I replied.

'About three hours Sir' he barked.

'Have they not taught you how to salute?'

'No', I replied.

'No sir' he said. 'Where are you going?'

'Home to Sliema-sir'

'Now' he said 'As you walk through the streets of Valletta you will come across officers of all the three services who will expect you to salute them' By this time a small crowd had gathered. I was panic-stricken. In a loud voice he gave me his instructions. 'You place the closed fingers of your right hand on the bottom button of your jacket and then you move your hand, through the shortest distance, up to the peak of your hat and salute'. You can imagine my horror as I searched for the tips of my fingers hidden by the sleeve of my over- size jacket. I sensed his unease as I rolled back my sleeve to shorten it. As I moved my hand quickly upwards, so the sleeve rolled back again. I had to go through this ordeal three times before he was satisfied. So I thought! As I walked away, he called me back 'Don't forget to change your uniform when you go back to St.Angelo, and remember to address an officer as 'Sir'. I walked through the streets of Valletta, meeting what seemed to be hundreds of officers who I had to salute, repeating the drill of rolling up my sleeve and saluting. That was the somewhat inauspicious start to my naval career and the beginning of my training.

I waited for a ship at the transit camp HMS Ricasoli, a dingy old fortification, built by the Knights. After two weeks I embarked on a troopship, one of many converted Liberty Ships. Thousands of these ships were mass-produced and assembled in American shipyards on a kit basis during the war. They were all given a number but no name. Because I was registered as a naval rating, I was given a berth amongst the sailors at the forward hold which was converted to an accommodation space. The ship was packed with servicemen returning home from the Far and Middle East, one of many used to ferry them from Port Said and Malta to Toulon in France, on what was called 'The Medlock Route'. My bunk was close to the anchor cable locker and alongside the Starboard anchor. It was assumed that sailors could endure the rough weather at the most vulnerable part of the ship and would not suffer from sea-sickness. The fact that I had never been to sea didn't make any difference. Throughout the journey between Malta and Toulon the sea was at its worst, taking three days on a voyage which should have taken two. I was, needless to say, violently sick and spent most of the journey on the weather deck amidships avoiding looking at the mast as it swayed about in the storm. In any case there was no chance that I would get any sleep, as the anchor, noisily and with regular monotony, banged against the ship's side. From Toulon, where I saw snow for the first time in my life, we were transferred to a Transit Camp in Hyres to the East, waiting for three weeks until the railway lines across France were cleared. The train journey, my first ever, in a captured German wagon without any form of heating over snow and ice made worse by the gaps on the floor of the wagon, which we blocked with blankets, took 36 hours in a bitter winter. During the journey I made many friends. They were tired of the war and were looking forward to their 'demob'. They were on their way home while I was going away from mine. Their expressions of 'Roll on my Demob', 'To hell with the Andrew (the Navy) ', 'I'll be glad when I see the back of Portsmouth Barracks', my destination, filled me with gloom, as I wondered what the hell I was doing joining the Navy for life.

We spent another three weeks at Dieppe waiting for the sea in the English Channel to calm down before we crossed to Newhaven with much discomfort. The gloom turned into horror as we arrived at Victoria Station in London on a bleak Saturday evening with snow and ice in abundance. Black smoke from thousands of chimneys filled the London sky, an unfamiliar sight for someone who had lived on a Mediterranean island all his life. The evening papers headlined the tragic events at Bolton Wanderers Football Club where more than 60 people lost their lives when a stand collapsed. At Waterloo Station I boarded a train for the third time in my life to head to the South coast of England. The bitter weather, the likes of which I had not experienced before, and the sight of Portsmouth Naval Barracks added further to my gloom, bordering on depression. The barracks with its large brick buildings surrounded by about two feet of snow, and what seemed a thousand chimneys belching black smoke, looked like a prison. The climax to the first stage of this dismal experience came when everybody, including all those with whom I had made friends during the journey from Malta, disappeared to go home. I felt very lonely. The authorities at the barracks had not received my papers or any advance notice of my appearance. So, for the next two months, I was detailed to act as a messenger. One of my duties was to escort new entries HOs (Hostilities Only]) around the various offices on their joining routine.

Throughout my childhood, during my school days, I had heard about three famous sporting events, the Derby, the Grand National and the University Boat Race between Cambridge and Oxford. Before I left Malta I looked forward to seeing these events for myself. The time in barracks waiting for a draft to a Training Establishment presented an ideal opportunity. I was lucky that I was in barracks at the right time in1946, when one of the three events was to take place. I travelled to London to see the boat race, the first since1939, and my first visit to that amazing Metropolis. The race, which was described by Alistair Cooke in his first 'Letter from America', was won by three lengths by Oxford. It took another four years before I achieved my ambition to see all three.

When my papers arrived from Malta I was posted to HMS Gosling, a Fleet Air Arm Training Establishment in Warrington, Lancashire, for a six-week course in square-bashing, a course of discipline, military drills and limited weapons training with hundreds of HOs. As I will describe later, I discovered after two years on my first ship, that I should not have been sent to Warrington but to an eight-month Marine Engineering Course at Portsmouth. From Camp No1 at Warrington I was transferred to Camp 5, at a place called Lowton St Mary's, where I joined a class of broad Glaswegians and Geordies. I could hardly understand a word they were saying. While at camp I not only learnt parade drill and how to fire a rifle and a Bren Gun, but also started taking an interest in the opposite sex. Hundreds of girls from the adjoining cotton mills came round the camp perimeter fence looking for boyfriends, who were at that time, in that locality, a scarce commodity. I had my first skirmish when I met one of these girls at the NAAFI Club. On one occasion, when I was on sentry duty late in the evening, she came over to see me carrying a bowl of trifle. I was wearing a heavy greatcoat reaching down to my ankles and holding a rifle. The Divisional Petty Officer was due on his rounds to check whether all sentries were alert. What was I to do with a 9-inch diameter bowl full of trifle? I hid it behind a bush and told her to disappear. When I found the trifle next morning it was obvious that it had attracted a few creatures which had had a feast. I found it very difficult to cope with a situation of this nature. After I returned the empty bowl and thanked her for the delicious trifle, I thought it best that I ended my relationship before I became too involved. She was a lovely girl and I felt guilty ending what was becoming an embarrassment, being chased by a woman.

After two or three weeks and with some difficulty, I began to get accustomed to the dialects of my fellow classmates. Inevitably, I finished up acting as a referee whenever Scotland played England on the playing fields. I was nicknamed 'The Scholar' because I spoke good grammatical and clear English, despite my Maltese accent. On being put through an Educational Test I couldn't understand why the questions were so easy. The Instructor Officer sent for me to tell me that I had passed with a 100% mark and wanted to know where I was educated. He advised me to sit the Higher Educational Test, an examination equivalent to 'A' level, to qualify educationally for officer rank, which I subsequently did when I joined my first ship.

At the end of my 6-week square-bashing I was sent back to Portsmouth Barracks to wait for a draft to my first ship, HMS Chaplet, a wartime Emergency Class Destroyer attached to the Mediterranean Fleet at Malta. I looked forward to going home to relate my experiences to my family. With several other ratings I was to travel to Chatham to take passage on the Repair Ship HMS Woolwich. We started on the tortuous drafting routine around the barracks, where crossing the parade ground had to be done at the double. At that time, before the age of computers, the joining and drafting routines consisted of about ten visits to different departments, the sick bay, dental surgery, hammock store, regulating office, pay office, gas mask store etc. This often meant crossing the parade ground, at the double, from one place to another only to find that the next destination was near to the one you just left. The GI's(Gunnery Instructors), wearing their black shiny gaiters and holding a stick in one hand would bellow away at you 'Double up there', 'Move faster'. Exhausted at the end of a gruelling day, I would settle down in the mess with hundreds of others waiting for transport and the beginning of a long journey.

There was a lighter side to the drafting routine. Reporting to the various locations was a source of amusement to me and my colleagues. At every department I had to recite my full name and number. You can imagine the look on the Master-at-Arms' face as I slowly rattled off my names, Daniel Francis Xavier Henry George Salvatore Marks. Later on, when they discovered that I was mistakenly given an HO (Hostilities Only) official number, they changed my number to PMX 666666. So I finished up with six Christian names and six sixes. This led to more fun at subsequent visits to the Naval Barracks.

On the 10th June 1946, while I was waiting to leave for Malta, I went to London to watch the Victory Parade where I had the privilege of seeing Winston Churchill, the King and all the famous Generals who had participated in the war. It was a spectacular occasion with thousands of troops from the Empire and the Allied countries wearing their distinctive national uniforms taking part. London was packed and I was finding it difficult to find a place to watch the parade. Every road seemed to have been blocked. A steward who was controlling the crowds by the Mall gently told me that I couldn't get through. I pleaded with him. When I told him that I came from Malta, which was at that time held with great affection by the British people for the part it had played during the war, he broke the rules and led me to an excellent vantage point on the veranda of a large building overlooking the Mall in full view of the main platform where the King and all the VIPs were standing. As the Maltese contingent marched past they got a terrific cheer from the crowd. Malta was still very much in the minds of the British people. I felt very proud that I was one of thousands of islanders who had withstood and defied the savage air bombardments by the German and Italian Air Forces.

Before leaving to join my first ship, while at Southsea with a colleague, we met two attractive girls and plucked up enough courage to introduce ourselves to them. Unfortunately, there was not much time left prior to my departure to meet the girl I fancied again before leaving. I asked for her address and promised to write to her. This short acquaintance led to almost two years of correspondence between us. The outcome of the romance that followed will unfold as I progress with my story. With rationing still in force I took every opportunity to send her food parcels on a regular basis. Through our correspondence I painted a picture of the kind of girl she was. I looked forward to our next meeting when I returned to Portsmouth, anxious to find out whether I had pictured her correctly.

We left for Chatham in the middle of July 1946 to board HMS Woolwich. In addition to its own ship's company of about 400, she was carrying another 150 officers and ratings on passage to join various ships attached to the Mediterranean Fleet. I had my first taste of living in a mess and sleeping in a hammock. During the journey I was required to undergo training attached to a Boiler Room crew. At sea I kept watches at all times of the day and night as we sailed through a reasonably calm Bay of Biscay, stopping at Gibraltar for three days before proceeding to Malta. At the Rock, the bars in the main street were packed with sailors as they were entertained to some high quality Flamenco dancing by reputable dancing groups on their way to or from Tangiers. But a visit to Gib was not complete without visiting the monkeys. As we entered the Mediterranean, the Captain stopped the ship for swimming on a number of occasions. As the goal posts were lowered into the water I played my first water polo game in the Navy. I was completely out of practice at a game which I had played regularly since I was a young boy at my Aquatic Club in Malta. Later on I was to play for the Navy at the highest levels. There were several chess enthusiasts on board and on one occasion I managed to beat the Ship's Commander. Using the experience which I'd gained from my father, I continued to play unbeaten throughout my Service Career.

HMS Woolwich duly arrived at Malta where I was given special permission to go home before joining my first ship. I couldn't wait to show my new suit to mum. I was by now an Engine Room Artificer belonging to a breed nicknamed 'The Gentlemen of The Lower Deck'. We were allowed to wear doeskin suits without any badges. I had learned how to salute, and with the pride of a new recruit, I saluted everyone in sight as I walked through the streets of Valletta. I wish I could have met that Royal Marine Colonel who chided me for failing to salute him three hours after I joined the Navy. I was greeted like a long lost sheep by my parents, and the whole family turned up to greet me. The pride of the Marks family had returned. Sadly, one of my sisters was seriously ill, having contracted Tuberculosis during the war. She was living at home where strict precautions had to be taken to ensure that this contagious disease did not spread to the rest of the family. In addition, my father was suffering with an acute heart condition. I was shocked at seeing them looking so unwell after only six months.

CHAPTER 3

MY FIRST SHIP

From Venice to Sevastopol
Palestine

On the following day I returned to HMS Woolwich to collect my kit and transfer to my first ship, HMS Chaplet, a Wartime Emergency Class Destroyer with a crew of about 240. She was berthed alongside in the Royal Naval Dockyard where I served my apprenticeship. I was led to the ERA's mess, a small compartment where nine men slept, ate, wrote their letters, read and studied. I soon discovered why I lacked the necessary training to be let loose amongst the machinery and boilers. The square-bashing at HMS Gosling had served me to no purpose, so much so that when the Chief Engine Room Artificer asked me to go and crack open the main stop valve I started looking for a 20-pound hammer instead of a wheel spanner.

It was summer and the atmosphere in the ship was hot and humid. With space limited there were two sittings for meals and there was no room for me, as the most junior artificer, to sling my hammock. I hung it in the passageway or on the upper deck when possible. Every day at 11a.m. a tot, an eighth of a pint of 100% proof Jamaican rum was issued. Senior ratings and artificers received theirs undiluted while junior ratings had theirs mixed to a proportion of two of water to one of rum. A neat tot was so strong that it needed to be followed immediately with a glass of iced water. I declined to draw my ration and opted for three pence a day instead. However, pressure was put on me by the Chief ERA to start drawing it. I refused to drink it, whereupon he promptly stored it in the gash bottle, a totally illegal act, and hid it away to be consumed later on special occasions or to offer to visitors. One tot of water was added to the mess daily issue adding another extra tot to the bottle. It was the only way that senior ratings could offer alcoholic drinks to their guests. Officers were only issued with a tot when the Monarch ordered 'Splice the Main Brace', on rare occasions such as the birth of a Prince or Princess, victory after a major battle, the end of the war or a Fleet Review. On these occasions, ratings received an extra tot at 5pm. It was also customary that when anyone celebrated a special occasion, such as a birthday, his messmates offered him 'sippers' from their tot. 'Gulpers', a hefty swig, could also be offered. The number of sippers offered would depend on the number of messmates. On one occasion, at a shore establishment, I had over 50 messmates but, of course, only close friends were expected to give me sippers. The issue of rum ceased in 1973 when new technology and the introduction of computers necessitated the need for operators to be very alert. Pressing the wrong button could cost thousands of pounds of wasted trial missiles or, in the event of an engagement with the enemy, missing the target altogether. After drinking one eighth of a pint of rum, it was all too easy to drop off.

There was a more serious problem. Drinking the tot followed by several sippers accounted for about four deaths a year and accidents of all kinds were likely to happen. A Stoker Petty Officer in a ship in which I served fell from a gangway into a dry dock and a sailor who jumped from a liberty boat into the Bitter Lakes was caught by barbed wire under the water. Another fell from the gun deck while we were dressing ship. Soon after I joined the ship, the Chief ERA gave me the job of removing a small drain valve from a steam pipe. He was responsible for ensuring that the pipe was drained of all steam and that at least two valves were closed between the drain valve and the rest of the steam system. Standing on a stool, as I unscrewed the valve, it shot out of my hand followed by a jet of high pressure steam which missed the top of my head by about three inches. Had it hit me, I would have been killed. The valve, a bronze casting, was later found flattened against the ship's hull. I was the only person in the boiler room. At the pipe 'Up Spirits' everyone had disappeared to drink his tot. When steam was seen ejecting from the exhaust fans on the upper deck, a rescue party was sent down the boiler room, by this time completely engulfed in steam. They lifted me out of the Boiler Room, strapped on to a Robinson Stretcher, and took me to the Sick Bay to be attended by the ship's doctor. It took a long time before I regained consciousness. The upshot of all this resulted in the Chief ERA being severely reprimanded. On one occasion, on my birthday, I too became the victim to the 'Sippers' culture.

I found life in the cramped conditions of the mess, the unruly behaviour of a few, the swearing, drunkenness on returning from shore leave, the crude and filthy jokes and stories of exploits with loose women at places of disrepute, quite distasteful. My strict upbringing had not prepared me for such an environment. I learned to choose my friends carefully. However, the majority of my messmates were well educated and decent fellows. Unfortunately, in such restricted conditions it takes one or two bad apples to make life difficult. The environment was made more unpleasant by thousands of little beasts crawling all over the place. The ship was infested with cockroaches. I couldn't believe my eyes when a cockroach dropped from the deck head into the soup plate of someone sitting next to me. He calmly scooped it out on to his side plate and carried on with his soup as if nothing of any consequence had happened. It was quite common for the messman to announce the first course as 'Cockroach Soup'. Before the introduction of air-conditioning in HM ships, these insects thrived in the hot and humid conditions. Every three months the ship's company was evacuated for a long weekend to allow the ship to be fumigated. Millions of these creatures were swept away and incinerated.

The months away from home in England gave me a freedom which I had not experienced before. I became more independent and was beginning to get accustomed to the British way of life. After a strict family upbringing, when I had to account for every move I made, my parents found it difficult to understand that I would no longer put up with such restrictions. After a few days at home I told them that I was to visit the ERA's club, of which I had heard so much before sailing from England. The transition that had taken place since I left home had not registered until I asked for the door key. I told Mama that I was not likely to return until the early hours of the morning. The 'Prodical Son' was back, but not as the innocent boy they had known. I struggled to establish my independence from my shocked parents, especially when they discovered that I liked a drink as well as the company of the opposite sex. They just couldn't come to terms with this transformation.

The ship, having finished its boiler-clean and self-refit, was now ready for sea and sailed for the summer exercises and the cruise that was to follow. The Mediterranean Fleet left the Grand Harbour with the pomp and ceremony which was customary when we had a Navy to speak of. Every ship from a cruiser to larger ships carried a Royal Marine Band which paraded on the upper deck on leaving harbour. Bugles sounded off as ships crews were called to prepare to leave. Ships were manoeuvred out of harbour by their Captains with the precision seamanship skills expected of the Royal Navy, witnessed by thousands of people cheering from the bastions surrounding the Grand Harbour, including families of sailors, and my mum, wiping away her tears as she said farewell to her little boy turned into a naughty sailor!

Six weeks of exercising was a gruelling experience. As soon as we left harbour the ship went into Action Stations. Airplanes started practising attacks on the fleet, while we searched for submarines with our ASDIC equipment and the main propulsion engines were subjected to continuous fluctuations from full to low speed, to full astern, back to full speed and so on. Each day was allocated to a specific exercise such as submarine warfare, communications, gun-firing, air attacks, replenishment of fuel, ammunition and provisions at sea by jackstay transfer, engine room breakdown drills, manoeuvring during the day or in pitch darkness, fire and damage control exercises and how to deal with casualties. Towards the end of the exercise, the ship was subjected to all the exercises combined, simulating wartime conditions. In rough weather the ship heels and pitches violently as crockery and loose objects fly all around. After a time the noise of the engines, the air circulation and exhaust fans, hydraulic systems and diesel generators become the norm. The stress and strain incurred only becomes apparent when you reach harbour as the ship's engines go silent, the diesel engines are shut down and the ship stops rolling and pitching. Getting ready to go ashore, to walk on dry land, to sit down in a restaurant, drink in hand, brings enormous relief.

At that time, the Mediterranean Fleet sailed from Malta three times a year, for the Spring, Summer and Autumn exercises each followed by a cruise. At the end of a gruelling six weeks the ships dispersed by squadrons or individually to various ports to show the flag and enjoy a break. It was my ship's turn to visit the French Riviera and the pretty bay of San Tropez. I soon learned that encounters with the opposite sex can't be avoided. At a reception at the local Town Hall I met a Swiss Italian girl who originally came from Montreux in Switzerland and lived in Menton on the Italian border. On the following day I invited her and her girlfriend to come and visit the ship. With one of my messmates we made a foursome for the duration of the visit until the ship moved to Monte Carlo closer to where her parents lived. She followed the ship and we met again when she asked me to meet her parents at their residence at Menton, a pleasant seaside resort on the Riviera. With father driving a posh car, I was shown round the town and treated to dinner at a typical French restaurant. Martese and I went to Cannes and Nice. At

Cannes we went for a swim on the famous beach, seeing at first hand the glamour and freedom of the body beautiful for which Cannes was noted. My short courtship with Martese was interrupted when I, with another three engineers, had to respond, by order of the Captain, to an invitation by a widow of an ex-Naval Engineer Admiral living in Monte Carlo. We were taken to her fabulous villa overlooking the harbour by chauffer-driven car, then lavishly entertained and taken to tea at the Café de Paris and a tour of the Casino.

The visit to the French Riviera was too brief to allow for any long term relationship with such a charming lady. The ship moved on, and after a few letters exchanged with Martese any affection which had developed between us ended. At the next port of call there would be another equally charming lady waiting. I'm often asked about a sailor's relations with girls met in different parts of the world. Many sailors headed straight for the nearest brothel on stepping ashore. Having been heavily involved in sporting activities when I was young, girls took second place, but I couldn't get away from them altogether. They were everywhere, at receptions organised by embassies, consulates, civil authorities, nurses, teachers, lovely and not so lovely! A Naval Warship and a sailor's uniform acted like magnets to girls looking for a good time.

From the French Riviera we sailed for Aranci Bay in Sardinia where the Fleet re-assembled for a Wash Up and to hold the Annual Regatta and other inter-ship sporting activities. I took part in rowing in the ERA's two-man dingy race where we were the favourites. Unfortunately as the race progressed and we were leading, my oar started slipping and the pulling length got shorter and shorter. Having to stop pulling to adjust it, we lost the lead, finishing a very disappointing last. I captained the water polo team, encouraged by the Captain of the ship who played at the highest level for 'The Otters' back home, and held the record for swimming the English Channel in both directions. We beat most ships including aircraft carriers.

After we left Aranci Bay we were ordered to proceed to Palermo in Sicily which, at that time, was dominated by the Mafia and the notorious bandit Guglielmo, who was reputed to be killing the rich to feed the poor in a murderous campaign which lasted many years before they got him. Here I witnessed poverty, starvation and deprivation such as I had never imagined.

Children, bare-footed, wearing hardly any clothes, descended on the rubbish bins which we placed by the gangway for collection. They scavenged for food which we had thrown away and ate it as adults tried to chase them away so that they could take the waste food themselves.

Those who have read about the Invasion of Sicily during the Second World War will recall how the two generals, Patten leading the American forces and Montgomery the British, raced to the city of Palermo in a bid to get there first. The rivalry between these two Generals was partly responsible for the pounding of the city into submission with heavy artillery bombardments from both sides. The rivalry was so great, and the disagreement as to who should enter Palermo first so intense that the two armies threatened to cross each others path to enter the first major city in Europe. After surrendering, the city became ungovernable. The Mafia took over, and the notorious Guglielmo started on his murderous campaign. Returning from shore on one occasion we had to run for our lives led by a man through the back streets, during a gun battle. We ended up in a bombed out building, witnessing a sight that I have never forgotten. Old and young men, women and children, their faces showing the signs of fear and deprivation, slept and sat on straw. We emptied our pockets and gave all we could to these poor people before we were led away, running as fast as we could to the safety of the ship before the curfew began. Sadly, I was to witness much more poverty and cruelty as I travelled to the Indian Sub-Continent, Calcutta, Bombay, Africa and other parts of the world.

From Palermo we sailed through the Straits of Messina to shadow the SS Santa Maria, a large motorised sailing ship which was on its way to the Black Sea to load with illegal Jewish Immigrants due for Palestine, their 'promised land'. We shadowed her for about a hundred miles East of Palermo at about seven knots and handed her over to another ship of the same squadron. A few months later we were to board and arrest the ship as it entered Palestinian Territorial Waters, and towed her into Haifa. Our next stop was Bari in South East Italy in the summer of 1946. Most of Italy was still occupied by Allied Forces and subject to curfew restrictions which we had to observe in most occupied territories. Jack, always eager to go ashore at the earliest opportunity, would find that just as he was settling down with some pretty girl late at night, he had to return to his ship by midnight. It was not uncommon to see sailors approaching the ship with their girlfriends, running towards the gangway breathlessly kissing their girls good-bye, wrestling with their trouser flaps as they went. Some couldn't care less and stayed ashore overnight, fully aware that they would be under stoppage of leave at the next port of call.

From Bari we sailed to Venice. They say 'See Naples and Die'. I'd say see Venice and you will never forget it. We anchored in the Grand Canal to witness an unforgettable spectacle. The Venetians were preparing for the visit of Eva Peron, the wife of the Argentinian President. Gondolas were decorated with coloured lights and bunting, floating bandstands lit with Chinese lanterns and surrounded by floral decorations. The canal bridges were spectacularly profiled by coloured lights and decorated with flowers. A carnival atmosphere hit the whole city. It was like being in Wonderland. At that time Venice was not as crowded with tourists as it is nowadays. During a recent visit I noticed how crowded the place had become. I am led to believe that in July and August the people visiting the city outnumber the total population of the historic centre of the city. For a break from ship's life, we were sent to Welfare Centres, and this is where I struck lucky. I was sent for a week to the Hotel Daniele close to the Ducal Palace, where I lived in luxury. I have since discovered that it's one of the most expensive hotels in Europe. At the hotel I became friendly with the Area Welfare Officer who was friendly with an Italian lady who had a daughter working in the hotel. To have breakfast brought to me in bed by this beautiful creature seemed like a dream. My knowledge of the Italian language was bearing fruit. I was given the daily programme, which included a vantage point from where I could watch Eva Peron's procession, the times our speedboat was to leave for Lido Island, as well as complimentary tickets for visits to Isola San Michele, the Ducal Palace and Murano Island. In restaurants everybody seemed to know the Area Welfare Officer where he received special treatment. I was so overwhelmed by all this hospitality that, like Jack at Bari, I was tempted to overstay my liberty. Venice was not subject to curfew making our visit so much more enjoyable.

Sadly our Venetian dream couldn't last for ever. We moved on to Trieste where the ship berthed alongside the jetty, not far from the main square, for the next three weeks. Here the city was under a strict curfew. It was close to the Yugoslav border, and Marshall Tito had not yet taken full revenge over the Italian Fascists. Our task, and that of the Americans who were occupying Italy, was to stop the Yugoslav partisans from crossing the border to take their revenge. On one of my duty days, as I was on my rounds of the machinery spaces, I noticed a small queue by the Gearing Room hatch. This compartment was situated aft of the Engine Room. It housed the main engines gear boxes and the two main propeller shafts leading into the shaft tunnels could be seen. It was always immaculately clean, and in harbour, when the engines were shut down, very quiet. The temperature was ideal in all sorts of weather. The platform around the gear boxes, made of bright aluminium plates was spacious, the brass fittings shining and the lights could be adjusted to suit any occasion. In fact it was once used by the Engineer Officer for a Cocktail Party. I asked one of the sailors in the queue why there were so many around the hatch. He took me to one side and said 'It's like this Danny. To tell you the truth there are two or three women down there'. It transpired that three prostitutes had been smuggled on board and were performing for the benefit of the duty watch and men under stoppage of leave. I discussed the matter with the Duty Petty Officer and we decided to give the Duty Watch a quarter of an hour to clear the ship of these women. Hammock mattresses were seen coming out of the hatch, together with three females. Who needs to go ashore to a brothel when you can set one up on board! Jack has a way of overcoming such small difficulties as stopping his liberty!

From Trieste we sailed for Pola, now called Pula which was being prepared for handing over to Yugoslavia. Our task was to assist the Occupation Forces with policing. The city and most of the Adriatic Riviera had been occupied by Mussolini and the Yugoslavs had a score to settle with the Italians. One of the biggest problems was to identify and rehabilitate the known members of the Fascist Party and to protect them from the Partisans. Despite this delicate situation, we still managed to enjoy the visit, thanks to the hospitality we received from both the British and American Armies. I became directly involved when the Captain learned that I had been heard speaking Italian with the locals. He asked me whether I was willing to spend some time with an American Army Corps who were short of interpreters. Living in the Sergeants Mess was quite an experience. They certainly knew how to let their hair down in the evenings and there was no shortage of 'signorine' to lift their spirits. Hospitality was exchanged between us and the occupying armies. At Malta we were warned by members of the ship's company of a ship in the same squadron as us, that at Pola, a British Army Sergeant

Major would visit the ship at about 11am, tot time. He would expect to be offered 'sippers'. We prepared some strong tea which we cooled down and put in a bottle and offered him a full tot. He drank it, but didn't react in any way. Before he left the ship he invited us to the Sergeants Mess. During the evening, over a pint, he told us why he hadn't reacted when he drank that tot of strong cold tea. Somebody from another ship had already played that trick on him. We invited him back on board and returned his hospitality by giving him a real tot.

From Pola, we sailed south through the Adriatic to join the Fleet at exercises in the Eastern Mediterranean where we were assigned to a task force, joining in a series of exercises. As we approached Turkey we joined the main fleet in a predetermined formation. With the Commander-in-Chief flying his flag in HMS Liverpool, we sailed through the Sea of Marmara and anchored off Istanbul. With the Royal Marine bands on the four cruisers playing, and the sound of the guns, as they fired a 21-Gun salute, we approached Istanbul in ceremonial mode with the Captains manoeuvring their ships with their usual skill.

Here I learned that Istanbul, the Capital of Turkey, with a population of about seven million, is the only city in the world situated on two continents on both sides of the Bosporus. Constantinople, the part on the European side is the ancient city which, in AD 330, was the capital of the Roman Empire. At the height of the Ottoman Empire, when Turkey occupied a vast area of Eastern Europe, the city was ruled by Suleiman the Magnificent. With the advantage of swimming and playing water polo for the Fleet I soon made friends there. I was shown around Istanbul, visiting the Blue Mosque of Sultan Ahmed, the Hagia Sofia Basilica and other places of interest. Sadly there was not enough time to explore more of the city's history.

At the end of the visit the Fleet was to depart, carrying out a manoeuvre in which HMS Liverpool, Chequers, our Flotilla Leader, and my ship Chaplet were to head North in the opposite direction to the rest of the Fleet for the first post-war goodwill visit by a Naval Squadron to Russia, the main Naval Base of the Black Sea Fleet at Sevastopol. It was, at that time, part of the Soviet Union in Ukraine, now an independent state. In 1854 it was besieged by the French and British during the Crimean War. As well as being a sea resort, it has been, for many years, a Naval Base. The three ships were to detach themselves from the rest of the fleet in a skilful manoeuvre in line ahead, following the Commander-in-Chief. Down in the engine room, as the throttles were opened, my ship wouldn't move. The Chief of the Watch forgot to give me the order to open the main steam stop valves fully to allow sufficient steam to move the ship. The Captain was not amused, especially as he had to appear in front of the Admiral on reaching harbour, with sword and medals, to give his reasons for the delay in leaving harbour. He had to tell the Admiral that the Chief of the Watch was suffering from an enormous hang-over after a heavy drinking session ashore on the last day at Istanbul, for which he was charged, found guilty and heavily punished. As we sailed through the Bosporus very close to the shore, from both sides of the ship, our Intelligence 'guests' were clicking their cameras at anything that resembled a military installation, through the portholes below deck. The cameras continued to click as we came within range of one of the biggest concentrations of warships imaginable, an awesome spectacle of aircraft carriers, battleships, cruisers and warships of all description. We were greeted with a 21-gun salute. As soon as we berthed the Captain cleared the lower deck and spoke to the Ship's Company. He told us that we had to go ashore in fours and were not allowed to carry cameras. He also warned us to avoid drinking vodka as we could easily get drunk on it. Naturally, Jack, on stepping ashore, went looking for it, but could only find soft drinks in the numerous kiosks. Apparently the officers drank gallons of it at the various official receptions.

The Russians had arranged a programme of sports events, including sailing, rowing, soccer, and water polo. A tiny unit of the Royal Navy was to face the best sportsmen of this formidable fleet. We rowed, with both teams of rowers using each others boats and they lent us their sailing boats to sail against them. We were heavily beaten in every event, except that we were fortunate to have an officer on the flagship, Lieutenant Patterson, an Olympic yachtsman, who won both his events. I played water polo against the pick of the Black Sea Fleet made up of seven players all over six feet tall. Before the match started they exhibited their skills on land by spinning the ball on their finger tips and passing it to each other with their elbows, showing off to such an extent that we were demoralised before we jumped into the water. Before the game started the Sports Officer of the Black Sea Fleet, a four-ringed Captain, came into our dressing room to greet us. The Captain of my ship, Lieutenant Commander Forsberg, a member of

30

our team, asked him jokingly whether we were going to play against the champions of Russia. Pointing to a map of Russia hanging on the wall, and to a line across Russia just south of Moscow to the southern border of the USSR, he replied 'Oh no you are not playing against all Russia, you are only playing against the champions of this part of Russia'. During the game they ran circles around us and, seemingly to humiliate us, they took two players out of the water. We were completely outclassed. Before the game they presented us with a water polo cap each. After the game they lined us up on the jetty and presented us with a bunch of flowers. For us the humiliation was complete. The Black Sea Fleet Football team included three Russian Internationals. After they scored the sixth goal, I and my other three shipmates, started walking out of the ground when a Russian male spectator confronted us with the comment 'Ah! British sportsmanship, you lose, so you go'. On an excursion, we visited seven cemeteries as the guide explained 'This is the cemetery of three American airmen'. 'This is the cemetery of the first defenders of Stalingrad'. '....the second heroes of Stalingrad' and so it went on and on. We couldn't wait to get back to the ship.

The visit to Sevastopol was quite an experience at a time when the friendship that had developed in the combined effort to defeat Hitler had started to fade. The Cold War was just beginning. We were not sorry to leave the place, deprived of their national drink! As we sailed back through the Black Sea, the Bosporus and the Sea of Marmara, and as the cameras continued clicking from all directions, the three ships headed for the open sea. While Liverpool and Chequers turned westward to Malta, we turned to the east towards Palestine. Our turn for the Palestine Patrol had arrived.

One of the country's first post war peace-keeping roles was developed in early 1946. This was a requirement for the Mediterranean Fleet to patrol the sea areas off Palestine to detect and detain unauthorised ships carrying illegal immigrants to Palestine, a British Protectorate. As far back as 1880, Jews had started emigrating to Palestine. By the end of the First World War, the population was made up of 104,000 Jews and 800,000 Palestinians. Today, there are about 7 million Jews in Israel. After the end of the Second World War, thousands upon thousands of homeless survivors of the Holocaust had nowhere to go. Palestine was their obvious destination. The Jewish community had organised themselves sufficiently to demand that the country be handed over to them and renamed Israel. But that meant that we had to abandon the right of the Palestinian Arabs to retain what they, with

31

the support of the surrounding Arab States, considered to be their land. It was felt that this position should be maintained until our mandate expired, in May 1948. In the meantime, we had to deal with organised Jewish terrorist organisations, determined to claim their land by force. They attacked military installations and inflicted heavy loss of life on the specially trained Palestine Police. There was carnage when the King David Hotel in Jerusalem was blown up, killing 91 people, including about sixty British Police and wounding several others. Our Servicemen and Police were constantly shot at.

The need to carry out the peace-keeping role of preventing illegal immigrants from reaching Palestine was covered by a Flotilla of Destroyers, led by the Senior Captain on board the Destroyer HMS Chequers, the ship on which the Duke of Edinburgh later served as First Lieutenant. This Flotilla included my first ship, HMS Chaplet. We took it in turn to patrol the Coast of Palestine and intercept any suspicious ship of whatever size. It was an unpleasant duty but, as one would expect, it was efficiently carried out. Each patrol lasted about two months with an occasional break at the Welfare Centre at Port Fouad in Egypt, or at Beirut, in Lebanon, which was, at that time, a stable Westernised City. Ships were not air-conditioned then and living on board for long periods, especially in summer, was most unpleasant. Our water distillers produced water to feed the boilers, and for the ship's company for a limited period without replenishing from shore or tankers. It had to last until we refuelled at Haifa, and was rationed. At times we had to wash with sea water using salt water soap. To amuse ourselves as we sailed up and down the coast with regular monotony, we passed the time by playing games of chess, draughts, cards, tiddlywinks or whatever. Occasionally this monotony was interrupted by stopping and searching suspicious craft. To refuel we berthed alongside the jetty at Haifa, spending just enough time to have a game of water polo against the Palestine Police, with me as the captain of the ship's team. We had one spell of four days alongside at Haifa, where my Uncle Albert then a Naval Officer, was stationed. We found time to go out together, dressed in civilian clothes, to meet some of his Jewish friends, including the Fishman Family of Russian origin. I was particularly impressed by the daughter, Sarah. They invited us to a friend's wedding where I had the opportunity to witness the traditional Jewish celebrations and the customary singing and dancing, a very pleasant occasion.

On my next visit to Haifa about a year later, by which time my uncle had left, I walked in uniform with a friend up Mount Carmel to visit the Fishmans, Sarah in particular, in an 'out-of-bounds' area. As soon as Mrs Fishman saw us, she was aghast and urged us to go back to the ship as we were risking our lives. At that time British Servicemen were being regularly shot at. She gave us a plastic bag each to hide our caps and jackets. We bade a sad good-bye to Sarah and Mum and ran in fear for our lives, back to the ship. I never saw them again.

It wasn't long before we were involved in our first confrontation with an illegal immigrant ship. The Santa Maria, escorted by HMS Childers, appeared on the horizon. We took over the escort duties, while Childers sailed into Haifa to fuel and store ship, and trailed her at 6 knots. Before boarding, we made every effort to do so peacefully, seeking their Captain's permission to board before entering the territorial limits. I well remember the First Lieutenant using the loud hailer asking the question 'Please, will you let us board you?' The reply was always the same; 'If you promise to let us stay in Haifa, we will.' The First Lieutenant responded, 'Sorry, in accordance with the Geneva Convention, only those with a valid passport or visa will be allowed to stay in Palestine.' They refused to budge. As we approached the three-mile limit territorial waters, 'Childers' approached and took station on the port side of the Santa Maria with us on her starboard side. At this stage it hadn't been decided who was to board. The two ships' boarding-parties were hidden from view behind the ships' superstructures until the last moment. Knowing that previous boarding parties had been fired at, only personnel on essential duties were allowed on the upper deck. As soon the Santa Maria entered the three-mile limit, both ships approached on either side at high speed. We were ordered to board, while Childers was to prevent her from veering away from us. It required great skill on the part of the two Captains to avoid sandwiching the vessel. The order was given to 'Jump'. Our boarding party promptly moved from the starboard side of the superstructure to the port side, leaping on to pre-designated parts of the ship's rigging. Long before we boarded, we were shown detailed drawings of every part of the Santa Maria, every compartment, the type and number of engines, position of flooding valves and so on. Our Secret Service had done a good job. The task of taking control of the engine room was given to another ERA. I was the stand-by, in case of emergency. As he described later, the engine room was already flooded making it impossible to restart the engines. We towed the ship into

33

Haifa where the illegal immigrants were transferred to specially adapted ships called 'Empire Boats', fitted with steel cages on the upper deck. Men, women and children were locked in and shipped to Cyprus, an eight-hour journey, and accommodated in 'Repatriation' compounds, a reminder of the suffering they had experienced in the Concentration Camps.

On one occasion, about 5000 would-be Jewish immigrants aboard the 'Exodus' used tear gas, steam jets, smoke bombs, tins of food and iron bars to fight off the boarding party. The fight lasted nearly two hours before the immigrants were transferred to three waiting ships. Twenty five of them were taken to hospital where three died. The rest were taken to Cyprus to join another 20,000 detainees. The 5000 immigrants were embarked at the small French port of Sete, near Marseilles. The 'Exodus', previously the troopship, 'President Garfield' sailed from Baltimore with an American Jewish Captain and crew.

Malta, where we were trained in boarding techniques, was closely involved as patrol ships sailed in and out of Grand Harbour where the waterside bars were alive with lurid stories. Early in 1946, the immigrant ships were mostly Greek 'caique' type of 500 to 1000 tons gross. Their speed was about 7 knots and each was crowded with as many as 1000 immigrants. In later months, larger and faster ships were employed and, instead of attempting to evade the patrols, they openly tried to break through the blockade, seeking publicity. This made the patrol duty most distasteful and there were several cases of ramming of ships. On one occasion, shadowing one of the ships, the 'Smyrni', heading for Tel Aviv, and before she was boarded, our Captain called by loud hailer, 'Please steer a steady course or we shall hit one another and then we shall both be sunk.' The reply was not clear. We cleared our forward 'B' gun for action whereupon the migrant ship pulled her wheel hard over and lurched across our bows. HMS Chequers closed in and her Captain persuaded the 'Smyrni' to stop by crossing her bows and firing bursts from the 20m.Oerlikon Gun into the sea. 'Chequers' boarded and found the ship incredibly crowded but, as we heard later, the people on board were good-natured. Looking back at this sorry chapter, it is hard to believe that after all the hardship they had suffered, these people, with nowhere to go except what was to them their Promised Land, had to be herded like cattle, subjugated and propelled towards an uncertain future.

At that time the world was split between the plight of the Jews and the Palestinians. International opinion was mixed, with the Americans putting on heavy pressure for creating the State of Israel. So soon after the Holocaust, there was much sympathy for the Jews, less for the Arabs. At 4pm on the 14th May 1948, eight hours before the British Mandate in Palestine was due to end, the Jews proclaimed the new State of Israel. The Jewish Agency Leader, David Ben-Gurion, became Provisional Prime Minister until he was confirmed in October of that year by a General Election. The proclamation read, 'We members of the National Council representing the Jewish people in Palestine and the Zionist Movement of the world, met together in solemn assembly on the day of termination of the British Mandate for Palestine and, by virtue of the natural and historic right of the Jewish people, and by resolution of the United Nations, hereby proclaim the establishment of a Jewish State in Palestine to be called Israel.' No boundaries were proclaimed. The law limiting immigration, invoked in 1939 by Britain, was immediately revoked. British Forces started leaving immediately and the Arab Nations began massing troops to move into Palestine. Fierce fighting broke out in Jerusalem. Syria, Egypt, Iraq and Transjordan attacked the Jews from every direction. It was a touch and go situation. Severe casualties were inflicted on both sides during the fighting and by some horrendous atrocities. The Jews prevailed, mostly because of the doubtful motives of each of the Arab States. The only hope rested with the United Nations and the possibility of the Jews and Arabs agreeing to some proposed partition. Sixty one years on, this problem has not yet been resolved. There has never been any peace in that land since that declaration. Historians will, no doubt, hold Britain partly responsible for the present situation in the Middle East where the question is still being asked. Who really has the right to Palestine, now known as Israel? Those who took part in the Palestine Conflict were awarded a medal with a bar showing the name, Palestine. I don't wear mine. Although I was awarded this medal it is, to me, an episode best forgotten.

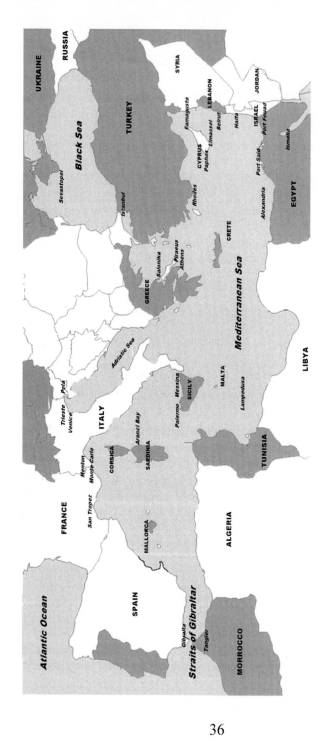

HMS CHAPLET COMMISSION 1946—1948

CHAPTER 4

ROAMING EAST OF MALTA

The Torpedoes and I are led Astray

Half way through the Palestine Patrol we were due for a break at the Welfare Centre at Port Fouad at the entrance to the Suez Canal. Berthed at Port Said, opposite to Port Fouad, liberty boats were laid on to ferry sailors to the Centre to enjoy the swimming facilities and entertainment. We also spent two days relaxing at the Army Headquarters at Ismalia in the Bitter Lakes. At both places German prisoners-of-war were employed as waiters, cleaners and cooks. We got the feeling that some of them were having a great time with our ATS girls and were not looking forward to their repatriation. At the Bitter Lakes I had my first experience of swimming in a sea temperature of 85 degrees F, perspiring as I played water polo.

The visit to Port Said was a welcome opportunity to meet several relatives on my mother's side. Her father was one of four brothers who between them owned the Malta Water Boat and Barge Company. As the Suez Canal was nearing completion they saw the opportunity to expand and improve their business activities. The brothers, together with their families and three sisters, left Malta with most of their boats and barges, leaving some behind with their business partners, to set up The Suez Canal Water Company at Port Said. By coincidence their surname was 'Said'. At that time Port Said was part of a desert, not a pleasant place in which to live. My grandmother didn't like it and persuaded her husband to go back to Malta. His brothers persevered and soon built up a fortune. They all went on to produce large families. So I had plenty of second and third cousins to visit, having already met many of them during their frequent visits to Malta. They were very generous with invitations to the Captain, officers and ratings to local functions and hospitality in their homes. It was at times embarrassing for a very junior artificer to be with the Captain and officers at these events where officers and ratings do not normally mix. Many other nationalities settled in Port Said where the French, who were jointly responsible for the control of the canal with the British, were predominant. Trained sea pilots from other European countries followed. Some of my relatives married into Greek, Italian, English and French families as a result of which they could all speak five or six languages, including Arabic, and continued to speak Maltese and English. By mixing with other European students at school, they learned other languages.

Over the years the Egyptians started questioning the monopoly and influence that foreigners were having on their country. There were no Egyptian canal pilots and most businesses were owned by wealthy Europeans who lived in luxury, while the locals became second class citizens. When King Farouk was deposed, the clamour to take control of the Suez Canal accelerated, and strict restrictions were imposed on Europeans. Some of my relatives realised that the time had come to transfer their assets away from Egypt and a few managed to sell their property and businesses and settled in Australia. Others had too much property to sell and owned businesses in Port Said, Cairo and Alexandria. They managed to transfer limited sums of money to foreign banks, but the bulk of their property was still unsold at the time of the Suez crisis in 1956 and they lost a considerable amount of their wealth. When the British landed in Egypt at Port Said, some of them openly assisted the troops by providing them with material and provisions. When the British and French retreated, they were evacuated on a landing craft, not knowing what was to become of them. Although they were Maltese with a British passport, Mr Mintoff, the Prime Minister of Malta, would not allow them to settle in Malta. They were flown to London where I met some of them living in the Imperial Hotel in Russell Square while waiting for an Australian Visa. I met them again at Maroubra and Paramatta in Australia when I called at Sydney in HMS Sirius many years later. With my wife, I also met some of them on recent visits to my son, who now lives in Sydney. After almost 40 years, they eventually received compensation from the Egyptian Government amounting to a small proportion of the assets they left behind.

For our second break we went to Beirut. Sadly I didn't see much of the city. With a colleague we joined other members of the ship's company to dine at a restaurant where we all ate oysters, for me the first time in my life. To a man we all went down with dysentery. A few were flown to the Royal Naval

Hospital in Malta after they developed Typhoid Fever. That was the first and last time that I ate oysters.

Life in my first ship was full of excitement. At that time ships' Captains took great pride in manoeuvring their ships at high speeds. During an exercise off Malta we were involved in a manoeuvre in complete darkness which almost led to a collision with our Squadron Leader, HMS Chequers. I was happily sleeping in my hammock, slung on the boat deck. Without warning I found myself totally engulfed by a large quantity of sea water which took no time to fill my hammock. Woken up suddenly, and as the upper deck emergency lights were switched on, I saw another ship steaming alongside, only a few feet away, generating an enormous column of sea spray across the whole length between the two ships. The Captains kept their nerves, moving steadily on a parallel course, gradually disengaging to distance themselves from each other avoiding a catastrophic collision. Several odd sorties were undertaken. We were often required to act as attendant destroyer to aircraft carriers dealing with emergencies that may occur during flying exercises. On one occasion one of the airplanes crash-landed on Lampedusa, a small island south of Malta. We were ordered to retrieve the pilot who had a lucky escape, as well as the damaged aircraft. As the island was almost barren and there was no means of transporting the aircraft to the ship, we hired two horse-drawn carts and tied them together. By erecting a system of shearlegs and a platform on top of the carts, we loaded the plane, wheeled it to the jetty and transferred it to another wooden platform erected on the largest fishing boat we could find. We lifted the wreckage using the sea boat davits and secured it on top of the torpedo launching pads. Throughout this operation I acted as an interpreter in Italian agreeing on the hire charges for the carts and fishing boat.

It was not unusual that good times, such as goodwill visits, and exercises, were abruptly and dramatically interrupted by a series of unpleasant international incidents. While the Fleet was at exercises in the Eastern Mediterranean, we were informed that the cruisers Mauritius and Leander with the destroyers Saumerez and Volage were detached from the rest of the Fleet to negotiate the channel between Corfu and Albania, then a Communist country, where six months previously the cruisers Orion and Superb had been fired at from the Albanian shore. The British Government maintained that, as the Corfu channel was an International Waterway, their warships were entitled to the right of a peaceful passage. In 1944 when the German forces retreated from Greece and Yugoslavia, they left behind them a stockpile of sea mines. During the war hundreds of these mines were laid across the coast of those countries and Albania. In 1945 our minesweepers swept a mile wide area of the Corfu Channel in the Greek sector, but not off Port Edda in Albanian waters. This area, because of its proximity to their shores, was treated with great suspicion by the Albanians. All ships were warned to stand by and retaliate should they be subject to any firing from ashore. What they didn't know was that the Albanians had recently mined this small section of the sea passage with mines left over by the Germans. They decided to extend their territorial waters to twelve miles instead of the International limit of three.

After leading his ship safely through the passage Admiral Kinham, on board Mauritius, signalled that his ship was entering the open sea. Within minutes Saumarez hit a mine which destroyed several fuel tanks and the forward boiler room. Through a raging inferno the ship's company tried to save their ship and some of the dying and wounded, as the ship started drifting towards the Albanian coast. Deeply conscious of the risks to a second destroyer, the Admiral ordered HMS Volage to take the crippled ship in tow. Saumarez was dragged stern first into the swept channel. We were alerted to stand by in case we were needed to assist. As Volage was towing Saumarez she too hit a mine after which followed an enormous explosion. She continued towing but, with her bows blown off, she couldn't make any headway and had to slip the tow rope. Throughout all this, both ships had to deal with their casualties as best they could. Saumarez started drifting and was in danger of going aground. Volage, now in deep trouble but still steaming, reconnected a new tow line and the two battered ships agonisingly staggered southwards stern first until another destroyer, HMS Raider, arrived to stay off Saumarez starboard bow for three hours. By this time ships, including the aircraft carrier Ocean, which had steamed to the disaster area at full speed from all round the Adriatic, started arriving at the scene from all directions. Raider transferred the casualties to the RN Hospital Ship Maine, which had sailed from Malta in company with three tug boats. The seriously wounded and eleven dead were taken to Corfu by other ships. The two crippled ships made a sad spectacle as they moved stern first to the comparative safety of Corfu. Forty five officers and ratings lost their lives, sixteen of whom were buried in Corfu.

It is a remarkable co-incidence that Albania has been in the news so much in recent years. In his book *On the Shores of the Mediterranean,* the much travelled historian Eric Newley refers to this incident, and I quote 'After the war Albania became even more remote than it had previously, a sort of Communist Tibet. In 1946 the Albanians displayed their independence by running the Corfu Channel which resulted in the sinking of two British destroyers with the loss of fifty five lives'. In fact the destroyers did not sink. They were towed to Malta where they were repaired. The Albanians refused to pay 900,000 pounds awarded by the International Court. They settled a few years ago when they became what was supposed to be a Democracy. At the end of this sad episode, and when both Saumarez and Volage were well underway on tow to Malta, we returned to our base spending most of the winter months on self-maintenance followed by more exercises with the rest of the squadron.

Our next task was to sail alone to carry out Weapons Practice around the Greek islands. We were to practise launching our torpedoes fitted with dummy heads towards a group of little islands in the Greek Archipelago. The order was given and the torpedoes were duly launched, but not in the right direction. As they left the launching pads, they scattered in all directions, completely out of control. We had a whale of a time searching for them as we veered and zig-zagged around these beautiful islands at slow speed. Occasionally we anchored for bathing and picnicking. The Captain wouldn't dare leave his torpedoes behind him and face a certain Board of Inquiry. We eventually found the missing weapons, but not before many false hopes were raised as basking sharks and flotsam and jetsam were mistaken for our misguided missiles. We felt very sorry for the Torpedo Officer who had given the order to launch the torpedoes with the wrong settings.

Recharged and revitalised by the unexpected holiday, we arrived at Piraeus for an official visit where I took advantage of two guided tours to Athens, the capital of Greece, with its famous ancient buildings and unparalleled history. During two excursions, when we were guided around the Parthenon, the Temple of the Goddess Athena and the Acropolis Museum, there was not enough time to see all the famous sites that this city offered. There was no shortage of night clubs to visit, some very exclusive, with performances by top dancers and musicians. Life in Athens, despite the Communist threat, was gradually returning to normal. We ended the tours by relaxing in restaurants to taste the local cuisine. The rate of exchange was twenty five thousand Drachmas to a pound turning us into millionaires overnight. Unfortunately money was not of much value. We were encouraged to take chocolate, cigarettes and chewing gum ashore with us, items which were in short supply.

Conscious of the dangers that I could encounter ashore, I was very careful where I went, avoiding the Red Light area at every seaport. Hardly did I imagine that I could fall into a trap laid by a female in the most unlikely of places. But that is exactly what happened when I went to the cinema with a colleague and came across a pretty, innocent looking usherette. We decided to accept her invitation to go to a restaurant not far from where the ship was berthed in Piraeus. That was almost all that I could remember until the next morning, when the President of the mess came to wake me up as I lay on the dinner table still fully clothed, suffering from an enormous hangover and stripped off my wallet, thousands of Drachmas, my chewing gum and chocolate and everything else I possessed. I couldn't remember a thing of what had happened. My friend was tee-total and hadn't consumed any alcohol, but hadn't seen anyone robbing me of my belongings. I was thankful that he had remained sober and carried me on board. Whatever that pretty girl put into my drink must have been very potent.

From Piraeus we sailed for Salonika which was still under curfew and very much under the influence of the Communist Party. The revolution, started in 1944, was still in progress and sporadic fighting flared up in this part of Greece as the Socialist National Liberation Front attempted to seize power. Our movements ashore were restricted to the centre of the city in groups of four or more. After a walk around the shops, we settled down in a restaurant in sight of Mount Olympus to taste an assortment of Greek delicacies. From Salonika we were ordered to intercept the illegal immigrant ship SS

Paduca and to shadow her to the Black Sea where she was to load with Jews who had escaped the Holocaust. Another destroyer shadowed her as she came out of the Sea of Marmara, fully loaded on her journey to Palestine. I didn't imagine then that my ship would be involved in arresting the vessel off Haifa and I wasn't aware that while we were shadowing her, we were observing her closely because we were likely to board her at a later date. The secret was well kept. We proceeded to our next destination, Cyprus followed by Rhodes.

The demands of the British Crown Colony of Cyprus to sever its links with Britain were in their early stages. Archbishop Makarios, who with General Grivas led the Greek Cypriots the guerrilla warfare which developed into a state of emergency between 1955 and 1959, was not taken seriously. He was dismissed as a fanatic who was trying to cause trouble by demanding Union with Greece (Enosis), despite the wishes of a sizeable Turkish minority who were totally opposed. The island was at this stage comparatively peaceful. Our visits to Limassol and Paphos were delightful. Both seaside resorts were being developed as tourist attractions. At Paphos we travelled North by bus on an excursion through the Troodos Mountains until we reached Mount Olympus travelling through spectacular scenery. Night clubs provided good entertainment by traditional Greek dancers. At Limassol we were challenged to a swimming meeting against the island. For a small ship we had a strong team, encouraged by the Captain. In the pre-match meeting their club president suggested that we include an event of underwater endurance, one that we had never heard of. I looked at the Captain in dismay, but he agreed to accept the challenge. After the meeting he told me that he would take on what turned out to be Cyprus' champion sponge diver. We gave the island swimming team a good run for their money. They were astonished when our Captain surfaced from under the water a good 20 yards ahead of their man, staying longer under water. They couldn't believe their eyes. I then told them that the captain held the record for swimming the English Channel both ways, and how he had prepared for the swim in baths full of iced water in his London flat in the middle of winter. His feat in beating the champion sponge diver of Cyprus made the front page in the local newspapers. As far as we knew, the visit to Cyprus was made to show the flag and our good will. But then the ship's company would not have been privy to any diplomatic initiatives or military secrets.

43

The guerrilla warfare and killing that followed later resulted in the Archbishop's deportation to Kenya. He did not achieve his ambitions for union with Greece. In 1960, when he made peace with Britain and the island was granted independence, he was elected Head of State. Britain retained sovereignty over the bases at Akrotiri and Dheklia. Any hope of gaining independence ended when Turkey invaded the Northern section of the island in 1974, to come to the defence of the Turkish minority, who were constantly harassed by the Greeks still demanding Enosis with Greece.

We left Cyprus for Rhodes, the largest Greek island of the Dodecanese in the South East Aegean Sea, off the South West coast of Turkey, where the Knights of St John settled between 1309 and 1522, until they were driven away by the Turks to resettle in Malta. Rhodes is a fascinating walled city best known for its statue of the Sun-God Chares, one of the Seven Wonders of the World, generally known as the Colossus of Rhodes. With the Pyramids of Egypt and the Pharaohs of Alexandria, the statue was the third of the Seven Wonders that I had seen.

We departed from Rhodes to our second stint at patrolling the coast of Palestine, sailing along the whole coastline from East to West and vice versa with regular monotony, intercepting any craft whatever its size. On one occasion we came across an abandoned schooner. After a search by our boarding party we found no signs of life. The Captain considered it to be a hazard to navigation and decided to sink it, while at the same time using it for firing practice. Shell after shell was pumped into her, but she wouldn't sink. They entered from one side of the wooden hull and out of the other without exploding. Every available gun was directed at it. As a last resort the Captain decided to drop a depth-charge as we steamed past her at 24 knots when the schooner disintegrated into tiny fragments. Every three or four days the ship berthed alongside the fuelling jetty at Haifa to replenish and take on fresh vegetables. We had a break at Port Fouad and, as on the previous occasion, we berthed at Port Said where I had another opportunity to meet with my cousins.

During this patrol we were ordered to go and intercept the SS Paducah which had been shadowed for many weeks by several destroyers, including us. She was bought by American Jews in South America and converted into an illegal immigrant ship at Genoa in Italy. As in the case of the Santa Maria, the ship we had boarded on a previous occasion, our Intelligence Agencies provided us with every detail of the vessel which was carrying about 1500 Jews from Romania and Bulgaria. We went through the same routine as we had when we boarded the Santa Maria. The First Lieutenant, using his megaphone, pleaded with the crew to allow us to board peacefully, but they refused unless we gave them a guarantee that we would allow them to stay in Haifa. The reply was predictable. They could not stay in Palestine unless they were in possession of a visa or passport. The scene was set and as soon as they entered the 3-mile limit, another destroyer approached from the Port Side of the Paducah, both of us increasing speed for the approach. While the other destroyer was preventing her from veering away from us, our boarding party pounced on the Paducah, and within four minutes, took full control of the vessel. Her upper deck was almost level with ours causing our anchor to get stuck into her hull. The Chief Stoker, who was manning the anchor capstan engine, thought of a brilliant idea. He decided to let go the anchor and lodge it inside the ship. So we were stuck together unable to retrieve the anchor until the St Austin Bay, another frigate, towed the Paducah away from us.

This patrol ended with a major engineering breakdown when one of our two main boilers burst. After fuelling at Haifa we anchored in the bay to wait for the seaplane to deliver our mail. As we sat in the mess waiting, we heard a noise which sounded like an airplane, until the telephone rang to tell us that there was an emergency in the boiler room. One of the two boilers had burst one of its tubes. The noise we'd heard was the safety valve blowing steam which was opened as an emergency. I and another junior ERA were detailed to enter the steam drum to investigate the damage as soon as the boiler was cool enough. The heat in the boiler was so intense that we could hardly breathe once inside the steam drum. We could only endure two minutes at a time, gasping for breath on each occasion. It was evident that the damage was serious. We were unable to continue with the patrol and were ordered to return to Malta for repairs. At the Board of Enquiry, the Stoker Petty Officer in charge of the boiler room at the time of the accident was found guilty of negligence and severely reprimanded. We spent two months in

45

the Royal Naval Dockyard before the ship was ready to go to sea again. At the end of the trials we joined the squadron for exercises by which time I was coming to the end of my time on my first ship. As we left Malta my sister Winnie became very ill. Having been informed by my father, that the operation to treat her infection with Tuberculosis was unsuccessful, I feared she was going to die and that I would not be seeing her again.

We were assigned to one of two aircraft carriers on flying exercises between Malta and Gibraltar, often steaming at full speed to keep up with her. Watching aircraft landing and taking off always fascinated me. At times we acted as their practice target, but for most of the time I was busy in the bowels of the ship, working or watch-keeping day and night, a tiresome routine in the hot conditions in the machinery spaces. The watches consisted of a Middle Watch (midnight until 4am), Morning Watch (4am to 8am), Forenoon Watch (8am to 1200), Afternoon Watch (1200 to 4pm), First Dog Watch (4pm to 6pm), and the Last Dog Watch (6pm to 8pm). Supper, between the Dog Watches, provided a welcome break. In three watches, the Middle was the worst, followed by the Afternoon. In between, having to work for two hours left little time to rest. Drinking the tot after keeping the Middle Watch was unwise. An eighth of a pint of rum was not recommended, so it was saved until the evening. Keeping alert during flying exercises was most important as the main engines and boilers were subjected to continuous fluctuations. After four days we arrived at Gibraltar to refuel, provision ship and to relax. In company with my friends, I crossed over the border into Spain to the town of La Linea to watch my first bull fight. One of our Petty Officers, much the worse for drink, decided to support the bull with vigour, much to the annoyance of the Spanish spectators, leading to a confrontation at a time when our relations with Spain were strained. Some spectators were obviously getting annoyed directing their aggression at the Petty Officer, provoking him to give even more support to the bull with vociferous acclaim of 'Toro' 'Toro' 'Toro'. As the crowd became angrier, two of our Officers who were sitting nearby, with the assistance of some senior Chief Petty Officers, escorted the offender out of the bullring. At that time the town of La Linea relied very heavily on British servicemen, consisting of a large naval presence and a sizeable army garrison, for business at the bodegas and restaurants and for keeping the brothels busy. Despite the tense situation at the border it was comparatively easy to obtain a visa to cross over to Spain.

We sailed from Gibraltar en-route to Malta unaccompanied by other ships. The captain stopped the ship for swimming at regular intervals. Soon after we left he told me to prepare for a water polo match, so I organised two teams and mustered them amidships waiting for the ship to stop. We started tossing the only ball we had to each other when it accidentally fell into the water. I rushed to the bridge to tell the Captain that we had no replacement. He immediately gave the order 'Hard to Starboard' and turned the ship round, steering in the opposite direction following the wake left behind by the ship's propellers. All hands on the bridge focused their binoculars on the foaming wake until the ball was spotted when we picked it out of the water and the pipe was made 'Rig water polo posts, hands to bathe'. I was rescued from an embarrassing situation.

During the visit to Gibraltar, I had received bad news from home. My 25 year-old sister was dying and had received the Last Rites. I put in a request for permission to go home to see her which was rejected on the grounds that we were due to return to Malta within a few days. By the time the ship docked Winnie was dead. I was too late. I had been right in thinking that the last time I saw her would be our final meeting. The Captain sent for me to offer his condolences as well as to tell me that my Demob number had been received. This was puzzling as I was classified as a 'Continuous Service Entry'. It transpired that, when I was wrongly assessed as an HO, instead of having been sent for six weeks square-bashing, I should have been sent on an eight-month marine engineering course. Little wonder I was so lost when I was let loose in the machinery spaces. After saying farewell to my family, distraught at my sister's death and my leaving again, I flew to England in a Valetta aircraft to await my next draft at the dreaded Portsmouth Barracks.

Units of the Mediterranean Fleet anchored at the far end of Grand Harbour in 1936. Many more were anchored in adjoining creeks and harbours with the aircraft carriers in open bays to complete a formidable Naval force.

The famous tanker Ohio, barely afloat, nursed along by two destroyers, approaches the entrance to Grand Harbour, Valletta (Imperial War Museum, London).

A Maltese Dgħajsa.

My English grandfather and his wife Concetta with nine of their surviving children, my father aged nine sitting on the right.

The next generation, with me on the right.

HMS Chaplet anchored in the Grand Canal Venice.

In Piazza San Marco (on right).

In dirty overalls just after crawling inside a boiler.

'Clandestine immigration ship' Paducah, an ex-cross Channel steamer of 915 tons carrying nearly 1,400 passengers, seen from HMS Mermaid in September 1947. (Bernard Alkerman).

Lifting a Firefly aircraft off a makeshift platform erected on a fishing boat.

At a night club somewhere in Cyprus

CHAPTER 5

LIFE ON AN AIRCRAFT CARRIER

Norway and Denmark
Meeting Field Marshal Montgomery
Fatal Accidents

I was looking forward to my reunion with the girl I had met in Southsea, after two years of corresponding with her, and to finding out whether she was the girl I had imagined by reading her numerous letters. I arranged to meet her at Portsmouth and travel with her by train to her beautiful little village a few miles away. I was greeted by her parents as if I was an old friend, no doubt because they'd heard so much about me from their daughter. This first meeting led to almost two years of courtship. Her father, who was the Golf Professional living in a house allocated to him on the Golf Estate, gave me a set of old wooden-shafted clubs and a few free lessons, while his daughter took me out on the course to put the lessons into practice, showing me the secluded areas where we stopped to admire the surrounding countryside!

Soon after I arrived at the barracks I was informed that I had been drafted to HMS Implacable, an Aircraft Carrier, the biggest and fastest ship in the Navy at that time with a compliment of 3500. The ship was driven by four steam turbines of 50,000 Brake Horse Power each, with steam generated by eight boilers. At that time, before the introduction of the angled deck and the catapult, carriers relied on their speed to produce the necessary wind to fly their aircraft. It was not uncommon for the attendant destroyer to signal the carrier that it could not steam close enough to her in the event of an emergency. The distance between my mess and the Engine Rooms was so long that the passageway leading to them was called 'The Burma Road'. I had to allow ten minutes to go on watch, having to open and close several heavy watertight doors on the way. One of the reasons for this draft was to give me the opportunity for training under the supervision of a Training Officer to make up for the 8-month Engineering Course which I had missed on joining. With a school and study centre, in a quiet atmosphere away from the din and the mess environment, I was able to concentrate on my studies and to prepare for a series of examinations. It was hard-going qualifying for my first hurdle in obtaining the Engine Room Watch-keeping Certificate for promotion to ERA 3rd class, and three buttons on my arms. I failed my mock examination, but I persevered, and eventually passed the examination board with a good result. It wasn't long before I was given the responsibility of taking charge of the Controlling Engine Room, one of four.

I joined the ship at Portsmouth on the 1st December, 1948, and soon started making new friends. One of them became very interested when I told him that I came from Malta. As I was showing him my photograph album he gasped with amazement, seeing a wedding photograph of his sister. It transpired that Mary had married a second cousin of mine who she'd met at Port Said when she was in the Wrens during the war. Philip and I became close friends and later I was to act as best man at his wedding. A one in a million co-incidence started a lifelong friendship with him and his family. Some of my Port Said relatives attended his wedding in Blandford in Dorset. Sadly he died a few years ago with lung cancer brought about by asbestosis with which many ship engineers suffered. Although I too have some asbestos in my lungs it is not life-threatening. At that time the inhalation of asbestos dust was not considered dangerous. The main engines, auxiliary machinery and pipe systems were thickly covered with this material. During a refit, while carrying repairs and maintenance, asbestos dust was scattered all over the machinery spaces. There were several fatalities in the Royal and Merchant Navies and among shipyard workmen, until precautions were introduced to prevent the inhalation of the dust.

Unlike my previous ship, a destroyer with a crew of 240, serving in a carrier was like living in a small town. Fifty years on I keep meeting people who served on the ship at the same time as me but never met. The full crew is made up when the aircraft squadrons and their support groups join the ship. When the ship is in harbour the squadrons return to their shore bases, in our case Culdrose in the South of England and Lossiemouth in the north of Scotland

We left Portsmouth on the 17th January, 1949 and anchored off Spithead, sailing for exercises daily and returning to anchor in the early evening. We headed for Devonport where we embarked 220 Fleet Air Arm personnel, the squadron support group. A day later, as we sailed for Invergordon, we took on 10 Sea Hornets. Due to a faulty wing mechanism, when the wings of one airplane failed to open, the rest of the aircraft were sent back to Culdrose. Later on we took on 10 Firebrands. From then on the ship seemed to be on flying exercises ad infinitum around the north coast of Scotland. It became a floating training unit with all departments working at full stretch, the main propulsion engines subjected to constant speed changes to accommodate the flying conditions. Engine Room personnel employed on the flight deck manned the barriers and the arrester wires, with emergency crews and fire fighters on the alert to deal with any unforeseen failures or accidents. We moved from Loch to Loch around Cromaty Firth, Scapa Flow, Aberdeen, Brodick Bay, Lamlash, Bangor and Lock Ewe, returning on week-ends to Invergordon which had for long been the assembly point for the Home Fleet.

Invergorden is remembered for a notable episode in the Navy's history, when the biggest naval mutiny took place in 1931, with sailors from 25 ships refusing to take their ships to sea in protest at the new pay rates which were reduced by six pence to twenty five shillings a week. Led by Able Seaman Len Wincott, they occupied the shore canteen, held unofficial meetings and prevented the ships from sailing for two days. However, although they could have used firearms, violence was limited to a beer glass hitting an officer's head. They returned to their ships singing 'The more we are together the merrier we will be'.

There was no respite from the intensive flying and landing of aircraft, repeated over and over again, night and day, to ensure that the pilots were fully capable of operating effectively before the ship joined the Home Fleet. Taking off and landing on an aircraft carrier is a hazardous operation and sadly, accidents occur from time to time. Crash barriers were provided to prevent an airplane overshooting the flight deck and diving into the sea were it to miss the arrester wires designed to help the plane stop on landing. I could not help admire the skill, courage and daring of those pilots. The rest from the repetitive exercises came at the week-end when sports of all kind were organised at the many playing fields. I played water polo in a swimming pool dug out of rock at a temperature of 54 degrees F, feeling more comfortable when we travelled to Inverness where we played in the local warm swimming pool. The golf clubs which my girl friend's father had given me proved useful when we played on a 9-hole course at Alness, about three miles away, weaving around the sheep droppings. At the end of the game we retired to the nearby Commercial Hotel for a typical Scottish tea and warm scones.

The ship's company, the young pilots in particular, were now well trained in readiness to join the fleet and our NATO partners at combined exercises. All of January and February, 1949 was devoted to more rigorous training. As we sailed from Rosyth in late February we joined the fleet and headed for Gibraltar with other units who joined us from Chatham, Portsmouth and Plymouth as we sailed through the English Channel. Together, we navigated the Bay of Biscay until we reached Gibraltar. A visit to the Trocadero to watch the Flamenco dancers was inevitable, as was the walk up the Rock to stretch our legs and see the monkeys. With my friends, we crossed over to La Linea, into Spain, to revisit Dick's Bodega and sample sherry served with his delicious 'Tapas' followed by a tasty dinner, in contrast to the boring and monotonous menu on board. The Admiral joined the ship and hoisted his flag on the 6th March, 1949, the first Admiral to use an aircraft carrier as his Flagship. On the next day we were joined by the Mediterranean Fleet for combined exercises, meeting with one of the last line of battleships HMS Duke of York and two cruisers. We kept returning to Gib after each spell at sea for the next two weeks.

Although I served as an officer for twenty one years, and was aware of the manner in which an officer is reprimanded, I was not familiar with the procedure for 'logging an officer' until I visited The National Archives at Kew in London. Reading from the log book, on the page allocated to the 11th March, 1949, I came across an attached fly sheet with a warning to an officer, signed by the captain and countersigned by the offending officer, which I copied. For this purpose I have called this person 'A. N. Other'. It reads as follows:

HMS Implacable
At Gibraltar
11th March, 1949

'Did this day reprimand Mister 'A.N. Other', for his disregard of my written instructions regarding Officers wine bills and of my previous verbal warning concerning his excessive daily consumption of spirit.

Signed

Read and understood   *Captain*

A.N. Other
Lieutenant Royal Navy.

Later on in the commission a Commander was logged as follows;

HMS Implacable
At Dornock Bay
Date

'The Commander-in-Chief, Home Fleet, has this day had occasion to admonish Commander 'A.N. Other' DSO, Royal Navy for delaying, without reasonable cause, his return on board after completing the duty assigned to him.

Signed
Captain

Read and understood
A.N. Other
Commander Royal Navy

Since he was admonished by the Commander-in-Chief (C-in-C) he must have been a member of his staff.

Flysheets attached to log sheets are not confined to the logging of officers, but are also used to register events of a serious nature. One such event was the loss of a young pilot, Lieutenant Shepherd, who died when his Sea Hornet crashed into the sea while taking off.

We left Gibraltar in the company of HMS Duke of York, two cruisers and five destroyers, arriving at Portsmouth just in time to prepare for Navy Days, when all ships in harbour are dressed overall and open to visitors. Displays by Ships Companies and the Royal Marines are laid on for the general public. Navy Days are a means of advertising the Navy, while at the same time, giving an opportunity to the crews to entertain their families and friends. Our visits to Portsmouth, our home port, where most of the crew lived, were a welcome relief, giving the sailors some time with their families while the ship was repainted and the machinery and electronic equipment was put through servicing routines. It gave me the opportunity to resume my relationship with my girl friend. I invited her to the ship for a party with other colleagues and their partners. A standard routine developed of meeting her after work, sometimes travelling with her to her village or alone to meet her after she got home. Looking back on those days it now seems a monotonous routine, despite her pleasant disposition.

The Commander-in-Chief returned on board and hosted a reception for local dignitaries and Senior Service Officers just before we sailed again. The Royal Marine Band rejoined and the C-in-C's flag was hoisted. We sailed for Invergordon, following what had become a standard routine, of anchoring at Spithead and then proceeding to embark the two air squadrons. We anchored at Cromarty Bay for a short stay at Buck. The next month was spent in the Invergordon area on similar exercises as before, by which time we were due for a break, which came as we sailed for Oslo in Norway.

We arrived in Oslo on the 6th of June, 1949 for one of the highlights of the commission. Judging from the headlines in the local press, it was evident from the outset that we were very welcome, and as British, very popular. It took no time before we embarked on the protocol and ceremony befitting the arrival in harbour of the largest ship in the Royal Navy and the Commander-in-Chief of the Home Fleet. Throughout the week a steady stream of VIPs called on the C-in-C. Visits started as we approached the city when we embarked the Naval Attaché and the British Liaison Officer. As we approached our anchorage we fired a 21-gun salute in honour of the Kingdom of Norway. At 1100 the C-in-C left the ship to call on the Lord Mayor.

The visit to Oslo illustrated the importance of such visits and the influence and friendship they generated across many countries at a time when the Royal Navy and Britain were held in great esteem. The Commander-in-Chief exchanged visits with the King, the British Ambassador, the Lord Mayor and Lord Lieutenant of Oslo, ministers, the Police Commissioner and other high ranking officials. VIPs were greeted with graded gun salutes according to their status, with the highest honour of a 21-gun salute to the king. At the end of our visit they all assembled in one of the hangers for an 'At Home'.

During my time in Implacable, we had a Navy large enough to show the flag in many parts of the world with enough ships to sustain fleets everywhere. We had fleets in the Mediterranean, East and West Indies, Far East and the South Atlantic. There were also numerous Resident Naval Senior Officers scattered all over the world where Britain had an interest. As the Navy has reduced in size so has our influence. I feel privileged to have seen the Royal Navy in its grandeur, during its glory days as I grew up in Malta, and then to have served in it, when it was still large enough to exercise its influence across the world.

I found Oslo to be one of the loveliest cities among hundreds of inland and seaside towns and cities I visited throughout my twenty nine years service. The reception we were given by its inhabitants was unforgettable. There were a number of excursions organised including one to Holmenkolen, the steepest and most difficult ski jump at that time which, three years later, was the venue for the 1952 Winter Olympics. Other places of interest included the City Hall, where the Nobel Peace Prize ceremony takes place, and the Viking Museum. A few of us, all in our early twenties befriended a few university students among hundreds who descended on the capital from all parts of Norway, wearing coloured caps with logos to distinguish them by cities, presenting a colourful and cheerful atmosphere in the main streets of Oslo. They invited us to their university campus where we joined them at their social activities. In return we took some of them on board, a visit they particularly enjoyed. We were sorry to have to say good bye as they came to see us off at the quayside. They jumped on the liberty boat and wouldn't leave. As the coxswain and the boat's crew removed some from the forward end more of them jumped astern, and as the stern was cleared others jumped forward. The ship was anchored in Oslo fjord and the Captain was becoming concerned that the last liberty boat was going to be late for the time of departure, timed to perfection with pomp and ceremony with the Royal Marines band playing and the guns roaring their 21-gun salute. Signals were exchanged between ship and boat. We had, until the situation became critical, watched with amusement. It was with much reluctance that we decided to assist the boat's crew. Kissing the girls good bye, and shaking the boys by the hand for the last time, we bade a sad farewell as we sang 'Now is the hour when we must say Good Bye'. We waved and waved again until we could see them no more. For a brief period we exchanged letters with some of the students. We wrote to say thank you for the memories and their kind hospitality knowing that it was highly unlikely that we would ever meet again.

We sailed for the open sea to Bergen, the second largest city in Norway, situated in the county of Hoodaland between two groups of mountains. It was the base for the country's fishing vessels known for its unique open air fishing market, occupied by the Germans in April 1940. As we turned back inland we approached at slow speed through the tranquil waters of the fjords, a magical experience. As we entered Bergen Fjord we fired a 21-gun salute. As soon as the ship was secured at Bergen jetty a stream of VIPs came to pay courtesy visits to the C-in-C with the Britannic Majesty's Consul leading the procession. An 'At Home' was given by the C-in-C for the local dignitaries and a press conference was held, presided over by the Admiral. It was a busy time for all on board with the ship open to visitors. A number of parties were given for children and several visitors were entertained by the sailors in the messdecks. The hospitality offered by the people of Bergen was just as warm as that which we had received at Oslo. At a restaurant, a gentleman dining with his wife and daughter, who was very keen to talk about England, invited us to his table and offered us a drink. I invited his daughter and wife to dance as did my friend. They kindly asked us to dinner on the following day at their luxurious home.

No visit to Bergen is complete without a tour of Edward Grieg's house at Troldhaugen, about eight kilometres from Bergen, a Swiss Style house, with its authentic interior and cabin where he worked, amid lush surroundings. After visiting the two largest cities I fell in love with Norway, the magic of its fjords, the beautifully clean cities and above all, the scenery as you travel inland. On leaving Bergen we knew that we were to return to see more of this beautiful country.

As we left Bergen for Scapa Flow no time was lost before flying exercises were resumed and lasted until we arrived at Oban in Scapa Flow, an opportunity for a walk in fresh air along the promenade. Then we headed south for Penzance for exercises with NATO ships from Holland, Belgium, Norway, America and France anchored at Mounts Bay. We exchanged a 21-gun salute with the French cruiser Montcalm. During the next four days, a constant stream of personnel from our NATO allies arrived on board where a conference of Senior Officers and Captains of ships was held to plan a convoy exercise. As we left harbour, we split up into task forces with part of the combined fleet acting as the enemy. While all the other ships steered a zig-zag course, a precaution against submarine attacks, we kept a straight course while aircraft were taking off and landing. Mock attacks by submarines and aircraft developed into a battle of wits. In the meantime the whole of the ship's company closed up for Action Stations with all watertight doors closed. The damage control parties practised damage repair techniques, flooding control, casualty clearance and first aid. Down in the machinery spaces the engine room crews practised machinery breakdown drills. Extensive communication drills were conducted between ships, one of the main objects of the combined exercise. At the end of the exercise the combined fleet assembled in Weymouth Bay, for the final Wash Up (post mortem). There was no doubt that the communication problem was foremost in the discussions that took place at the conference attended by the First Lord of the Admiralty, the Naval Secretary and the Vice Chief of Staff.

Prior to sailing Field Marshal Montgomery, Deputy Supreme Commander of NATO forces in Europe, and Prince Bernard of the Netherlands arrived on board. During manoeuvring practice, as I was watch-keeping in charge of the Controlling Engine Room, I had a visit from the Field Marshal, surrounded by reporters and what seemed like hundreds of photo lamps adding to the heat in the compartment. Time after time, I had to ask reporters to keep away from the control equipment while trying to cope with the questions from the distinguished guest. He pointed to a number of gauges on the control panel asking me what they were registering. In the subsequent broadcast that was shown to the nation, the reporter stated that 'the Field Marshal was driving the fastest and biggest ship in the Royal Navy at full speed'. In fact he had his hand on the Astern Throttle! I eventually received a picture with me and the Field Marshal which hangs proudly on the wall of my study together with other naval memorabilia.

From Weymouth we headed for Portsmouth, flying off all aircraft on the way for a short break. But we were soon on the move again to Sandown Bay in the Isle of Wight, when the aircraft flew back on board, followed by visits to Weymouth Bay and Torbay where the sea was warm enough prompting the Captain to order 'Hands to Bathe'. On the way back to Weymouth we exchanged greetings with a Swedish Squadron of one cruiser and three destroyers sailing in the opposite direction, returning to Portsmouth for our second Navy Days week-end, where the C-in-C opened the event. The Royal Marines and a number of ships laid on displays showing the Navy at work and I brought my girl friend on board to join other wives and sweethearts for a mess party. We remained at Portsmouth for a month to catch up with the maintenance and servicing routines of machinery and the preservation of the ship's hull to make the ship 100% ready for yet more exercises. We sailed from Portsmouth in early September for exercises in the Invergordon area anchoring regularly at Cromarty and Moray Bays. For the Engine Room Department it meant a tedious and monotonous routine depriving us of fresh air for five days at a time. A break from this tedium came when we anchored off Aberdeen for four days and then to Rosyth, giving the Scotsmen the opportunity to see their families, after which we sailed for Portland to join the Home Fleet for ten days of exercises before returning to Portsmouth for a 2-month docking.

At the end of January 1950, with units of the Home Fleet we sailed for Gibraltar for a month's combined exercise with the Mediterranean Fleet, anchoring frequently at Gibraltar. A few of us paid a visit to Dick's Bar at La Linea across the Spanish border where Dick greeted me like a long lost brother. At the end of February we sailed for Palmas Bay, a favourite anchorage for ships sailing in that area. Sporting events were organised between ships and the usual conferences were held to discuss the outcome of the exercise and the remaining programme.

Palmas Bay, in Sardinia, was a safe and accommodating anchorage, used regularly by ships to shelter from heavy seas, including those commanded by Nelson. With my colleagues Dick and Ned, we travelled to Cagliari. After walking around the town outskirts, through barren terrain we were more than relieved when we came across a restaurant packed with local people where we met with more shipmates. By general consensus we ordered a local delicacy, something different to the food produced in the ship's galley. Acting as an interpreter, I asked the restaurant manager to oblige. Half an hour later he re-appeared with two large plates piled high with tiny plucked raw birds, heads and beaks included, but legless, sprinkled with olive oil, vinegar, garlic and parsley. We looked at them in horror. Nobody would dare make the first move and raise enough courage to touch them. It fell to me to apologise for our cowardice, and order Spaghetti Bolognaise. Showing the flag in this instance proved rather embarrassing!

Our next port of call was Villefranche-Sul-Mer on the French Riviera, four miles from Nice. It brought back memories of my first visit to that part of the world in my first ship. This deep natural harbour provides a safe anchorage for large ships. The town, surrounded by hills rising up to 1750feet, had a population of 7000. Fort Mont Alban offered an incomparable view of Cap Ferrat at the Eastern coast of Italy with its small church of St Michael, housing various works of art. From here a visit to Nice was a must, even if it was just to sit in one of the attractive cafes, sipping coffee and tasting the exquisite French cuisine. Stops in between extensive exercises across a large area served to boost the morale of the crew and provided breaks from the constant, repetitive drills and manoeuvring at sea day after day. One advantage was that, unlike my previous ship, a small destroyer, Implacable was much more stable with less discomfort from pitching and rolling.

The next port of call brought memories of the Second World War and the awkward situation in which Britain found itself when France capitulated in 1940. It was in Mers-El-Kebir and the nearby bay of Oran that a Naval

Task Force sent by the Commander-in-Chief, Admiral Somerville ordered the attack that destroyed much of the French Fleet on the 3rd July, 1940. The French were asked to surrender their ships or join in the war against Germany. They declined, and Churchill did not hesitate to give the order to sink the French Fleet, an action that shook the world, seeing Britain attacking one of her recent allies. The attack was called 'Operation Catapult'. The British feared that the Germans could take control of the ships. The potential use of the French Fleet would have caused a sizeable shift in the balance of power that would have seriously threatened Britain's ability to protect her supply lines. Some French warships managed to escape only to be scuttled later in 1942 when the Germans attempted to capture them in Toulon. British warships which took part in the attack included HMS Hood, Valiant, Resolution and the aircraft carrier Ark Royal. 1297 French sailors were killed and many injured. Some ships stayed at Mers-El-Kebir. The French Admiral agreed to disarm them and eventually joined the Allies in 1943. From Mers-El-Kebir we sailed for home arriving at Portsmouth in mid-May, from where, after more training, we joined the French for another NATO Exercise at improving communications, and ending in Brest.

Early June saw us returning to the North of Scotland via Spithead for 'Operation Shopwindow', also known as the 'Summer War'. With units of the Home Fleet, we operated around the usual areas in the North of Scotland. In the machinery spaces we practised how to steer by alternative means, providing different means of electrical power and ventilation, routines that we practised time and time again. There is no end to the limits of training that takes place in a warship. During this period we experienced our first fatal accident when a Sea Hornet crashed on taking off with the loss of its pilot, Lieutenant Shepherd aged twenty two. Despite the efforts of our attendant destroyer, the rescue attempt failed. When an accident like this occurs an eerie silence descends on the whole ship. Our fellow ERAs employed on the flight deck described the incident witnessed by everyone on the Bridge and Flight Deck. Although flying was temporarily suspended during the rescue attempt, it continued until the exercise was completed. As described earlier in this chapter this accident was noted in the ship's logbook by a brief report signed by the Captain. More accidents were to follow when we took on a squadron of fixed wing Vampires, the first generation of jet fighters, for testing on an aircraft-carrier. In the space of half an hour we lost three aircraft and their pilots as their aircraft nosed-dived into the sea or hit the flight deck island before flying was suspended.

After anchoring in Dornoch Bay we sailed for a short cruise to Trondheim and Copenhagen. There was no respite on the way, as flying training continued. We anchored at Movihen to transfer the C-in-C to the destroyer Battleaxe in Namsem Fjord before proceeding into Trondheim, occupied by the Germans between1940 and 1945 and used as a U-Boat base when it was frequently bombed by the Allies. Sailing through the fjords, surrounded by breathtaking scenery in flat calm waters, was a delight. Between watches every opportunity was taken to spend as much time as possible on the flight deck with camera and binoculars in hand. On arrival we were treated to the usual Norwegian hospitality with excursions to the ski slopes and the country inland. At dinner at one of the hotels, I sat at a table with the ice skating and skiing instructor of Sonja Henie, the famous ice skater and actress. The account of his experience and relationship with the actress was quite fascinating. Sonja Henie was the winner of three Olympic Gold medals and won a record of ten individual world titles between 1927 and 1936, when she turned professional and went to Hollywood. She made several films and became an American citizen in 1941. She died in 1969. In describing how he put her through a rigorous training programme, he told us of the part he played in convincing her to turn professional and go to Hollywood.

On the way to Copenhagen the airplanes took to the air again until we were in sight of Denmark. Copenhagen turned out to be another highlight of my two years on this remarkable, floating airfield. Thousands of Danes turned up to greet us, waving and cheering from several vantage points as we approached the harbour. Past history dating back to1801 when Nelson put his telescope to his blind eye at the Battle of Copenhagen, in order to ignore Admiral Parker's signal to cease fire, was long forgotten. As if that wasn't enough the British returned in 1807 to gain control of the Danish Navy when great damage was inflicted and hundreds of people died. But that didn't matter. It was just history. What mattered was that we were very popular and the Danes loved the British. The Scandinavian people had not forgotten the part Britain had played in ridding them of Hitler's grip.

This was a high powered visit on the scale of Oslo. No sooner had we fired a 21-gun salute and berthed alongside, (the first aircraft carrier ever to do so), than the VIPs started arriving to pay their respects to the Admiral. Rear Admiral Lunsteen was followed by the British Ambassador, Major General Knotzen and the Vice Lord Mayor. The Admiral went ashore to dine with King Fredrick of Denmark. The King returned the visit on the following day when we laid on an exhibition for him by driving a damaged aircraft into the crash-barrier, setting it on fire demonstrating how to put the fire out, followed by a march past of the pilots and crews and support personnel on the bomb-loading carriers, jeeps and anything that moved.

Among other highlights was a visit to the Tuborg Brewery where Jack showed his skills at sinking gallons of beer in the hospitality reception area, as waiters pushed trolleys loaded with cans and bottles of the liquid around the tables. By the time the waiters came round for the second time the glasses were empty, as they were the second, third and fourth time, until the senior officer present requested our hosts to stop replenishing. In the large hospitality area a Swedish contingent of tourists sent a message asking us to sing some English songs. Jack was in the right mood and obliged with renderings of 'Tipperary', 'I belong to Glasgow', 'All the Nice Girls love a Sailor' and one or two other familiar songs. When our tables fell silent the Swedes stood up and sang our National Anthem 'God Save the King'. We returned the compliment by applauding them for the gesture.

The Old Vic Shakespeare Theatre Company was performing in the city at the time and a special performance of Hamlet was arranged at Helsingor Castle in the presence of the King, the British Ambassador and the Commander-in-Chief, Admiral Sir Roderick McGregor and other VIPs. On the last day, Prince Axer of Denmark dined with the C-in-C. The Royal Marines 'Beat Retreat' on the jetty watched by thousands of cheering crowds. There were so many visitors watching from the starboard side that the ship developed a three degree list. The next morning, with the Royal Marines parading on the flight deck and the band playing, with all our airplanes laid out on the flight deck in impeccable order, we sailed away from Copenhagen after yet another memorable visit.

No sooner had we left harbour, into the open sea, than our aircraft were up in the skies. The ship's integrated organisation was put into action. The main engines started roaring again, the boilers generated their superheated steam, the communication and navigation systems reverted to operational mode while the air crews busied themselves guiding their airplanes on and off the flight deck. We arrived at Margate four days later. By this time my two years on HMS Implacable were drawing to an end. The ship came to rest at Portsmouth at the end of July 1950 for a major refit and docking and I left the ship a month later.

The end of my time on the ship was soon followed by the end of my relationship with my first love. After almost two years it was evident that we were getting nowhere. I saw her for the last time at her parents' house. It was an emotional farewell as I left the house and walked down the village lane, just like Rhett Butler in the last scene from 'Gone with the Wind' but without bitterness or anger. As I strolled slowly to catch the train I heard her calling me. We spoke for a few minutes before agreeing that there was no point in continuing with our relationship. There was no future in it and so I said good-bye to a very lovely lady. The relationship was an experience which stood me in good stead. With travelling around the world, and my love for the Navy, I avoided getting involved in any long term friendships with any woman until later on in life. Although I had a few skirmishes with other girls, I was lucky that I pursued that course. When I eventually met the ideal person, I knew that the time had come. I married a most talented and wonderful woman, my wife for the past 50 years, of whom you will read more as my story unfolds.

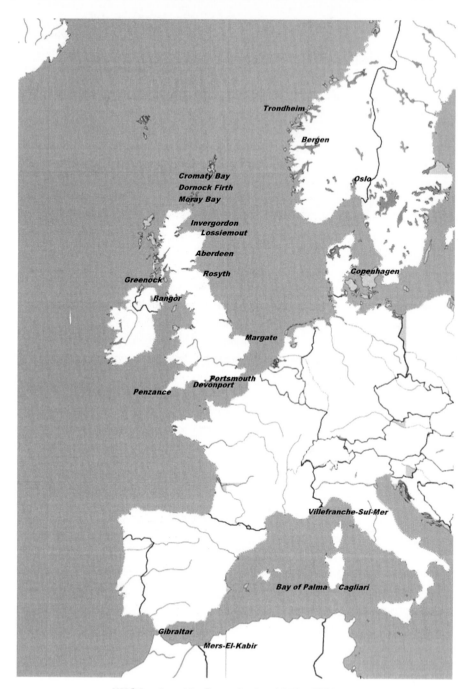

HMS Implacable Commission 1958—1960

The island floodlit with a Hornet in the background.

With Norwegian University students on the flight deck.

With Viscount Montgomery in the Controlling Engine Room, HMS Implacable.

HMS Implacable enters Portsmouth Harbour, passing HMS Foudroyant, a Sea Cadets training ship.

On the Flight Deck.

Thousands queue to visit the ship in Copanhagen.

Royal Marines 'Beat Retreat'.

Airplanes lined up on flight deck as ship prepares to leave harbour.

CHAPTER 6

LIVING WITH SUBMARINERS

Trevor Howard-An Encounter

I was drafted to the dreaded Naval Barracks at Portsmouth to await my next assignment to HMS Dolphin, the submarine base at Gosport, on the other side of the harbour. Serving at a shore base presents a contrast from living in a ship. There were no longer any middle watches to keep. For most of the next two years I slept at night, free from the pitching and rolling, war games and the continuous din of machinery and ventilation fan motors. My job at the base was to assist the submariners with the self-maintenance of their equipment. I spent most of the time in the workshop where I had the opportunity to polish my skills at the lathe. Occasionally I went inside the submarines or 'Boats' as submariners call them which, at that time, were all driven by Diesel Engines. The smell from these engines contaminated the clothes worn by the crews to such an extent that you could smell a submariner as soon as he stepped ashore.

The film 'Morning Departure', starring John Mills, Nigel Patrick, Richard Attenborough, James Hayter and George Cole, was at that time being produced at Dolphin and other Naval bases. It was the story of a submarine grounded at the bottom of the sea. Short of rescue kits, four members of the crew were trapped, running out of oxygen when the rescue operation failed. It may have been a coincidence that the name given to the ERA was Danny Marks, the part played by George Cole. I was told that the producer picked my name from a list of ERAs serving at the base at the time. It is ironic that soon after the film was produced the submarine Affray left Dolphin for exercises in the morning of the 16th April 1951, with a party of commandoes and twenty three officers under training, never to surface again. Seventy five men lost their lives. I knew most of the ERAs. An eerie atmosphere descended on the base as we mourned our friends and consoled their loved ones. Efforts made by the rescue vessels failed to locate the wreck which was found on an even keel off the Hurd Deep two months later on the 14th of June, when the Royal Navy salvage ship Reclaim used an underwater radar detector for the first time. Amongst the officers was Sub Lieutenant Frew, the son of an Admiral who had previously survived the Truculent Submarine Disaster in the Medway Channel when she collided with the Swedish tanker SS Divina in 1950. The Captain of one of the ships I served in, who was the navigating officer of Truculent at the time, saved him, swimming with him for over two miles. It seemed that the young midshipman, as he was then, was destined to die in the manner he did. Sixty four of the seventy six men on board died as a result of that disaster. The cause of the loss of HMS Affray was attributed to the snapping of the Snork mast which is used to draw air into the main propulsion engines, allowing them to be used while the submarine is just below sea water level, while at the same time charging the batteries used to propel the vessel under water. But the mystery has not yet been totally solved. As recently as 2007 questions were being asked in the House of Commons and the demand made for a more detailed engineering explanation.

On the lighter side, there was more time for sport, in which I participated to a great degree, captaining the ship's water polo team and playing for Portsmouth Command. There was plenty of time in the evening to practise, up to three hours a day on most days of the week. As a bachelor, I had plenty of time for pub crawling in well established pubs in Old Portsmouth and Southsea and I frequently lodged at the ERA's club in Southsea surrounded by pubs to the left and to the right. I made a number of friends who lived in the club with me, forming a formidable pub crawling team. At one of the more memorable crawls, I was in the company of Trevor Howard, the actor, who at the time was understudying a friend of mine, a Captain in the Royal Marines, for his part in the film 'Cockleshell Heroes'. At the 'Still and West', a famous pub in Old Portsmouth, Trevor felt hungry and insisted on ordering Chrysanthemum sandwiches from flowers decorating the bar. Unwilling as we were, we had to eat them as the actor insisted with loud vocal persuasion. Astonishingly there were no after effects! The pub crawl lasted into the small hours at a night club in Southsea. Trevor was just mad. In one of his exploits in London he was arrested for being drunk and disorderly and was taken to a police station where he was made to walk over a straight chalk line, the recognised test at the time. Drunk as he was, he walked over the line without veering one way or the other without any difficulty at which the police burst out laughing and took him home in one of their cars. I avoided Trevor for the rest of his stay at Portsmouth.

During my time at Dolphin I was under consideration for selection to officer's status. On the 10th of July, 1951, my birthday, I went on night leave after several sippers of rum from my messmates. By the time I stepped ashore I was feeling quite happy. Unfortunately, on the same day, Randolph Turpin, an ex-Naval steward, was to fight Sugar Ray Robinson, the Light Heavy Weight Champion of the World. The pubs were granted an extension until 1130pm. Needless to say, I was feeling much the worse for drink, as was my friend Dick. Randolph beat Sugar Ray and we were determined to celebrate this famous British victory. We walked out of the pub singing when a police car approached and we were given a warning for disturbing the peace. Assuming that they had gone away, we started singing again. As if from nowhere, the police reappeared and gave us a second warning. We walked to the ERA's club, where I was staying at the time, and knocked on the door. The secretary, still drinking with a few others, no doubt also celebrating Randolph Turpin's victory, opened up. We had no idea that we were being followed. A policeman standing behind us asked the secretary whether we were entitled to use the club. The secretary told him that I was allowed because I was a member, but my friend wasn't. I told the secretary that if my friend wasn't allowed in I would not desert him and wouldn't go in either. The policeman disappeared and we started walking to Dick's home, about three miles away, stopping at a demolished building site on the way. My friend suggested that if we climbed over the rubble we could claim that we were in an uninhabited area and would be entitled to sing. As soon as we started singing, two black Marias arrived and we were shoved into separate cars, arrested and taken to Southsea police station. From the little I can remember, it was quite a humiliating experience as they stripped us off to our underpants, called out our possessions one by one and logged them before locking us up in separate cells. When I was woken in the morning, with a mug of tea and a chunk of bread, I discovered that I was at Fratton police station. It transpired that the police share their prisoners equally to ensure that there is always someone to clean the lavatories and polish the brass every morning. Fratton police were short of prisoners and were duly provided with those from Southsea. At about 11 am we were taken to the magistrates' court. My Divisional Officer was sitting in the front row and was called to testify on my behalf, telling the court what an exemplary and responsible person I was, and that my behaviour was entirely out of character, which made no difference whatsoever. We were both fined two pounds and released. As I left to return to Dolphin I realised that I'd left my hat at the Apsley Hotel where we had watched the boxing so, with my friend, we went to collect it. I had to have it because at that time, when you returned from shore, you had to salute the officer of the day by doffing your hat. When the manager heard our story he felt sorry for us and gave us a good drink on the house. The effect of this drink was unfortunate.

By the time I arrived on board I was hardly sober. The president of the mess informed me that the Captain was holding a special session for defaulters to deal with my case. My friends, seeing that I was not quite fit to appear in front of the Captain, tried to sober me up by spraying me with the cold water firemain hose. By 3 pm, I was facing Captain Bomber Brown across the defaulters table. He told me later, at a mess social to which he was invited, that he was aware that I had told the magistrate that 'I was as sober as a judge'. I well remember the laughter that this comment raised in court, and the magistrate burying his head in his hands. As a punishment, I was given 30 days stoppage of leave with special permission to play water polo for the ship and the Command, under escort of the senior player in the team. I was also informed that I was no longer considered for selection to officer status. Unfortunately, I was soon to experience another setback which made matters worse. I was full of remorse at what had happened especially since I didn't think that I had committed a crime of any consequence. I thought my career was ruined and I started thinking the unthinkable, of leaving the service which I loved dearly. This setback cost me four years before I was considered for promotion again through another route. Out of loyalty to my friend I had ended up in court. My Captain 'Bomber Brown', as he was nicknamed, was a keen swimmer and water polo player in his young days. He attended most of the ship's matches and was a keen supporter. He knew me well as the captain of the ship's team and came to speak to me after one of the matches. I took advantage to tell him that my friend Dick, who had committed the same offence as me of 'bringing the service into disrepute' was only given fifteen days stoppage of leave by his Captain while he had given me thirty. He said he would look into the matter, but I never heard any more about it.

Dick and I were very close friends and, although I spent most of my time at the ERA's club I lived at his house for long periods. His parents treated me as one of the family. On one occasion, we travelled together to London on my Red Panther, notorious for loss of battery power and dimming lights. After a hectic week end, we returned to Portsmouth in the early hours of the morning in dense fog. The lights on my motor cycle kept dimming so I had to drive very close to cars ahead of me following their rear lights to keep on course. With Dick as the pillion rider we were travelling very close to danger. By 7am, tired and under pressure peering through the fog, we were not sure that we were close enough to Portsmouth to guarantee that we would arrive at our respective establishments on time. We just made it by a whisker.

For the remainder of my time at the submarine base, I led a bachelor's life with the ERA's club as my main place of entertainment where serving and retired artificers gathered daily. Sons and daughters of these gentlemen, in their late teens or early twenties, attended for the Saturday hop. In summer, I played for the club cricket team at friendly matches against village teams in the beautiful Hampshire countryside. Sports continued to play a big part in my life, with swimming and water polo taking precedence. In the winter months, in my capacity as a qualified FA and RN referee, I officiated at matches for all three services. At the mess in Dolphin I became proficient at Billiards and Snooker. I still play the latter regularly for my golf club in Bromborough in the Wirral about five minutes walk from my home. I befriended a daughter of one of the old boys at the club. As opposed to the situation with my first girlfriend, where it was I who was going away, this girl, in her late teens, was due to leave for India where her father was posted on an exchange service appointment. I met her four years later when she returned to Portsmouth finding her a completely changed person, matured and sophisticated. We dated a few times, until I was sent to the Royal Naval Engineering College at Crownhill near Plymouth, when we lost touch.

During my time at Dolphin, I learned a great deal about submariners and how they lived on board their 'boats'. I listened to their stories as they returned from their various sorties, for most of the time leaving in the morning and returning in the evening. From time to time they joined the fleet for combined exercises. On their return their crews came to live in the mess ashore bringing all their smelly clothes with them. In the evening, unless they happened to be on duty, they would go home to their families like most other naval personnel. They were, at times, under heavy pressure to take their boats to sea working at all hours to carry out last minute equipment repairs. The ships' Engineer Officers would not upset their superiors by keeping the boats in harbour.

Submariners are a special breed, specially selected from the surface fleet. I admired their loyalty and dedication to their service. They deserve every extra penny they get for the conditions in which they live and work. It was a privilege to be associated with them. During the Second World War, as a young man in Malta, I used to watch submarines sailing and returning to their base from one of the creeks. Some never returned. Their exploits are well documented, and accounts of the experiences of submariners as they came under depth charge attacks, are horrendous, vividly described in the book *Grey Wolf, Grey Sea* written by E B Casaway in the story of U-boat U124. He gives a reconstruction of the daily life of the officers and men in the cramped and complicated quarters, and the desperate chases and escapes as depth charges exploded all round them. Several submarines disappeared in mysterious circumstances in the Second World War, probably due to equipment failure.

Stationed at a shore base gave me the opportunity to fulfil my ambition of witnessing the other two world famous English racing events of the year, of which I had heard so much as a young man in Malta. I had already watched the Boat Race soon after arriving in England. I travelled to Liverpool to watch the 1951 Grand National, one of the most sensational in its long history. It started with an error, when Leslie Full, the starter, pressed the starting button with half the runners still milling around, creating a chaotic situation. The race was not recalled and most of the horses fell at the first three fences. There were only five left at the end of the first round and only three finished the race with Nickel Coin the winner. I was watching the race from the terraces listening on a radio held by a spectator next to me. The excitement was so intense that, while I was listening, I missed seeing the five horses as they went past. I managed to see the three that finished on the second round. My journey wasn't totally wasted, but I had a better view of the race on television later. It was well worth travelling to Aintree to see this spectacle with the holiday atmosphere and the festive mood of thousands of people. My ambitions were fully realised when the submariners organised a bus trip to Epson to watch the 1952 Derby. I was delighted when my horse Tulyar, owned by the Aga Khan, won the race and I, a handsome fifty pounds. That was the first time I attended a race meeting. A lifelong ambition was achieved and I had something else to write home about.

1951 was Festival of Britain year. I met my sister Ethel and her husband who were on their honeymoon in London, and together we watched a performance by the Royal Ballet Company at the Royal Festival Hall. I took them to Petticoat Lane where Albert was conned by a persuasive auctioneer into buying a set of cutlery of doubtful value as its usage proved over time.

Wherever you are in the Navy there is no shortage of humour. On my duty days I had to sleep on board in a large dormitory. One of the tricks played on colleagues returning from shore, was to tie the legs of their pyjama trousers in knots and then watch them struggling to put them on in semi darkness, as you pretend that you're asleep. Watching someone trying to get into blocked pyjama trousers when he is half drunk is hilarious. Another trick was to smear someone's socks with Limberger cheese, the smelliest on earth. Even the change of the Monarch was the subject of a good laugh. While I was stationed at HMS Dolphin, King George VI died and Princess Elizabeth was proclaimed Queen. The inscription on the rum barrel had to be changed, after which the original 'God Save the King God Bless Him' read 'God Save the Queen God Bless Him'. The photograph of the barrel was printed in the local newspaper. I have no idea what happened to the poor Shipwright Artificer who was responsible for this regal error.

My two years at my first shore base were now coming to an end and, as was normal in those days, I was drafted to Portsmouth barracks to wait for my next assignment. I was drafted to the destroyer HMS Saintes attached to the Mediterranean Fleet at Malta. While waiting for transit, I was due for two weeks summer leave when the unexpected happened. A few months earlier I had been introduced to a close friend of the wife of one of the Command Swimming Team who came from Bootle near Liverpool. I was asked to make a foursome on a number of occasions during which it became obvious that she had worked out some grand design for me. On one occasion she took exception to my preference to attend to my Royal Enfield motorcycle rather than meeting her. Try as I may, I couldn't convince her that matrimony was not yet for me. But I succumbed to her invitation to visit her in Bootle, near Liverpool. I started off from Southsea with a friend, Tommy, who had just been jilted a few weeks before he was due to get married. His pockets were stuffed with bank notes which he had saved for his wedding, which he was blowing away like confetti in an effort to relieve the pain in his broken heart.

After a few drinks on the train, he talked me into stopping at his home in Woolwich where he lived with his parents. I sent a telegram to the lady to tell her that I had been delayed. But there really wasn't much time left as I had to return to Portsmouth to act as best man for a friend of mine. I sent another telegram to say that I was not going to see her after all. On returning to the ERA's club in Portsmouth, where I was living at the time, I was told that the Naval Patrol was searching for me. I had been recalled from leave and they couldn't find me at the address I had given. Apparently I had missed my flight to Malta, arranged in my absence. My uniform was at the dry cleaners, and a friend, more or less the same size as me, lent me his. I returned to the barracks immediately. As soon as I reported to the Master-at-Arms I was seen by the Officer-of-the-Day who put me under close arrest. I was to report to the Regulating Office every two hours, from 8 am until midnight. He was not interested in my excuses and referred me to the Commander's defaulter's session on the following morning. I made a frantic effort to contact my friend in Bootle to find out what had happened. She rang to say that her sister received a telegram addressed to a Mr Daniel, who she didn't know. I told this story to the Commander at the Defaulters table but he wouldn't listen. At that time the Commander of the barracks was chosen for his qualities as a hard and heartless person without the slightest bit of compassion. Even though a copy of the telegram was produced, he refused to give me special permission to attend the wedding to act as my friend's best man. The bride and bridegroom were devastated. They came to see me in the barracks and were very understanding. But we had to find a replacement as best man. Poor Tommy, who had just had his wedding dreams shattered, and who hardly knew the bride and bridegroom, took my place with less than 24 hours notice. I understand that he was almost speechless at the wedding. The upshot of all this was that I was given a punishment of yet another 30 days stoppage of leave and fined thirty pounds.

CHAPTER 7

BACK TO THE MEDITERRANEAN

The Wonders of Aqaba and Much More
The Coronation and Fleet Review
The Empire Windrush
We Escort the Queen Home

A week later I arrived in Malta, still under punishment, assuming that I would be unable to visit my parents and the rest of the family, after an absence of almost four and a half years. But the Captain of my new ship was much more humane and understanding than the commander at the naval barracks. He quashed my sentence, whereupon I hastened away to Sliema to see my mum.

For the second time I joined a ship serving with the Mediterranean Fleet. She was berthed at the dockyard where I served my apprenticeship and attended the Technical College. A few members of the ship's company were accompanied by their families, but most were separated for the duration of the commission and relied on the daily flow of letters to keep in touch. At that time there was not much financial support to maintain two homes at home and abroad. Things have now changed, with very few accompanied foreign postings left in the modern Navy.

During the two years of this commission I visited Gibraltar, Marseilles, Toulon, San Rafael on the French Riviera, Aranci Bay in Sardinia, Naples, Palermo and Syracuse in Sicily, Navarin and Piraeus in Greece, Beirut, Port Said, Ismalia, Fayid and Suez in Egypt, Aqaba in Transjordan, Tunis and Algiers

Although there are hazards at sea which result in serious accidents and fatalities, dockyards present ships with many dangers, especially that of fire. It wasn't long after I joined that two nasty accidents occurred. A stoker mechanic fell from the forecastle into the dry dock. He survived with very serious injuries. A seaman had his hand trapped between the drums of the anchor capstan engine. Unfortunately, accidents of this nature continue to happen.

I didn't have long to wait before I was back at sea, keeping watches in the engine room during exercises off Malta. With another three ships, we sailed for Tunis in North Africa for a commemoration ceremony for those who were lost in the desert during the Second World War, where we provided part of the funeral party. The British Ambassador and a French Admiral paid a visit to the Captain. From Tunis we sailed northwards to join the fleet on the autumn cruise. At Naples, I was invited to dinner at the home of my brother-in-law's Italian cousin. After dinner he drove me back to the jetty, where hundreds of sailors were waiting for their liberty boats to take them back to their ships. As I was about to board the ship's cutter, to my embarrassment, my host put his arms around me and kissed me on both cheeks, prompting the waiting sailors to break into a chorus of whistling and hooting. At that time British men did not indulge in such demonstrative gestures. How times have changed! But my visit to Naples was memorable for different reasons. The Monte Carlo Opera Company came to give a special performance in honour of Lord Louis Mountbatten, the Fleet Commander-in-Chief. Senior officers turned up wearing their ceremonial uniforms with tailcoats, cocked hats and medals. Dignitaries from the Italian Government wore formal dress and decorations and their spouses looked gorgeous in their evening dresses. The few of us who were lucky enough to get a ticket wore our best uniforms.

The First Lieutenant was quite generous with granting shore leave, making up for the many days spent at sea. With my interest in the stage, a subject which features in other chapters of this book, I took the opportunity to go on a conducted tour of San Carlo Opera House. I was taken backstage, covering an area almost as big as the auditorium, where some spectacular performances of Grand Opera were staged. We were given a demonstration of the changing of scenery and the handling of equipment used to produce the required stage effects by members of one of the best resident stage teams in the world. The next evening, a special person came over from Capri, where she lived, to give an open air concert for the visiting fleet. Gracie Fields put on a great show, singing those familiar tunes for which she was so well known. She brought the house down as sailors joined in the singing. It was a memorable occasion and a fitting climax to the welcome we received from the Italian community.

During the visit, I joined an excursion to Pompeii, one of the most important archaeological sites in the world. At one point, in the brothel area, we came across a mosaic covered by a wooden frame fitted with a window which only the guide could open. He asked the ladies to move away while he showed the mosaic to the men. An American lady refused to budge. She stood on an elevated circular platform, excavated from the rocky road, with chariot marks on each side, and refused to move. The guide gave up pleading with her and opened the window to expose the figure of Bacchus weighing his penis against a pot of gold. She just smiled and showed no sign of embarrassment.

Before we sailed, the charismatic and charming Lord Louis was piped on board. He told the ship's company how pleased he was with the ship's performance. We moved on to Aranci Bay in Sardinia, a regular meeting place for the Mediterranean Fleet because of its safe anchorage, where we embarked on inter-ship sports and harbour communication drills. As soon as we left the anchorage we started playing war games again with a bombardment, anti aircraft firing and torpedo attacks. We were carrying two Admirals who were conducting the operation from our ship. Back in Malta, Sliema Creek was buzzing with destroyers and frigates going in and out of harbour, while ships' boats ferried senior officers from ship to ship. Bugles sounded at regular intervals to convey messages to the crews.

As if we hadn't had enough, we were out at sea again. The Tannoy blared out 'Gas Gas, Gas'. We put on our gas masks and left them on until the Captain decided it was time to breathe again. Wearing the gas mask in the engine room was almost unbearable. Testing time approached as the Flag Officer boarded with all his staff for the sea inspection. Out in the blue Mediterranean all hell was let loose as we came under attack by the 'enemy'. The anti aircraft guns opened fire at the same time as a submarine was detected trying to sink us. The main engines were subjected to continuous changes from full ahead, to slow, to full astern, to half ahead changing revolutions from 200 to 150 to 40 in an effort to track the submarine. In the meantime, we were preparing to fuel and take on stores by jackstay from supply ships as they steamed alongside. Inside the ship, the Admiral's staff were planting 'explosives' to simulate damage, fire and flooding of compartments and casualties. From 8am to 5pm we were closed up at action stations, living on wartime emergency rations. On the following day we were subjected to the harbour inspection to check our records, making sure that between inspections we had been carrying out the proper training of the crew, that the manuals and instruction books issued by the Admiralty had been updated, and that we had used the statutory amount of ammunition. The stores inventories were checked and the condition and availability of equipment spare parts assessed and examined. The whole evolution was completed on the third day with Divisions, when we all donned our best uniforms for inspection by the Admiral. When it was all over we were glad to see the back of him and his entourage.

Port Said was the next port of call in October 1952 involving endless manoeuvres with another three ships of the squadron. We split up as we neared the Suez Canal, taking fuel at Port Said and proceeding to Famagusta in Cyprus, an ideal place with plenty of sandy beaches and night clubs. This visit was made at a time when the Greek Cypriots' demands of union with Greece started gaining momentum, creating serious friction with the Turkish minority. Our task was to reassure the latter of our protection against growing Greek provocation without appearing to take sides. Football, running and swimming teams were landed by a motor cutter which lost its rudder, making berthing at the jetty a rather hazardous operation. The divers were called to retrieve it. The swimming party camped on the beach for the night. On our way back to Port Said, with fifteen soldiers for passage, we practised at creating a smoke screen using our two boilers for the purpose, polluting the atmosphere with thick black smoke with its dense CO_2 content. I wonder how this would have gone down with to-day's Green campaigners. Nowadays, ships don't use this poisonous device to conceal themselves from the enemy. We stayed at Port Said for ten days where I had plenty of opportunity to call on my relatives. The Governor made a courtesy visit on the Captain.

The next port of call was Beirut to the North East. Here we found plenty to entertain us at the night clubs and restaurants in what was, since the First World War, a Westernised city, a French Protectorate, until it gained independence in 1943. Sadly there is a limit to the exploration of cities like Beirut. There was no time to spend at the many art galleries, museums, churches and other places of interest for which the city is well known. But a visit to the 'Souk el Barghout' was not to be missed. At that time there were no sectarian problems and we were allowed all night leave. The ship was open to visitors throughout the six days stay. On the 26th November the ship was dressed overall in honour of Lebanese Independence. An official reception was held on board at which only officers participated. I had to wait until I became an officer to participate in such events and enjoy the privilege of meeting local dignitaries and guests. I travelled on an excursion to Damascus, reputed to be the oldest inhabited city in the world since 5000 BC. We climbed over narrow hilly winding roads, on a bus of doubtful suspension, as it jerked and twisted dangerously around sharp bends until we mercifully reached a crowded city with its interminable array of small shops selling crystallized fruit, brass and copper ware, silk and an assortment of woodwork. The guided tour took us to the old walls and gates of the city followed by a long stop at the main Souk Medhut Pasha, named after one of the Governors. The return journey was equally hazardous, especially since we had to travel in darkness for part of the way. But relief was at hand when we hit flat ground at Beirut. I enjoyed my second visit to the city more than I did the first when I was poisoned with oysters. From Beirut, we sailed south through the Suez Canal. Since last meeting my relatives, many of them had left Egypt as terrorism escalated, sensing that a bleak future lay ahead, as the events of 1956 proved. As we proceeded through the canal we passed El Qantara Station, El Ballal, Lake Timsah, and the Great Bitter Lakes where we anchored overnight on the way to Suez. The governor was invited on board for lunch in the wardroom while the ship was checked by the Quarantine Doctor.

As we emerged out of the canal into the Gulf of Suez and the Red Sea we headed for Aqaba in Transjordan, berthing at the far end of the Gulf of Aqaba. A visit to this city is not complete without a guided tour of Petra. A rock in the Greek Archeological site in South Western Jordan on the slope

87

of Mount Hor, in a basin among the mountains by the Dead Sea, it was discovered by a Swiss explorer in 1812. It was described as one of the 'New Seven Wonders of the World, one of the most precious properties of man's cultural heritage'. It has become one of the main attractions for tourists from all over the world. It is an unforgettable site with its carved streets, numerous temples, tombs, shrines, altars and a theatre carved out of the red sandstone cliffs. Apart from the magic of this world heritage site, the manner in which we travelled from Aqaba was quite unique. We were driven by the army to a camping area by Moses Well not far from the Bedouin Police Headquarters. We took provisions and camping equipment with us and hung our hammocks between trees. Having been warned of the very cold nights, we immediately started collecting fire wood from fallen tree branches to light our night fires. We were also warned by the army of the looting likely to take place at the site. True enough, after the first night, when we got out of our hammocks we found all sorts of things missing, including strands of hammock lashing and shoe laces. To cap it all, the Bedouin Police came to tell us that the Bedouins had complained that we had pinched their firewood. We had to deal with a protesting group who demanded compensation. They were not interested in money, just cigarettes and lighters. Breaking Her Majesty's Customs and Excise Regulations, we mustered enough duty free cigarettes to appease them and they departed into their fields. How they sneaked between the hammocks and the sentries without detection remains a mystery. It would appear that the sentries were too cold to move away from the fires to carry out their rounds of the camp. On the following night, security was tightened and we asked the police to provide us with some firewood for which we were prepared to pay. The same Bedouins who had complained to the police brought a cartload of firewood and sold it to us for yet more cigarettes.

There was no other way of getting to Petra other than to travel through the narrow crevices dug into the rocks on the back of a mule. So we assembled at the starting point where the Bedouins were hiring their animals. Again they demanded cigarettes and would only accept money as a last resort. I had never ridden a mule or a horse. Looking at the narrow and steep tracks I was in two minds whether to ride one at all. I was helped to mount by the owner and led to the track road for about five minutes, then left to fend for myself. I travelled down to Petra and back without any mishap. However, a colleague was not so lucky. His mule went berserk, run up a hill and tossed him off its back. Luckily he got away with a few bruises and scratches. What we saw at this site was simply awesome as we moved from one temple to another and to the theatre and shrines. I can understand why it has been called one of the 'New Seven Wonders of the World'.

The main object of sailing through the Suez Canal was to escort convoys of British ships and protect them against attacks by Egyptian terrorists. We were to sail through several times. At that time, the demand for the British to leave Egypt was intensifying and terrorist activities were on the increase. Power was seized by General Neguib, who led an army coup on the 26th July, 1952, leading to the abdication of King Farouk in favour of his nine month-old son, leaving all effective power in the hands of Neguib. Known as the Playboy King, his departure in his luxury yacht was celebrated with dancing in the streets. Infighting within the Egyptian army between Neguib and Colonel Nasser led an army coup and took over power. In July 1954 the 80,000 British troops and airmen started pulling out of the Suez Canal base after an agreement with Nasser. They were to leave Egypt altogether by 1956. As soon as the British forces left, Colonel nationalised the Anglo French Suez Canal Company leading to the ill-fated invasion of Egypt by the French and British.

As we left the Gulf of Aqaba, we shifted berth to carry out a bombardment exercise before re-entering the canal. We refuelled at Port Said and sailed for Malta in time for Christmas and the New Year where we settled down to a more peaceful routine, renewing the ship's paintwork and servicing machinery and gunnery equipment. The ship became quieter, and the mess emptied as most of its occupants, at the end of a day's work, went on liberty. Except when on duty, once every four or five days, I went home to my parents. On my duty days I caught up with my studies while my messmates were ashore. As they returned to the ship, peace was often disturbed by high spirits, the effects of more than a few drinks. At sea I often used an unmanned electronic compartment for studying. There were times when messmates who didn't wish to go on liberty volunteered to stand in for me. On one occasion I had the opportunity to reciprocate their kind gesture.

One, who was to be on duty on Christmas Day, had his family in Malta so I volunteered to take his place to let him enjoy Christmas with his family. Christmas in Malta was treated as a Holy Day rather than a day to party and we had no particular celebrations planned at home. The Squadron Engineer Commander had his girlfriend, Diana Lynn, a Hollywood actress, as his guest on board for the evening entertainment in the wardroom. He and the Engineer Officer invited me for a drink, to cheer me up and I was introduced to Diana, an unusual gesture by an officer that could only happen on Christmas Day.

After the New Year, we settled down to the normal routine of going out in the morning and returning in the evening, repeating exercises and drills as directed by the Flag Officer. Each department had to carry out a set of drills at regular intervals. During Action Stations, emergency procedures were rehearsed. We practised what would happen if an electric generator was put out of action, the provision of alternative power, how to lay emergency cables, stop water engulfing compartments adjacent to a damaged section and how to replenish oxygen to breathing apparatus. Down in the machinery spaces, we had to know what action to take if a boiler failed or the propeller shaft or the ventilation equipment was damaged. There are a multitude of eventualities that may occur during a battle for which we practise over and over again. At sea, and in harbour, classes were held for further advancement and the education officer prepared personnel for academic examinations to national standards. In harbour, every opportunity was taken to participate in sporting activities and the Fleet Recreation Officer organised inter-ship competitions throughout the year. Exercises and training in the Royal Navy are extensive and thorough, unsurpassed by any other navy. These rigorous and effective preparations for possible conflict still go on in the modern navy. Time and time again, our ships outmanoeuvre those of every other nation during combined exercises.

After almost six weeks in Malta, we joined the fleet in the South of France for exercises with the French, spending eight days at Marseilles. Numerous VIPs, including the mayor, admirals and generals descended on the ship. Leave was granted daily from 1600 to 0700 and whole days were allocated for excursions and guided tours. At Marseilles we berthed alongside the main square where the port offered facilities for cargo and passenger ships as well as warships. My main recollection was of meeting several Spaniards who had settled in the South of France during the Spanish Civil War and escaped the horrors of that cruel conflict. They spoke fluent French and Spanish. With my knowledge of Italian and broken French and their limited English I was able to communicate with them and listen to their gripping stories as they escaped the revolution. Guided tours were organised. We travelled North to Nimes and the beautiful city of Avignon on the banks of the Rhone, visiting the Papal Residence where Popes lived between 1309 and 1376, the Gothic Palace of the Popes, the ruins of the 12th century Pont St. Benezet, subject of the folk song 'Sur Le Pont d'Avignon'. Sadly, there was no time left to visit the many churches and museums and the famous Avignon School of Arts for which the city is so well known. On leaving Marseilles, we joined units of the French Navy in combined exercises, anchoring at San Raphael and Golfe Guan at night, ending at Toulon.

Toulon is the main French Naval Base in the Mediterranean. Like all naval ports it has a dockyard and a red light area. The usual advice was given to the sailors to be careful and to take the necessary precautions, preferably not to go to the brothels, reminding them of the risks involved. But sailors are not known for their celibacy. They were provided with the necessary 'armour' to wear if they had to. In those days sailors had to fall in on the upper deck to be inspected by the Officer of the Day before they proceeded on shore leave. As he walked along the lines of liberty men, a Sick Bay Attendant followed him carrying a tray full of condoms (French letters, as the sailors called them). They helped themselves to as many as they liked. Early on in my naval career I learned to avoid the pimps, prostitutes and criminals who strolled at the quayside. I chose my shore-going friends carefully, and always opted for the official invitations that came through the consulate or embassy or invitations from reputable organisations or tours arranged by the ship. As a naval city Toulon is, in many ways, identical to Portsmouth or Plymouth, with large shopping centres, parks and places of entertainment but without the attractive sea fronts of Southsea and Plymouth Hoe. It brought back memories of my first stormy sea voyage and the first time I saw snow as I waited for transit across France. The ship was now due for a long refit. On arrival at Malta, we de-fuelled and de-stored, rendering the ship non-operational at extended 'notice for steam' (the state of readiness of the ship's main propulsion engines). I was not looking forward to the dockyard routine and a dull period of three months in harbour.

As soon as the refit started a multitude of workmen descended on the ship. Chipping hammers, welding machines, cranes and an assortment of noisy machines were let loose, creating a continuous din and the accumulation of waste material and dust which had to be cleared daily to reduce the fire hazard. Down in the machinery spaces, equipment was dismantled for major overhaul and asbestos from the steam pipes and steam-driven equipment removed, causing its dust to spread. The whole of the ship's company was accommodated ashore. To my great delight, I was given the opportunity to swap ships with another ERA and to get away from the boredom of a long refit.

The Fleet Coronation Review at Spithead was due in June 1953. A fellow artificer, Andy, serving in the sister ship HMS St Kitts, wished to stay in Malta with his family and was looking for someone to swap with him while his ship was at the review. I wasn't particularly looking forward to the refit and I was also aware that my brother Bob, serving with The Royal Malta Artillery, had been selected to march with the Maltese contingent at the Coronation procession. I volunteered to change with Andy on a temporary basis. My brother was accommodated on the Fleet aircraft carrier HMS Theseus. His wife of only a few months, Terry, flew to England and watched him march in the procession on the 2nd of June from the Mall, where she was allocated a special place. I watched from Trafalgar Square, where I saw Bob marching with thousands of other service men and women from all over the Commonwealth. Despite the wet and cold weather everyone was in a festive mood, singing traditional, patriotic songs. With Terry, I watched the Queen and the Duke of Edinburgh waving to the large crowd from the palace balcony and the spectacular fireworks display on the Victoria Embankment. The announcement that a British Climbing Expedition had conquered Mount Everest made the occasion even more memorable. Among the various dignitaries taking part in the procession was Queen Salote of Tonga, a large beaming figure who waved to the crowd with her handkerchief with great enthusiasm. In her coach was a little man holding an umbrella over her head. It is reputed that when Noel Coward was asked, 'Who is the little man?' he replied 'That's her lunch'. Years later I met her son at his coronation in Tonga two years after her death. He was much larger, at 29 stones. The inhabitants of Tonga were devoted to their Queen mourning her for two years before her son was crowned.

At 3pm on Monday 15th June, 1953, the Queen, on HMS Surprise, left Portsmouth for the Solent to review the Fleet, accompanied by a thunderous gun salute from the ships waiting for her, lined at anchor in nine columns. There were 197 ships from the Royal Navy, 13 from the Commonwealth, 16 from foreign navies, 51 merchant ships and 4 RNLI lifeboats. HMS St Kitts was positioned with the destroyers, while HMS Theseus, with my brother on board, was anchored in a line of aircraft carriers. The Queen, standing on a special platform waved as each ship greeted her with three loud cheers. On the 16th of June she gave the order 'Splice the Main Brace' when an extra tot of rum was issued. At the end of the Fleet Review the ships dispersed and sailed to their various destinations. St Kitts sailed for Malta where we arrived on the 3rd July. I returned to my ship and Andy rejoined his. I thanked him for giving me the opportunity of a lifetime.

Saintes was half way through its refit and equipment started returning from the workshops and the hull was painted with a rust-protective, orange coloured coating. Just before the ship's company returned to live on board, the ship was closed down for fumigation to get rid of thousand upon thousand of cockroaches which had hatched during the summer season. By the time the ship's company returned, the testing of the propulsion machinery had been completed. We sailed for sea trials anchoring in Marsaxlok bay, best known as the place where the Italian Fleet surrendered in 1943. After swinging around the buoy to correct the magnetic compass, we tied up at our normal berth in Sliema. For the next few days we went to sea each day except weekends until all the armament was tested. No exercise is complete at Malta without pumping a few shells into the tiny island of Filfla. This little rock, jutting out of the water, had been used for bombardment practice for the past hundred years. Every ship stationed at Malta must have had a go at it. In between target practice, Maltese fireworks manufacturers took the opportunity to collect cordite dust to use for their pyrotechnics.

Our first task, on completion of trials, was to act as attendant destroyer to the aircraft carrier Theseus on our way to Palermo for what was my second visit since I joined the navy. The Mafia's influence was still very much in evidence, although I didn't witness the deprivation and misery that I did on my first visit in 1946, just after the war. Many of the bombed buildings had been restored and homelessness eliminated. The curfew was lifted and I felt much safer during my shore leave. My forays into the city were confined to shopping and eating out at restaurants, tasting the beautiful Italian cooking which the British had yet to experience on any scale. We returned to Sliema for a few days but were soon off, accompanying Theseus to Phaleron Bay in Greece, anchoring for one night at Vatika Bay on the way. On arrival at Phaleron Bay, as we approached Piraeus, Theseus fired a 21-gun salute in honour of the King of Greece. After my previous experience, when I was robbed of all my possessions, after my drink was doctored, I was determined to avoid Piraeus at all costs. I took advantage of an organised tour of Athens. I didn't mind revisiting the Parthenon and the Acropolis for the second time. We sailed east for a brief stay at Paphos in Cyprus before returning to Malta. The frequency of visits to the Turkish region of Cyprus by naval units had been increased as the conflict between the Turkish and Greek communities intensified. Since my last visit in 1947 the situation was being taken seriously. Our main object was to try and restore peace between the two communities, but as events proved later, we were not successful.

We were soon off to Navarin Bay, now known as Pylos, in Greece, to meet the Fleet during the autumn cruise. The usual harbour drills were conducted under the auspices of the C-in-C. The annual regatta was held and ships companies faced each other on the playing fields at all kinds of sports. Lord Louis Mountbatten called on the captain and spoke to us. He was obviously briefed by the captain that I was the captain of the water polo team and played for the Fleet. He was quite a flatterer and, as if he knew me intimately, he said 'You have excelled at sports and you have one of the best water polo teams in the fleet led by ERA Marks.' He looked around 'Where is Marks?' I put my hand up. With great charm and confidence, he went on to mention a few others by name. He remained on board for the night and transferred to HMS Surprise, a small frigate specially converted to carry his staff and used as a hospitality ship to entertain foreign dignitaries. It was used by the

Queen at the Fleet Review during the Coronation, acting as the Royal Yacht while Brittania was being built.

In company with Theseus, we dropped anchor at Soudha Bay in Crete. The carrier embarked on flying her airplanes while we kept on the alert in case of any accident, while at the same time acting as her practice target. The area covered by this exercise was subject to great activity during the Second World War. In March 1941, British warships destroyed a large part of the Italian Fleet south of the island. The Germans launched an airborne invasion on the 20th of May of that year. The landing was preceded by heavy bombing of the island's airfields.

We rejoined the fleet to continue with 'Operation Weldfast', one of the many names given to specific exercises, after which the whole fleet headed for Malta, where we stayed for a fortnight before we were off again to Port Said, where we stayed long enough to give me the opportunity to visit my relatives before sailing with a south bound convoy. We escorted the merchant ships as far as Ismalia where shore leave was granted. Other escorts were present to take up different positions among the ships making up the convoy. Ismalia, founded in 1863 as a base for the construction of the Suez Canal, is situated by Lake Tismah. A heavy concentration of British troops was stationed in the area. As we waited for a convoy going northwards, we were entertained at Army Headquarters. After a night out ashore, one of our stokers, who was wearing a raincoat to protect him from the bitter desert cold, and probably having had too much to drink, jumped from the liberty boat into the lake and was caught in the barbed wire used to defend the Garrison against possible attacks by frogmen on the Army Headquarters. Despite being a competent swimmer, he failed to surface. In the log book for 5th November 1953, the Officer of the Day recorded 'Stoker Mechanic Terence Johnson. O. N. PSKX 867322, missing, presumed drowned (Ismalia, Egypt)'. The statement was signed by the ship's Captain. On the 6th November another statement was added, 'Search for Stoker Mechanic Johnson discontinued.' In the Log Book, on the 11th November, 1953, an entry by the Officer of the Day added, 'Captain of HMS St Kitts piped on board to lead a Board of Enquiry into the presumed death by drowning of S.M. T Johnson PSKX 867322'. On the 3rd December, the Log Book reads, 'Body of Stoker

Mechanic Johnson recovered at Lake Timsah. Cause of death uncertain, possibly drowning, buried, Military Cemetery, Fayid.' However, the general opinion on board and at Army Headquarters was that, almost certainly, he was caught by the underwater barbed wire laid along the shores of the lake. The Board of Enquiry may not have wished to reveal this method of defence to the enemy. When the convoy assembled we set off northwards stopping at Port Said. Two of my male cousins who I was to meet again in 1968 in Sydney, after they were forced out of Egypt during the 1956 Suez War, came on board.

Christmas and New Year saw us back in Malta, where we reverted to the usual routine of going in and out of harbour. On the 17th December, Warrants No 21, 22 and 13 were read as a result of a fracas at the naval canteen. The offences must have been serious to authorise Warrant Classification. For December 21st, the Log Book reads, 'Dance Patrol landed', no doubt to avoid another fracas. On the 15th February, we sailed for Gibraltar.

As well as preparing for a possible conflict, the Royal Navy, not only acts as an ambassador for the country, but also as protector of the sea routes, prevents contraband activities, assists at natural disasters across the world and goes to the rescue of ships in distress. In early 1953, we came across an abandoned small cargo ship carrying fertiliser products and towed her to Port Said. In August, 1953, we observed what appeared to be a large flare in the sky which was later identified as an air collision between a Valetta aircraft, carrying service families en route from the Middle East to UK, and a Lancaster Bomber. We sailed into the area and spent a considerable amount of time recovering floating debris from the wrecks. On the 29th March, 1954, the order came to sail at full speed from Gibraltar to the aid of the troopship 'Empire Windrush' which, after an explosion in the engine room, had caught fire off the coast of Algiers killing four of her engine room crew. Efforts to control the fire had failed. The 700 servicemen and their families, many of whom were seriously injured and hospitalised, were disembarked at Algiers. As soon as we sighted her in the early morning, a boarding party was sent to investigate and an attempt to tow her began. At midnight the list had noticeably increased. The fire had spread and was out of control. The side of the ship around the funnel was gradually turning red and eventually, with the intense heat, the funnel collapsed. As I came out of the engine room after the first watch (8 to 12 pm), I was told that we were about to slip the tow line. Before we could slip, it came apart and the ship began to sink, stern first, disappearing below the waves, leaving a whirlpool over a large area. Nothing remained of the HMT Empire Windrush. There is no sadder or wretched a sight at sea than the sinking of a ship.

HMT Empire Windrush, 14651 tonnes, was built in Kiel, in Germany and named Montersoa. She had been used for cruises by the Nazi 'Strength through Joy' programme and as a German troopship during the Second World War. In 1945 she was captured at Kiel, taken as a war prize and renamed 'Empire Windrush'. In 1948, she was in the vanguard of today's multi-cultural Britain, bringing the first wave of West Indian Immigrants. Before becoming a passenger ship, bringing servicemen and their families home to Southampton from Singapore and elsewhere, she made a few more trips carrying West Indians to work and settle in Britain. On her last trip she was bringing families back from South Korea. As we towed her we were looking forward for a share of the prize money, a dream dashed as the stricken ship sank 14 miles from Gibraltar. There were no reporters on board, but members of the ship's company took several photographs. It was rumoured that a number of sailors were paid handsomely for negatives by reporters waiting at Gibraltar. The survivors lost all their belongings but were lucky to be alive, due largely to the orderly manner in which they had been directed into the lifeboats by Captain Wilson and his crew.

We returned to Malta just in time to join the fleet for the Spring Cruise, mainly in the Western half of the Mediterranean. After the usual rigorous war games, we were off to the Riviera anchoring at San Rafael. I found time to travel to Nice and take advantage of an excursion to the Maritime Alps, stopping at beautiful Grasse and St Auban and then north to some breathtaking scenery. From San Rafael we were led to Naples by Lord Louis flying his flag on the cruiser Glasgow. On stepping ashore we were surrounded by numerous rogue traders with their fake Rolex watches, cameos and other suspicious looking objects. I joined a tour of the city, calling at the Galleria Umberto directly opposite San Carlo Opera House, an area buzzing with activity and restaurants. The tour took us to Castel Nuovo, built during the time of Charles the First, the first King of Naples. To my disappointment, the guide decided that there was no time to look inside the Museo di Capodinonte to see the paintings of Caravaggio and Rafael. I took advantage of every organised excursion to see as much of Italy as possible, a country endowed with so much beauty, history and art. The Bay of Naples presents a lovely view in sight of Capri, Posidi and Ischia.

The many visits to Italy during my naval career made me fall in love with that beautiful country. With my wife, I revisited Naples and drove along 'La via de mille Contri', (the road of a thousand bends) also known as the Amalfi Coast, calling at Positano, Sorrento and Amalfi for lunch at an enclosed restaurant on the pier where we treated ourselves to a fabulous meal such as only the Italians can cook. We have many happy memories of Italy and will never forget our stay at San Mamete, a village on the shores of Lake Lugano, within easy reach of the lakes of Como and Maggiore and the surrounding scenic areas of northern Italy. Two weeks at the hillside village of Artimino overlooking Florence were equally as memorable, where we travelled by car to San Giminiano, Siena and Pisa, not forgetting the visits to the villages in the surrounding area to taste the locally made Chianti at the wine cellars.

Back at Malta we started preparing for a Royal occasion with great anticipation. The Queen and Prince Philip were returning from Australia on the Royal Yacht Brittania and we were to escort them all the way to England. For three days we practised at high speed to execute 'The Precise Manoeuvre', the name given to a spectacular meeting with the Royal Yacht. Three loud cheers echoed across the sea as each ship sailed past the yacht at 25 knots. Lord Louis, on HMS Glasgow, led the yacht into Grand Harbour to a tumultuous reception, with bands playing and the Maltese people cheering and waving frantically to a much loved queen, who had lived on the island as Princess Elizabeth, when Prince Philip served there not long after their marriage. She may have felt nostalgic as she reminisced about the happy times spent on the island. I will never forget the warmth and affection with which the Queen was received during her four days stay and the excitement her visit generated across the whole island. When she finally left, the crowd gathered on the bastions of that famous harbour to wave her good-bye in their thousands. We waited in the Channel between Malta and the sister island of Gozo, until the Yacht was within sight. At 2020 on the 7th of May, 1954 we took up position with HMS Glasgow, Lord Louis Mountbatten flying his flag as Commander-in-Chief, and another two destroyers. As we approached the Yacht we greeted the Queen with three loud cheers. With Glasgow leading, we sailed past Malta on our next stop, Gibraltar, where the Queen was again enthusiastically greeted by her loyal subjects. There was just enough time for a reception on the Royal Yacht before we were off to Portsmouth. The voyage couldn't have been better staged-managed, with uncle Dickie leading Elizabeth on her way home as Brittania sailed away over the horizon escorted by HMS Chequers, in which Prince Philip had served.

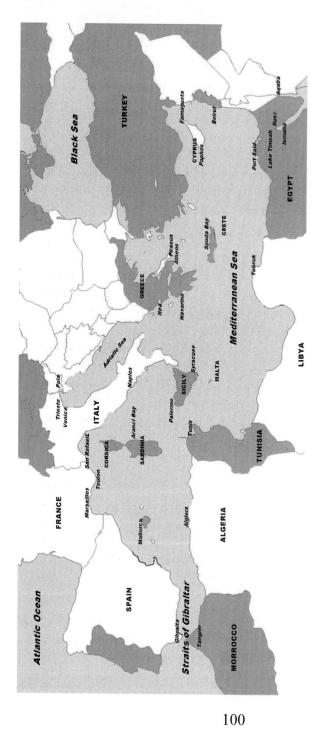

HMS SAINTES
Commissioned 18th December 1951
Paid Off 14th May 1954
46,365 miles logged
3145 hours steamed

CHAPTER 8

A NEW COMMISSION

Ship in Quarantine
Bremen, Oslo and Iceland
Promotion

When I joined the Navy, sailors were separated from their families during a commission away from home which lasted two and a half years. In 1950 this was reduced to two years. By the time we were due in England a commission was reduced to eighteen months. Saintes, the cruiser Glasgow and Aisne, another destroyer, were to embark on a new experiment. On arrival at Portsmouth the ships were to change the complete crew and return to the Mediterranean. I volunteered to stay and serve in the next commission. The experiment backfired badly and all three ships experienced great difficulty throughout the journey back to Malta, so much so that both Glasgow and Aisne came to a grinding halt at regular intervals. At one time, Glasgow was seen drifting in the middle of the Bay of Biscay. With me as the only continuity man guiding the new Engine Room crew, Saintes kept going. I spent most of my time trouble-shooting at all times of the day and night. By the time we got to Gibraltar I was exhausted. Machines have their own peculiarities. It requires experience and familiarisation over a period to operate them correctly. Before this experiment, the crew used to be changed gradually to maintain continuity. We spent a few days in Gibraltar for a much needed rest and sailed for Malta at a leisurely speed, giving the new crew a better chance to familiarise themselves with the equipment. By the time we arrived in Malta we had started to look more of a cohesive crew. One of the machines that gave trouble during the journey was the main freezer. It was touch and go whether food worth thousands of pounds was to be saved or ditched.

Although by now I had started revisiting places from preceding years, the new commission proved as interesting as the first, calling at major ports in France, Italy, Iceland, Germany, Norway, North Africa and UK. With the new system the ship could be deployed anywhere. We spent half the time in the Mediterranean and the other with the Home Fleet operating in the Atlantic, North Sea and the Skagerrak, as far north as the Arctic Circle. With hardly any notice we were directed to proceed to Tripoli in Libya. We were not told why we were being sent there in such a hurry. From time to time we visited places ostensibly to show the flag. As a rating, I was not to know that there was usually some diplomatic reason for these forays. Such information is only divulged to some officers on a 'need to know' basis. I had become accustomed to North African ports which all seemed to bear the same characteristics. Inevitably, I always finished up at the Suq. Tripoli specialised in sheepskin rugs and carpets with a Middle Eastern flavour.

Back in Malta the ship was put in quarantine due to a case of poliomyelitis, and the yellow flag was raised, but that didn't stop us going out on exercises. The Captain did his best to cheer us up by stopping the ship for swimming at some of the pretty bays around the island but we were not allowed to go ashore. Luck was against us. The water polo posts were slung over the side but as the game progressed, a heavy storm (most unusual for that time of the year) suddenly blew up. The water polo players and other swimmers were being taken away by the heavy seas. The ship's motor boat and the second whaler were launched and a rescue operation got under way. The ship's engines were brought to immediate 'Notice for Steam'. I had to use all my strength to make the gangway while others didn't. Fortunately, everyone was picked up some good way from the ship.

After two weeks the ship was cleared of the Quarantine restrictions and we returned to the Grand Harbour in time to cheer off three ships who were 'paying off' on their way home. We were due for canal escort duties and off we went to Port Said to protect two convoys, one to the south and another to the north. We took the south bound as far as Fayid in the Bitter Lakes where a special assignment was waiting for us. We were to assist the army, offloading ammunition from the cargo ship SS Fort Rosalie for the following five days where leave was confined to the army barracks where we were well entertained. After joining the northbound convoy we headed for the open sea to another trouble spot, Famagusta. Agreement with Archbishop Makarios, who was still detained in Kenya, had not yet been reached so we had to continue protecting the Turkish minority and assure them that we would not abandon them. In fact agreement was not reached until 1959 when Makarios was released from detention and elected president of Cyprus on the 14th December of that year. A Turkish vice president, Dr. Kutcheck, was elected as part of the compromise reached between the Greeks and Turks. Makarios, who was earlier deported by the British, met the Queen in January 1961. But trouble continued to flare up between the two communities in the Turkish area until Turkey intervened by invading the northern part of the island inhabited by the Turkish minority in August 1974. Back at Port Said the Egyptians painted the ship during a six day stay. Most evenings I relaxed at my cousins' homes, now reduced in numbers. As the trouble escalated many of them sold their businesses at cut down prices and fled to Australia to join other relatives. Back at Famagusta, despite all the trouble, we managed to enjoy our regular visits. We returned to an unscheduled call at Port Said to take Lord Louis and the Admiral in Command at Malta to Paphos, after they'd had talks with the Egyptian Government. Free from the Suez Canal convoy duties, we sailed to Palmas Bay to join the fleet on the Autumn Cruise just in time for the fleet regatta. While at anchor, I received news that my father was dying at the age of 59 and I was given compassionate leave to go home immediately. Unknown to me, a Surgeon Commander from the Royal Naval Hospital at Malta had gone to see him to check on my sister's accounts of his state of health. A place had been reserved for me on an airplane due to fly to Malta but as I was packing, I was informed that my place had been taken by the Fleet Recreation Officer. No other reason was given. I was then told that I was to travel to Malta on the Pakistani destroyer Tippu Sultan.

My Engineer Officer had long been urging me to sit the examination for promotion to officer rank. The closing date for application for the next examination was imminent. Before I left the ship he produced a request for me to sign. Having been deprived of an attempt at promotion earlier in my career for no significant reason, I was at that time still undecided as to whether I wanted to remain in the Navy at the end of my contract, in three years time. I was also aware that I had promised my father that I would work hard to achieve my earlier ambition to achieve officer status. I thought that it would please him if I told him that I had applied to qualify before he died.

So, with that in mind, I signed the request presented to me by my divisional officer just as I was about to walk down the gangway. I joined Tippu Sultan on the day she sailed to find myself in a strange environment. Before we sailed, the Pakistan Chief ERA told me they were experiencing difficulties in the machinery spaces and I volunteered to help. The ship was in serious trouble and had to slow down and stop in very rough weather. The engine room bulkheads were painted dark green and I could hardly see the dark bodies against the background. Unfortunately, many of them were sea sick as the ship rolled and pitched violently. I spent hours on end during the day and night, trouble-shooting. To add to my discomfort they only served curry for lunch and supper every day. The president of the mess noticed that I wasn't eating the main course. As I intimated that curry disagreed with me, until we arrived in Malta I was served with Irish stew, in other words curry without the curry powder. I was glad that I had something to occupy my mind creating a distraction from the prospect of what was waiting for me when I got home. Miraculously we just managed to make Malta without a major breakdown. By the time we arrived, my father was dead. I arrived just in time to see him buried. Had I been flown on that airplane I would have seen him while he was still alive.

My social life in Malta was divided between the English way and the one which I had been accustomed to until I joined the navy. I retained my Maltese friends who I knew through my sporting activities in my younger days. One of them, Eddie Cole, also a British descendant, was a Maltese International footballer and one of the best tennis players on the island. Occasionally we met at Paul's bar on the sea front at Sliema where my ship and several others berthed. I introduced him and other Maltese friends to my shipmates. Paul was an excellent barman. He specialised in Rainbow Cocktails, laying as many as six or seven layers of different liquors on top of each other without mixing them. He took us frequently to his holiday house at Mosta. With my Maltese friends we found time to mix with the opposite sex. A friendship which I developed with a pretty girl with black hair and black eyes was becoming too serious. Since I had no intention of letting our relationship develop deeper I had been considering ending it. She was a particularly nice person and I didn't wish to lead her into thinking of a permanent association. But my mother had other ideas. While I was away she discovered that I had been dating her on a regular basis and invited her home, forming a close relationship with her, to such an extent that she started knitting a jumper for my little nephew. Somehow, I had to get out of this messy situation. I plucked up courage and ended my short-lived love affair, telling the girl that I had no matrimonial intentions while I was sailing around the world. As for my mother, as far as she was concerned, it would have been ideal for me to marry a good Catholic, Maltese girl and one who lived just round the corner.

The ERA's club had a reputation as the best service social club in Malta and has featured in a number of books about wartime Malta. For about two years I was the Sports and Social secretary, a task which occupied much of my time. I acted as link between our sports teams and the Maltese Civil Service Sports Association, taking part in local competitions. On the social front the programme included combined evenings with other service associations. One of the regular performers at the club was Stuart Wagstaff who later became a professional actor and a household name in Australia with the television series 'Beauty and the Beast'. There were occasions when the social programme was taken too far when for instance, after a bet, two of the members wheeled a gharry horse into the bar and fed it with Blue Label ale, a favourite Maltese brew.

While I was attending my father's funeral I missed the ship's visits to Palermo and Porto Liscia. I rejoined the ship when she returned to the Grand Harbour. On the same day we were off to Civita Vecchia, the port of Rome. The highlight of this visit was the audience with Pope Pius XII. In one day we managed to see a little of the many sites of ancient Rome, the Colosseum, Castel St Angelo and the Seven Hills of Rome. Back at Malta we had just enough time to pump a few more rounds of ammunition by bombarding the tiny island of Filfla, yet again. A week later we were off to Gibraltar to start a six-week refit. There was ample time to watch the Flamenco dancing at the Trocadero and to relax at the Rock hotel. La Linea provided the opportunity for tasting the Spanish cuisine and sherry back at Dick's bodega. During this stay at Gib, I sat the examination for promotion to officer rank with other candidates. At the end of the refit we headed across the straits to Tangiers for two days. I didn't form a very good opinion

105

of this port. I have never known so many pimps on the jetty all bent on leading the way to the red light district. It was most unpleasant to have to fend off so many of them. I had heard of this city's reputation as a place for seedy bars and debauched night life and as a spying and smuggling centre and I decided that I certainly wouldn't venture ashore alone. Second only to Casablanca in importance within the Kingdom of Morocco, it was governed by the Portugese for a long period until it was partitioned by the French and Spanish before gaining independence. Cafes seemed to dominate the social life.

In keeping with the new policy of reducing the length of time away from home, we headed for Portsmouth for Christmas leave, although, in my case, I was going further away from my home. There was a special scheme for people like me called Domcol (Dominion and Colonial Leave). After a brief work-up at Portland, we headed back to Gib with a troublesome electric generator which the dockyard had repaired, so we thought. We joined the fleet for yet more war games, but not for long. The generator broke down and we headed for Marseilles prematurely, with only one other generator in service, a situation which for safety reasons was not acceptable. We had no option but to try to repair it using our own resources. Unfortunately, we didn't have the spare part to replace the broken item and one couldn't be sent from UK in the time period acceptable to the Captain. The mechanician responsible for the boiler room, where the machine was situated, didn't feel that he could repair the broken item. The Engineer Commander asked me to take the job on so I selected my team and we set about working round the clock. The repair of a broken mitre gearwheel required great skill in drilling, tapping, brazing and filing to precision against profile gauges, which we had to make ourselves. We worked from 7am to 8pm for four days, with special permission to go ashore outside the liberty hours. After the successful trials, the two Engineer Officers produced a large glass of whisky and a special recommendation from the Captain. The repaired item was eventually exhibited at the Royal Naval Engineering School at Portsmouth as an example of what could be achieved in an emergency.

Despite a busy time during the first four days, I still managed to enjoy Marseilles, living up to the engineers motto of 'Work hard, play hard and drink hard' and in any case, there were two days left after we had finished the job when we were given all day leave as a reward for our hard work. The officers were invited to a reception by the mayor. As they couldn't make up the numbers, they invited two of us to join them in an enjoyable evening of music, dancing and refreshments. We said good-bye to Marseilles and hello to the next port, Sete, a pretty little resort to the west, with a population of about 36,000. It straddles a network of canals and had a fishing port and several good quality restaurants on the quayside. On the way to Golfe San Juan, we carried out a full power trial to test the engines to their maximum speed, and headed for Malta, acting as guard ship for the aircraft carrier Centaur. On arrival, we dressed ship in honour of the Duke of Edinburgh who was on a visit to the island.

On the 27th March, 1955 we sailed for Portsmouth to spend the second half of the commission with the Home Fleet. Captain Talbot took command after a three hour hand-over from his predecessor, just in time for Navy Days. The new Captain's first task was to take the ship to Bremen in Germany, making it the first to visit that country after the war. It was a delicate assignment which had to be executed with great tact. The Germans made it easy for us with an enthusiastic welcome. Senior ratings were hosted by ratings of equivalent rank, some of them retired from the German Navy. My host, Hilde Klaus was very proud that he had served on the battleship Bismark, before she was sunk. He was also proud of the sixteen bullet marks he had on one of his legs, inflicted on him when he served on a torpedo boat. We had expected the war not to be mentioned. After a game of tennis and dinner at Fritz's home, the subject came up again. I was presented with a signed photograph of the Bismark. Hilde had a good sense of humour. He came up with expressions like 'When I was cruising up and down the Cornish Riviera in 1941'. There was no doubt that despite being our adversaries in war, they showed great admiration for the British. At a reception by the Marine Association, the main speaker, a retired Admiral, told us that he couldn't remember the number of times he had discussed the Battle of Jutland in British naval wardrooms and was still not sure who had won that battle. After telling us how much he admired the courage of the British he ended his speech by saying 'I hope that if there is to be another war, we will both be fighting on the same side' to which Captain Talbot replied with typical British diplomacy 'Let's hope there will not be another war'. We were fed with an excellent variety of German sausage and, in the beer cellars were overwhelmed by the hospitality from local people with beer provided by the gallon. In one cellar, where a number of the ship's company had gathered, we were requested to sing some English songs. When the beer started having its effect, we obliged with the rendering of traditional songs which they were probably familiar with having heard British troops singing them during the war.

Bremen, one of the principal seaports in Germany with access to the North Sea, has a naval academy and is one of the main naval training bases. The first German steamship was built in Bremen. The city was subjected to heavy bombardments by air and land forces and was captured by the British in 1945. The Town Hall, severely damaged, was being restored to its original architecture and beauty. We were taken to the Schnorr, an area surrounded by crooked lanes, fishing houses, cafes, artisan shops and art galleries. The town is also known for its Beck's brewery. From Bremen we sailed to Londonderry in Northern Ireland followed by Invergordon, where I spent so much time in HMS Implacable. Exhaustive manoeuvres with units of the Home Fleet followed.

The highlight of May 1955 was my second visit to Norway, beginning with Oslo, bringing back memories of my first visit to this beautiful city in 1949. It hadn't changed much. The people were just as hospitable and we were very well received. Visitors queued by the thousands for guided tours by the sailors, the ship being open to visitors throughout our stay. I revisited the ski jump at Holmenkollen which by now had been made more famous at the 1952 Winter Olympics. The views around the ski jump exposed the beautiful features of the Norwegian countryside and the fjords in the background. My second visit to the Viking Museum was followed by a walk round Frogner Park to admire the hundreds of sculptures.

From Oslo we sailed on a special mission to Tromso in the Arctic Circle, where I earned my first Blue Nose Certificate. In June, Tromso is not as cold as in January when the temperature averages -4 degrees C, but is warmer than most other places in the Arctic Circle due to the effect of the Gulf

Stream. The city has the highest number of wooden houses in Norway with a population of about 60,000. There is no real darkness between April and August, while from November to January the sun is absent. As we steamed through Tromso Bay we could see a large part of the wreck of the battleship Tirpitz, the biggest built in Europe before the Second World War. She was put out of action by British midget submarines off Tromsay Island and subsequently sunk by Lancaster bombers flying from Lossiemouth in the north of Scotland.

At Tromso we were to present the bell of the wartime cruiser HMS Devonshire to the city from where she had evacuated King Haakon in 1940 as the Germans were invading his country. For this purpose we took Admiral Sir John Cunningham out of retirement with us, who at the time was Captain of the cruiser. The bell was presented at the end of a football match which we played against the city with me as the referee. The game was due to start at 9pm in broad daylight, by which time most of our football team, having been drinking for most of the evening, were in no fit state to take part in such an important event. As the opposition started piling in the goals it was pretty evident that the goalkeeper was legless. It was so embarrassing that at half time the Captain sent me a message asking me whether I would make the second period shorter. It was a difficult proposition for an FA qualified referee to make, but I had to weigh off the rules against an international crisis. I must confess that I broke the rules by five minutes. The final score was in the region of 8 or 9 to nil. I, with some of my colleagues enjoyed the usual Norwegian hospitality with an invitation to a family home where we noticed that the curtains were closed and lights switched on to simulate evening darkness. After disembarking the Admiral at Rosyth in the Firth of Forth, we sailed through Scapa Flow en route to Reykjavik in Iceland where the fishing row with the Icelandic Government was about to begin. There was no doubt that our visit was part of a strategy to foster good diplomatic relations between the two countries. We were well received by the local population finding time to look at the Blue Lagoon, the most famous attraction in Reykjavik, consisting of a stretch of water surrounded by lava walls, heated to lukewarm temperature, and at Gulfers we saw the country's famous waterfall.

My time in HMS Saintes was by now drawing to a close. We were on our way to Portsmouth down the east coast of England making courtesy calls to Great Yarmouth and Hastings where the Royal Navy proved just as popular in British ports as it was in Oslo and Copenhagen. Thousands flocked to see the ship and children enjoyed the two parties we gave for them in both places. There was no shortage of volunteers from among the sailors to dress up as pirates to entertain them. Hundreds of pretty girls milled around the ship and many friendships developed as the sailors joined them ashore at the local hop, bars and at functions organised by the local authorities. The aircraft carrier Bulwark joined us off the coast of Hastings to give an exhibition of flying aircraft with Saintes as the attendant destroyer. My mother, who was in England at the time, was watching the spectacle on television. When I met her in Portsmouth she remarked 'It was so interesting to watch, especially when the black smoke started coming out of your ship's funnel'. She was not to know that, while the smoke was belching out, we were fighting a fire in the boiler room requiring us to cut down the air supply, preventing the proper combustion of the fuel by starving the boiler furnaces of oxygen. On Saturday morning the Lord Mayor of Hastings was invited on board. As he was about to step into the ship's boat he slipped and fell into the water. The Sunday newspapers had a field day with photographs, one showing a sailor dragging him out of the water and the caption 'The mayor takes a ducking'.

The climax of my three years in the ship came when I met the Stores Petty Officer ashore. He congratulated me and told me that he had seen my name in the latest Admiralty Fleet Order on a list of successful candidates for promotion to officer rank. I immediately returned to the ship to seek confirmation from my Engineer Officer. It so happened that the new Squadron Engineer Commander, who was on the Examining Board, had a private copy of the result. After confirmation that I had indeed been successful, I was invited to the wardroom to celebrate with a stiff gin and tonic. The ship paid off at Portsmouth where I left and headed for barracks for further instructions and the beginning of a new life.

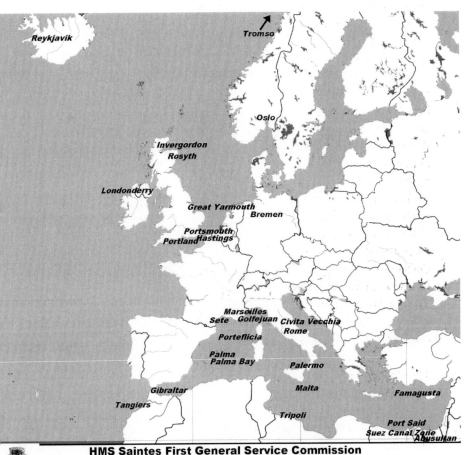

HMS Saintes First General Service Commission
May 1954—August 1955

HMS Saintes.

The Bedouins guide us on our way to the passage leading to Petra (on mule left).

112

First batch of West Indian immigrants to Britain arriving on the Empire Windrush.

The ship on fire seen from the starboard side.

Shackling on the tow line.

On tow.

Ship starts to list.

A scorching Hull.

At the Bremen Marine Association reception, fourth from left.

The battleship Bismark.

CHAPTER 9

THE ROYAL NAVAL ENGINEERING COLLEGE

I spent four months at the Naval Barracks in Portsmouth waiting for the beginning of a new stage in my Naval career and my officer's uniform. Throughout this period I, with several other ERAs in transit, was employed at the Royal Naval Marine Engineering School and Repair Base at Portsmouth doing odd jobs. I knew that the course which I was to undergo at the Royal Naval Engineering College at Manadon, Crownhill, in Devon, included subjects containing a large element of calculus so I attended the Portsmouth Polytechnic to brush up on this aspect of mathematics which subsequently served me well during the course. On changing uniforms on 1st February, 1956, together with the other successful candidates, I was transferred to the Barracks Wardroom to acclimatise to the new life until our transfer to college.

Life in HMS Thunderer, in Crownhill was pretty relaxed. There was plenty of opportunity for sports and relaxation in between what was to be an advanced course in Marine Engineering. As part of the General Knowledge syllabus we were taught wardroom etiquette, including how to hold a knife and fork at the dinner table, to stay sitting during the toast to the Queen and how to make a bow tie, reminding us of the penalty to be paid if caught wearing a ready-made one, costing several drinks to fellow officers.

The tradition of remaining seated during the Royal Toast dates from the days of Queen Victoria. One evening while dining with the Commander-In-Chief and Officers on HMS Victory at Portsmouth, she noticed that some tall officers were standing uncomfortably, bending as they stood up, struggling to avoid hitting the deck head. She beckoned them to sit down, granting a privilege which has prevailed to this day.

We had to learn how to parade as officers and how to march while holding a sword, taking it in turn to lead the class at the weekly Divisions on the parade ground. One of the drills was to march past and salute the Captain as he stood on the dais. During the drill the class had to perform a delicate manoeuvre when the officer in charge, using his sword, ordered the class to turn left at a position only a few feet from the pavement. When it came to my turn, I was late giving the order, 'Division turn left in single file' resulting in everyone marching a few steps over the pavement and the slope beyond. They scattered like confetti before they turned around and formed ranks again. Blushing with embarrassment, I just managed to salute the Captain with my sword and give the order, 'Eyes right'. Obviously, at that stage, I was not a candidate fit to replace the Gunnery officer.

The Course at College was intensive and complex, requiring total commitment and a great deal of concentration during lectures by some of the cleverest brains in the Navy. At that time the college was not classified as a University. It was granted that status three years later. Although I'd prepared for the course with some hard work at the Portsmouth Polytechnic, I struggled to absorb the Advanced Theory of Thermodynamics. The theory was put into practice at the Steam Plant at Keyham, which formed part of the old college at Plymouth Dockyard. Results of machinery performance had to be proved against the theory by the completion of charts and trials sheets. It was an entirely different world to that which I had been used to, working against the background of my training as an apprentice at the Royal Naval Dockyard and Technical College and the numerous Courses in Practical Marine Engineering. To keep up with classroom work and tuition I had to swot hard in the evenings and at week-ends. The General Engineering lectures, given by specialist lecturers, covered a variety of machinery likely to be fitted in most RN Ships, with a totally different approach to what I had been used to. I enjoyed the course, but felt it a pity that it didn't last longer. We were given a short course on public speaking when we all had to speak on a chosen subject. I selected the visit of the Russian President and the Secretary of the Communist Party, Bulganin and Khrushchev, and the embarrassing situation when the frogman Commander 'Buster' Crabb was discovered under the cruiser Ordzhonikdze which was carrying the two leaders of the Soviet Union, ostensibly 'carrying out trials of certain equipment' in Portsmouth Harbour. Commander Crabb disappeared during the operation and was presumed drowned. I did not fare too well. I quoted the wrong place where they'd landed in Britain. When the speech was relayed back to the class I was surprised how noticeable my Maltese accent was. I was brought up speaking English and Maltese in equal measure. I'm often thought to be Welsh or Irish.

Each class had to take part in inter-class and staff competitions and make up the numbers. I had to play in my first rugby match where I was completely lost and have never played the game since. However, I soon started captaining the college water polo team, playing all the league matches in the Plymouth Command, just missing winning the competition at the final. I joined the cricket team, playing village cricket against several teams at some beautiful Devon villages around the college and against the Plymouth Constabulary, who escorted us back safely to college after a heavy drinking session. The college had a number of tennis courts where I enjoyed playing in the evenings. During that year, 1956, when England was playing Australia for the Ashes at Old Trafford, word was passed around that the Aussies were collapsing. We were given special permission to watch the match on television before we attended afternoon lectures. Jim Laker, in one of the most memorable matches against Australia, took 19 of the 20 wickets. There was keen interest in sailing. Two 35 foot yachts, which were taken from the Germans as part of the war reparations, were in the custody of the college. I was asked to join the crew of 'Gauntlet' for the Plymouth to Teignmouth race as the cook and deck hand. Our skipper decided to head way out in the open sea while the other skipper on 'Gallahad' decided to race close to shore. He won the race and returned to Plymouth. As for us, we found ourselves sailing in thick fog in a choppy sea, landing in the midst of the tall ships flotilla during their first ever race from Torbay to Lisbon. Emergency stations were called as we took it in turn to sound the fog horn repeatedly. Life for the two midshipmen became almost intolerable as the sea got rougher, compounded by the smell of sausages and bacon which I was cooking. When it was realised that we were overdue in Plymouth, alarm bells sounded at college and a search was ordered. We could hear the sound of a helicopter hovering over us but couldn't see it. We were completely helpless as we drifted along. After three days and when the fog had cleared, we headed for Teignmouth to finish a disappointing last but able to communicate with the college. On return to Plymouth we discovered that worried mothers and sweethearts had been anxiously seeking news of our whereabouts as we faced the perils of the sea! Of course nobody bothered about me. Thousands of miles away, my mother wouldn't have known that I was lost in the fog!

During my time at college, I bought an old 1936 Austin 12 for £40 from an Australian officer who was leaving. It was falling apart and the engine needed a major overhaul. The whole class, knowing that a car would be quite useful for travelling around, descended on the engine and renewed all the moving parts. When we finished the overhaul, the engine was as good as a new, but the body was in a bad state. All this was well before the MOT was introduced. It was my first car and, as a learner, I relied on friends to teach me how to drive. I was at that time commuting from Plymouth to Portsmouth at most week ends, driven by a different driver on each occasion. After taking some lessons I was ready for my test. At the last minute, the person who was to take me for the test couldn't make it and a midshipman, a complete stranger, took his place. During the test the car kept wobbling all over the place, the effect of missing and loose wheel spokes, the signal direction indicators kept sticking and the back doors were firmly held together by a half inch rope. I had to resort to winding down the window to give hand signals and I feared that I may have failed. When the examiner gave his verdict he said 'Mate, if you can drive this, you can drive any car'. I was duly pronounced a qualified driver.

On one occasion, while I was still a learner, driven by a colleague on the way to Portsmouth, we were approaching Dorchester following an ambulance. The driver remarked 'We'll be OK now if we have an accident' after which he lost concentration for a moment and crashed straight into the back of it, carrying a woman being driven to hospital to give birth. On another occasion, as I was driving from Portsmouth, the car in front stopped abruptly. I took evasive action but still managed to rip across its whole length. I couldn't find a scratch on my car. They used to make them out of thick steel in 1936 and the running board had the ideal cutting edge. But the car became useful for other reasons. I even lent it to a friend as a wedding present. Later it played a prominent part in my courtship with the girl who eventually became my wife. I was sad to have to dispense with it when I was due to join my next ship. I left it in the hands of the Roman Catholic padre at Rosyth who sold it for me for £50, making a profit of ten pounds.

Crownhill in Plymouth was surrounded by beautiful countryside and picturesque villages with small pubs presenting a peaceful, quiet and relaxing atmosphere. The social life at college was excellent with frequent mess dinners, cocktail parties, treasure hunts and a variety of other activities, with or without ladies. At one of the pubs we met two New Zealand girls who were in the UK on a promotion visit to advertise a particular brand of butter. We nicknamed them 'The Butter girls'. They were great fun. My 1936 Austin 12 was proving useful!

On one occasion Lord Louis Mountbatten, The First Sea Lord, came to speak to us about the future of the Royal Navy and the new generation of ships to be built refusing to start speaking until the press reporters left the auditorium. He described how on one occasion he went to see the Prime Minister, Harold Wilson, to ask for his approval to build eight Guided Missile Cruisers equipped with a new system of propulsion and the introduction of the Gas Turbine. The Prime Minister rejected the idea on the grounds that cruisers were now too heavy and cumbersome unsuitable for modern warfare. Mountbatten told him that he would go away, reconsider his proposal and consult the designers and the Board of the Admiralty. Six months later he called on the Prime minister to tell him that the Board had decided to build eight destroyers instead. He told us that those destroyers were the same eight cruisers of the same tonnage and equipment. He had just changed the name from cruiser to destroyer. The Prime Minister agreed, the decision giving birth to the eight Guided Missile Town Class Destroyers.

The Suez Canal crises flared up while I was at college. Four Egyptian officers were under training. With my knowledge of the Maltese language, I was asked to sit next to them at lunch and dinner and listen to any discussion which may be of use to our Intelligence. I had already spoken to them on a few occasions to experiment with speaking to them in Maltese to gauge the similarity between the two languages. But they were soon on their way to Egypt.

The course was nearing its end and we were all waiting anxiously for our results and our first Captain's report as officers, as well as the Admiralty Appointment List showing our postings. I was given a good report. We were advised that two of us would be transferred to the Submarine Service. Having had the experience and pleasure of serving with submariners I would not have minded joining that distinguished service. As it turned out I was appointed to the cruiser HMS Gambia which was undergoing a major refit and modernisation at Rosyth Dockyard in Scotland. This appointment was to have a significant effect on my future life. At our last meeting as a class we wished each other good luck and parted, going in different directions to our respective ships as officers.

Divisions on the College parade ground.

The College water polo team including Chilean, Canadian and Australian
midshipmen and the PT instructor, a sergeant in the Royal Marines
(front row left).

123

CHAPTER 10

MY FIRST APPOINTMENT AS AN OFFICER

Meeting the Perfect Partner
The Fleet Review at Invergordon
The East Indies Commission

After loading my belongings into my Austin 12, and replacing the loose spokes in the four wheels, I travelled to Rosyth in Scotland, some four hundred miles away from Plymouth. I had been appointed to HMS Gambia which was refitting in the dockyard. The skeleton crew standing by the refit were accommodated at HMS Cochrane, a shore establishment at Donibristle, a few miles away from Rosyth. On arrival I was greeted by the Senior Engineer who came to meet me from Dunfermline where he lived. It was a kind gesture by someone who I came to know as a fine gentleman. On the following day I took the bus, with others, to see the ship for the first time and meet the officers and ratings with whom I was to work for the next two years. The ship was undergoing modernisation to deal with the nuclear threat as well as a major overhaul of its main machinery. I was given the junior engineer's job of looking after spare parts, motor boats, domestic equipment and machinery outside the main machinery compartments. I soon got used to the routine of boarding the bus from Cochrane to the dockyard, returning for lunch, back to the ship and returning to Donibristle at 5pm.

HMS Gambia was built at Swan Hunters in Wallsend on Tyneside and launched in 1942. She had a displacement of 8000 tons and was driven by two steam turbines with a total of 72,000 shaft horsepower with a complement of 650. In 1943 she was loaned to the New Zealand Navy until 1946. Her refit began in early 1956 and I joined her in July of that year. She was the first ship to be based in Rosyth. The thinking behind this idea was that Scottish personnel, and those living in the North of England, would welcome the opportunity to be closer to home rather than in the three home ports of Portsmouth, Plymouth and Chatham. As it turned out, the authorities could only find 25% of the crew to volunteer to serve in her. It was evident that most Scots who were drafted to the other three ports married English girls or were quite happy to be stationed down south. However, the ship had the advantage of being adopted by Rosyth, receiving special treatment.

Life at Cochrane was pretty relaxed with plenty of sporting activities and entertainment in the wardroom as well as some attractive pubs in the area. I had to use my car sparingly as the Suez Canal war had just started and petrol was rationed. On one occasion the General Manager of the dockyard paid us a visit while we were having coffee. He was the President of the Rosyth Dockyard Operatic Society and had come to recruit some men for the chorus of their production of Gilbert and Sullivan's 'Yeomen of the Guard'. He was sure, he told us, that some officers would enjoy the chance to join while the ship was refitting. A few officers could read music and were keen, but getting to Dunfermline from Donibristle for rehearsals was difficult. As I was the only one with a car they tried to talk me into joining. The only trouble was that I couldn't sing a note and I was adamant that I wouldn't join.

One evening, after a cocktail party at Cochrane, we all met at the Officers Club in Rosyth and after a few drinks they had talked me into it. Needless to say, on the following morning I woke regretting my decision and dreading my first rehearsal. Little did I know at the time what effect that decision was going to have on my future life. On the day when I had to 'face the music' I didn't have a clue what the musical director was saying. I pretended that I was singing but I wasn't. I volunteered to serve drinks and sandwiches from the top of a grand piano during the break. I was very impressed, however, by the standard of singing and I expressed my views to one of my colleagues who said 'Wait till you hear the leading lady.' That leading lady was a pretty, young girl of seventeen. Her name was Margaret McRae, well known for her singing across Fife and beyond. I wasn't looking forward to dressing up and was mortified when I found myself wearing a pair of yellow, baggy trousers, a frilly jacket and a flat hat with wavy trimming. On her first entrance I, accompanied by a group of men, had to drag Elsie, the leading lady, on to the stage. That young girl eventually became my wife. We celebrated our golden wedding anniversary in 2009.

I introduced myself properly when, on Christmas Eve I saw her preparing the crib for Midnight Mass in the little church in Aberdour, not far from Donibristle. According to my wife, while she was walking down the drive to catch her bus home, I rattled up beside her in my old Austin, wound the window down and said, 'You don't know me but I know you. You're Elsie in the Yeomen of the Guard. Would you like a lift?' Apparently, she took a chance on me, as she knew I'd just been to confession and assumed I was of sound character. She has since teased me, reminding me that, when we reached Donibristle, I admitted that I didn't have enough petrol to take her to Rosyth and left her at a bus stop, miles away from where she wanted to go!

My courtship with Margaret made progress as she started joining me at wardroom functions and meetings at the Officers Club. Our friendship developed to such an extent that I plucked up the courage to ask her to marry me. I had never met her father who was, at the time, serving in Malta with the Admiralty. When Margaret's mother wrote to him telling him of my intentions, he couldn't believe that his little girl who he had left behind two years earlier, still at school, was planning to get married. I arranged for my mother and the rest of my family to meet him in Malta which they did on several occasions. He was so impressed by my family that he wrote giving his blessing for our engagement.

The Yeomen of the Guard was a roaring success with full houses for six nights at the Carnegie Hall in Dunfermline. Margaret was applauded by the Fife newspapers and the Scottish Daily Express for her singing. Soon after the show, I took her to Leeds where she was to audition for the Doyle Carte Opera Company. After they'd heard her sing, she was invited to re-audition in a year's time. In the meantime, she had a decision to make. With me sailing round the world and she travelling with an opera company, normal married life would have been difficult. She had a choice to make. She decided to go ahead with the engagement, making the day she told me one of the happiest of my life.

Having a car was a big advantage during the refit. I was able, with friends and Margaret, to take advantage of the beautiful Scottish scenery, travelling to the Trossachs, Pitlochry, Fort William and Braemar. Occasionally, in the company of the Dental Officer, carrying his shotgun, we went shooting hares around Gleneagles which he did through the open car windows. The wardroom was treated to jugged hare ad infinitum. The car engine was performing remarkably well, but I was experiencing problems with the body and the wheels in particular. I took Margaret on a long drive to Southsea to meet one of my uncles, an ex-naval officer, and his family. On reaching Guildford, I came to a roundabout when the car seemed to bear heavily to one side. The police, who were following, stopped me and proceeded to check the steering system which they duly found to be tight and passed the test. What they didn't know was that several spokes in the wheels were loose causing the car to weave about as it turned. I stopped at the nearest garage to have them tightened, preventing them from causing more punctures to the inner tubes of the tyres. On another occasion, on our way back from a tour of the Trossachs, smoke started to rise from under the passenger's seat where Margaret was sitting. Due to a short across the battery, which was located under her seat, the lead contacts were melting away and had set the seat on fire. I stopped the car, smothered the fire and hammered the lead contacts from my spare battery on to the melting lead, arriving back just in time to get to a cocktail party at HMS Cochrane.

The ship was now nearing the end of the refit. Once the engine harbour trials proved satisfactory, the crew moved to live permanently on board, the complement gradually grew to full strength, and the ship was painted and cleaned in readiness for the Commissioning Ceremony. On the 1st of May, 1957, watched by hundreds of guests and families, at 1355 the Captain and the Commander, his second-in-command, took their post on the quarterdeck facing aft. At 1400 the signalman reported 'Four Bells Sir'. The Officer of the Watch ordered 'Make it so'. As the first bell was made the Commissioning Pennant was broken at the foremast and the National Anthem was played. Then the Ensign Staff was hoisted. No commissioning is complete without a service, held immediately after the parade, conducted by the Church of England Chaplain, followed by the Captain who addressed the ship's company. To end the proceedings, the band from HMS Fulmar, the Fleet Air Arm base at Lossiemouth in the North of Scotland 'Beat Retreat'. The next fortnight was devoted to training the crew at sea and testing the propulsion equipment and weapons to prepare for joining the Fleet which we did at Invergordon in 'Operation Steadfast', employing all the devices of warfare, including submarines, aircraft and all kinds of surface ships. With the rest of the fleet we anchored at Invergordon to tidy the ship in readiness for a special occasion. The ship was dressed with flags tied to a continuous wire rope, stretching from the bows to the main masts and to the stern as did all other ships. Intensive rehearsals commenced in preparation for the big event. The 27th May, 1957 was a beautiful day, one with 'Royal Weather' as one newspaper said, and Gambia found herself in a flat, calm sea and clear blue skies, following four aircraft carriers. The Fleet had formed into two columns with the C-in-C flying his flag in Apollo in the centre. At 1130, Britannia hove in sight with her escorting destroyers. The fleet closed range to two and a half miles and fired a co-ordinated Royal Salute. Immediately the two columns wheeled outward, increasing speed to 21 knots, then forming into a single column, manned and cheered ship, passing the Britannia at a distance of half a cable. The Glasgow Herald described the scene. 'Aboard the Gambia the bugles shrilled the Royal Salute, and as the cheers rolled across the short intervening distance, the Queen smiled and waved, while Prince Philip saluted. They were standing on the saluting platform forward of the bridge. The Queen was hatless and was wearing a dark blue coat'. The Fleet then formed up to escort Britannia into Cromarty Firth at a speed of 12 knots. On passage, four submarines passed through the columns on an opposite course, manning and cheering ship. The final salute was given by 71 aircraft from the carriers. Flying in perfect formation, the Sea Hawks and Sea Venoms displayed the Queen's cipher of EIIR, and the Wyverns and Gannets followed in diamond formation. Considering the different speeds of the various aircraft, their timing and co-ordination was perfect. Royal Divisions took place on the following day. A number of officers and ratings from each ship were ferried to the aircraft carrier Ocean to be inspected on the flight deck by Her Majesty. With Prince Philip, she was slowly driven in a Land Rover around the assembled divisions. That evening, after a reception in Britannia, Her Majesty was entertained in the hangar of another aircraft carrier by a combined Home Fleet Concert Party. Gambia was well represented by her own Skiffle Group, aptly named 'The Gambets'. It may be of interest to music lovers to know that a recording of 'The Gambets' was played on the BBC Light Programme and the European network, including the Iron Curtain countries, their efforts described in several languages.

The Dockyard civilian stores officer was still on board, finishing the storing of the ship in readiness for service in the East Indies. He was keen to watch the Review from the upper deck but was not allowed in civilian clothes, so I loaned him one of my uniforms and he took up his station. Fortunately, nobody outside the ship noticed that we had broken the Queen's Regulations by allowing an 'officer' to wear a moustache, breaking the golden rule that only beards may be worn. By co-incidence that 'officer' was the father of a close friend of Margaret's who was later to be chief bridesmaid at our wedding.

On the next day we said goodbye to the Queen and displayed our loyalty and affection by falling in on the Quarterdeck to give three cheers as the Royal Barge passed. Two days after the Review, we proceeded independently to Rosyth for six days, before sailing for Chatham where we arrived on Prince Philip's birthday when we dressed ship again. From Chatham we moved on to Portland for a short 'Work Up' with the Training Squadron, practising fuelling at sea, Jackstay transfers and war exercises of all kinds to prepare for possible hostilities when we deployed to the East Indies. We ended by anchoring at Spithead, giving an opportunity to the Portsmouth natives to visit their families as we had at Chatham. We then joined with an aircraft carrier and a small task force for yet more exercises in the Skagerak before returning to Rosyth. From Rosyth we proceeded to Buchie and Lock Eriball for firing practice, anchoring between shoots. There was not much for the sailors to do in this remote part of Scotland so banyans (picnics) were organised and a few sailors were taken ashore by the ship's boats. Our chief steward went ashore to buy fresh fish and lobsters. Jack has a knack for finding booze, even in a place as remote as Eriball. They discovered a whisky distillery. From what transpired when they returned on board, they must have drunk gallons of it. Fighting between the sailors was reported from shore and patrols were sent out to restore order. As the sailors started returning, fights developed on the Quarterdeck. The Master-at-Arms and his staff had to be augmented by seamen from the Gunnery Department. Several sailors were put under close arrest and the two ship's doctors, assisted by the dental officer, got down to the task of patching up the wounded, some very drunk and difficult to handle. This was not a good start to the commission and some of the troublemakers continued to cause disruption throughout our time abroad. On one occasion, at Aden, vital parts of the anchor capstan engine were thrown overboard, necessitating Admiralty detectives to be flown from UK to investigate. As heads became clearer and calm was restored, we sailed to Cape Wyatt for a bombardment and torpedo firing practice, returning to Rosyth prior to sailing for Bergen in Norway for my second visit to that beautiful city.

At dawn on Monday 22nd July, 1957, Gambia steamed up the Bergen Fjord in calm waters, quiet but for the sound of the engines of Norwegian fishing boats going about their business, to secure alongside at Skoltegrunnen Kalen. We berthed in the old part of the town, dominated by the Bergenus Fort. The cathedral there has an English cannon ball embedded in its wall dating from 1665 when the Earl of Sandwich bombarded the harbour. Our sight-seeing trips took us to the famous market in the large square, selling fish in the morning and flowers and vegetables in the afternoon. From the narrow, cobbled roads of this part of town, we saw a change of character when these opened out into broad, dual carriageways and the small shops gave way to large, modern department stores. Many of us were tempted by the souvenir shops and bought a variety of goods on offer. The Floyen funicular railway was popular from where we enjoyed a panoramic view of Bergen from a height of 1050 feet. We were treated to free showings at the cinemas, sightseeing tours daily and a dance every evening. But the most enjoyable part of the entertainment was the hospitality offered to us at private homes to which many of us were invited. Out of town, the most popular trip was to Edward Grieg's home alongside the beautiful Nordas Lake where I'd been on a previous occasion. I was happy to re-visit and was glad I did, because I learned much more about the life of this great composer. Seeing the place which had inspired his music made it easier to appreciate and understand it. Some 150 children attended a party on board and our sailors made a collection, enough to fill a suitcase with sweets to donate to the local hospital to children who couldn't attend. The Royal Marines sounded the Last Post and Reveille at a memorial service when the Captain laid a wreath at the British War Memorial. Besides playing on entering and leaving harbour, they played at the Captain's dinner party, they 'Beat Retreat' in the centre of the town and gave a band concert, drawing large crowds. Floodlit at night, the ship made a beautiful sight in the dark waters of the harbour.

Sporting events made up an important part of our programme during our stay. I captained the swimming team at an aquatic meeting. We had built up a good water polo team and I was anxious that we should test it against strong opposition. At first, the Norwegians were reluctant, but we managed to change their minds. The swimming pool had been erected alongside a jetty in the sea where the water was extremely cold. At that time, a game of water polo could last as long as 40 minutes. Although actual playing time was seven minutes, each of the two periods of play could go on for up to 20 minutes as the referee stopped his watch for every infringement. We managed to beat them, but at a cost. Emerging from the water, teeth chattering in the seemingly freezing temperature, we ran straight to the dressing room to warm up under a hot shower, where we were alarmed to discover that our nether parts had shrunk to such an extent that they had almost disappeared. Luckily the damage was not permanent! We realised then why the opposition had been reluctant to play.

Just as we'd learned to say 'tak' and 'skol', the ship was underway. On the last day, after church service, attended by several British residents, Gambia slipped away from her berth. As crowds waved us good bye from the jetty, we steamed out of Bergen down the fjord, as the Norwegian ensign, flown from houses, dipped in salute as if to say, 'Will ye no come back again'. We wished we could.

We arrived at Rosyth on the following day in time to give Summer Leave during the month of August. For my leave I stayed at the Officers' Club, a stone's throw from Margaret's home. In early September we sailed west to join in exercise 'Turtle and Mushroom' with the Home Fleet and American ships, attaching to a group of four aircraft carriers on a continuous zigzagging course ending at Helensborough, giving the Glaswegians and others living in the vicinity, some time to spend at home. On the 21st September, 1957 we crossed the Arctic Circle, which brought me my second 'Blue Nose Certificate'. An Asian Flu epidemic, which started at Helesborough, when a rating returned on board carrying the potent virus, had by now spread right around the ship, incapacitating a large proportion of the ship's company, including me. We were forced to break off from the exercise, flying the yellow quarantine flag. On anchoring in the Firth of Forth nobody was allowed ashore. The ship was thoroughly disinfected and medical assistance provided. When the epidemic subsided we moved into harbour and berthed alongside at Rosyth Dockyard for the final preparations before leaving for the Middle East.

The ship was now operating as an integrated unit with all departments fully trained to face any emergency during the next year as the last Flagship of The East Indies Station. All departments, including the seamen, engineering, weapons, navigation, communication, education, laundry, galley and other domestic facilities were functioning smoothly. The store rooms were fully replenished. Sports teams at cricket, soccer, hockey, aquatics, rugby, volleyball, and rifle shooting were formed. Before we left Rosyth we embarked Goenese wardroom cooks and stewards. Most officers said they looked forward to curried food every day, but as we sailed away from UK shores, the enthusiasts started dropping off one by one. Requests for curry were replaced by requests for salad. But the Goenese cooks were just as good at cooking English food. During my time in the service I tasted food cooked by Goenese, Indian and Chinese long before their national diets became popular in Britain.

On the 7th October, 1957, HMS Gambia slipped quietly from her moorings and sailed down the East coast of Britain, stopping at Chatham for nine days, giving a last opportunity to some members of the crew to see their families until our return in a year's time. Although the prevailing atmosphere was one of sadness as officers and men thought of their families and friends who they would not see for another year, we consoled ourselves with the thought that we were to be spared the rigours of winter at home in favour of the azure and gold of the Indian Ocean. We sailed between the mud banks of the Medway to the Channel across the Bay of Biscay, past the coast of Portugal close enough to see the mouth of the Tagus and the city of Lisbon. On the morning of the 21st, Trafalgar Day, we actually passed through the very waters where the battle had taken place over 150 years before. Later that same day we arrived at Gibraltar in bright sunshine and changed into tropical rig, for many, the first time in their naval career, wearing white shirts, shorts and socks. Although we only stayed for a few hours, most of the ship's company took the opportunity of a quick run ashore, for some their first experience of 'going foreign', for others, the revisiting of old haunts. In the wardroom we just had time to celebrate the traditional Trafalgar Night and drink to 'The Immortal Memory of Lord Horatio Nelson' over a glass of port. We left Gibraltar that same night and headed East across a flat calm Mediterranean under a clear starlit sky. The next few days were idyllic, as our skin tanned in the brilliant sunshine. On the 24th we passed close to Malta, unable to call in, to the disappointment of many, especially me, unable to visit my home. A helicopter delivered some long-awaited mail.

In the late evening of the 26th, we anchored for a short while at Port Said. All my relatives, who I used to call on regularly on previous visits, had gone. At just past midnight we led a convoy of tankers and cargo vessels into the Canal, the first warship to do so since the Suez debacle, observing the desert and its inhabitants. Midway, there was a welcome pause for a swim in the very warm waters of the Bitter Lakes. Many who swallowed the accidental mouthful of salty water can vouch for the aptness of its name. As we entered the Red Sea we could feel the hot air, made bearable by a slight cool head of wind. We anchored for a few hours off Kamaran Island, a port of call for many Mecca-bound pilgrims. After a voyage of about 5000 miles we arrived in Aden and began preparations to become the flagship. We embarked a number of local Somali stokers and seamen to be employed in keeping the ship clean and painted and preserve the machinery compartments' bilges during our time on the Station.

For the next year Aden was our main base. After the loss of the Suez Canal, it became the main British base in the region. A natural harbour lying in the crater of an extinct volcano, it was ceded to the British by the Sultan in 1838. Royal Marines landed there to protect British shipping, on the way to India, against attacks by pirates. Until 1937 it was ruled as part of British India when, at the Aden Settlement, it became the Aden Protectorate. Insurgence against the British started in December 1962, when the British High Commissioner was killed. Mass riots followed in 1967 and the British pulled out. It was renamed the People's Republic of South Yemen. In 1970, after unification with the north it was renamed the People's Republic of Yemen and in 1990 the Republic of Yemen. The ship was to return to Aden on a number of occasions, in one instance at full speed, to deal with an emergency.

We spent a few days in Aden, anchored at Steamer Point. We were invited to the RAF Officers messes, where we befriended a number of officers and their spouses who regularly invited us to their homes. On leaving, we sailed close to the coast which appeared to be baked, grim and desolate until we sighted the barren coastline of Iran and the Strait of Hormoz at the entrance to the Persian Gulf, and anchored off Bahrain in sight of HMS Ceylon, wearing the flag of the Commander-in-Chief. At sunset on the 6th November, 1957 we took over the flag, and on the following day we manned forward to give 'Ceylon' three mighty cheers to speed her on her way home.

Bahrain was at that time the only 'home from home' in the Gulf. The Sheik, a loyal old man who was very pro-British, was delighted to give the Navy a small piece of his island when the Persians asked us to vacate our base at Bushire in 1936, where we set up a small Naval Base which housed the Resident Naval Officer. There was a large compound on the island of Awali where thousands of employees from the British and American oil companies lived with their families in comparative luxury. They looked after us very well. Nothing was lacking. There were air-conditioned cinemas and a theatre, swimming pools, facilities for most sports, restaurants and cafes and shopping centres making it feel like a small town. We took every opportunity to visit the friends we made, even if it was just to get away from the hot and humid conditions on board. At that time ships were not air-conditioned. The heat and humidity in the Gulf was unbearable.

We sailed for Basra after a daylight passage up the Shat-al-Arab. The landline on the Iranian side of the river was formed by mountains, while on the Iraq side the desert stretched as far as the eye could see. At Basra, we could see what the Iraqis were doing with their oil revenue. Large buildings were under construction over a large area, mainly built by the British and Americans. We found time to socialise with the expatriate community enjoying the usual hospitality given and received, including a children's party held on board and daily visits to the ship for those interested. We gave our first performance of 'On the Quarterdeck', Gambia's contribution to the world of art and comedy, which improved with every performance throughout the commission. The ceremonial awning was rigged for a cocktail party given by the captain and officers to the British community and local dignitaries. A few days later, we moved about thirty miles downstream to Abadan past an endless succession of palm trees, mud huts and dhows moored to the bank of the river. Abadan relied mainly on its huge oil refinery due to be taken over by a national company within five years. Tours were organised to show us how a great refinery works. Wherever we went, the British community were delighted to see us, their hospitality unlimited. After five days of near-suffocation by a smell like rotten eggs coming from the refinery and a prevailing wind which had no mercy on us, we cast off and made our way down the dark brown river, twisting and turning past the lines of fishing stakes, fishermen's huts and dhows. Two days from Abadan, we arrived at Umm Said, anchoring just off the palace of the Sheik. One purpose of our visit to this Sheikdom, and other places around the area, was to reassure the British Communities that they hadn't been forgotten and that help was at hand in the event of any trouble. In fact, a strike was on when we arrived at Umm Said. The local Arabs complained that it was costing them too much to travel to work at the Oil Refinery. An over-nervous political agent, who couldn't look after us properly and deal with the strike at the same time, felt that our presence was causing him embarrassment so we left prematurely.

We were visiting several countries around the Persian Gulf at a time when they had started to feel that the time had come for them to take charge of their own destiny. A considerable amount of reconstruction was taking place everywhere we went, desert land being replaced by high rise buildings and wide boulevards. Already a worker in Doha was, by comparison, paid more than in any other country in the world. On the other hand, any local out-of-work spent his days living in a hut made of empty oil drums, tending one or two scraggy goats. During recent visits to Abu Dhabi, Dubai and Qatar I was amazed at the transformation that has taken place since I visited them some fifty years ago when most land was barren desert. We liked to think that our presence in one of the Navy's most unpopular parishes, with the raw material of much of the world's wealth but also its troubles, enabled us to foster some friendship with the local population while at the same time reassuring the British communities that we hadn't forgotten them.

We had to abandon the visit to Dubai, our next planned destination, as the place had just been devastated when it was struck by a tropical hailstorm.

136

We by-passed what was at that time a small town and made instead for Khasab Bay and the small but exclusive Arab Khor-Kwai on the Western side of the Musandan Peninsula. This was a fishing village with a community of about three hundred, presided over by a Wali who ruled from a large impressive mud fort flying his personal large, tattered flag. Nobody went ashore except the Commander who made a personal call on the Wali who in turn called on the C-in-C with his three young sons, one ten years old, and the inevitable fierce looking bodyguard who placed himself confidently, rifle at the ready, at the top of the ladder leading to the Admiral's quarters. In the meantime word had got out that all wasn't well at Umm Said. We weighed anchor and made for Bahrain at full speed with the intention of embarking a number of Cameroonians in case they were needed. But by the time we arrived at Bahrain the situation had improved making it unnecessary for the army to be taken on board. And so, after fuelling, we were on our way again, this time to join in 'Exercise Crescent' with nation members of the Bagdad Pact, including Turkey, Pakistan, Persia and the United States. Unlike the unpleasant and complex exercises in the Atlantic and Mediterranean, with numerous warships participating, this was a comparatively small exercise. The general idea was that we were protecting a convoy as it was attacked by aircraft and submarines. The tactical side of the battle was interesting, providing much needed practice for the guns crews and the Control and Operations Room personnel, but it was the men in the boiler and engine rooms who sweated most. To them, and many in the ship, the lessons learned were invaluable although at times tedious. By the fourth day everyone was pretty well exhausted and glad to make for harbour. That meant Karachi, where we arrived on Friday 6th December, 1957.

Karachi gave me my first glimpse of life in Pakistan. Ten years after partition, the city was undergoing a massive programme of expansion and reconstruction to become the gateway to that young country. Long wharfs were occupied by merchant ships where cranes busily emptied and filled their holds. Most products in the shops seemed to have come from behind the Iron Curtain. We gave a cocktail party under the ceremonial awning on the quarterdeck for local dignitaries and the British community. Knowing that I was the senior naval soccer qualified referee, one of the guests, the English captain of the main Naval Shore Base, asked me to referee the

Pakistan Navy cup final. After the match, a boat manned by a Pakistan crew, took me back to the ship. It is a tradition that when a foreign officer visits an RN ship he is piped on board. The Officer of the Day, a Royal Marine Lieutenant, looking through his telescope as the boat was approaching, informed the Commander that a foreign officer was about to visit the ship. A guard of honour, including the Commander and a piping party was formed. I ascended the gangway step by step. As my head popped out on the quarterdeck the order was given 'Pipe'. As soon as they saw my face the piping stopped and everyone burst out laughing. I had been, with my dark skin, mistaken for a Pakistani Officer. Another incident involved two young American officers who were guests at the cocktail party. American ships are dry and their officers look forward to coming to our wardrooms knowing they will be treated to alcoholic drinks. Two midshipmen had drunk more than they could take and got so drunk that they were incapable of leaving the ship. After consultations with their senior officers, they were kept on board until the following morning when a boat was sent to collect them in the early hours to take them back to their ships to face the consequences. We played soccer, cricket and tennis against Pakistan naval teams. At the regatta we won all the races. When their crews came on board for the presentation of the trophies, and in keeping with naval tradition, we greeted them with a guard of honour of sailors holding brooms over their heads to emphasise 'a clean sweep'.

The scope of entertainment ashore was limited by the high cost of living and the distance we had to travel to get to the city centre. We had to decide which mode of transport to use, a taxi, a horse-drawn gharry or a mechanical rickshaw. The owners of these three means of travel indulged in haggling for our custom with us as the principal victims. We opted for the cheapest and placed ourselves in the hands of the scootershaw. We passed by squalid squatters' shacks made of a few boxes and some sacking by the roadside, the price paid for a divided country. After partition, the population of Karachi was increased overnight by huge numbers of refugees who were penniless, having been unable to take any Indian money out of that country. The drive into the city was hair-raising. The driver decided to take the busier of two alternative routes, engaging in a continuous war of nerves with every other road user. We couldn't wait to get off the vehicle in the middle of a crowded road. Most shops seemed to bring everything from inside on to the pavement. The shopping area could be detected by the noise and a smell, as roadside fires under pans of beans were subjected to heat treatment and a great deal of smoke. There were a number of modern showrooms and large shops mainly selling mechanical products. I found a trip into the backwaters useful. There, the brightly lit shops were replaced by small open-fronted wooden huts lit by oil lamps, and workrooms, with craftsmen at work. Patiently, and working with simple tools that looked inadequate, these men carved and inlaid wood in most intricate designs. With a large variety of wooden articles, it was easy to find one which suited the smallest pocket. With my eyes on my forthcoming marriage when I returned to Scotland, I started collecting small items of furniture. I bought a collapsible hexagonal-shaped table made of chestnut wood with a pattern inlaid with ivory which has withstood the test of time and sits next to my armchair to this day. After walking the dusty streets and carrying my newly acquired bit of furniture, it was time for a rest and some refreshment in one of the many restaurants. The astronomical price of alcohol was enough to encourage anyone to turn teetotal. For entertainment I chose to go to an air-conditioned cinema before making the journey back to the ship. On the last day we were invited to an impressive performance of 'A Midsummer Night's Dream' at the University. We were to return to Karachi before leaving the station.

Wherever we were during our time on the station we kept in touch with Aden, our base, where the situation across the Yemen and infiltration by terrorists was worsening. Returning on the 16th of December for a 3-week stay, we were offered the usual hospitality at the RAF messes and at the homes of friends. I was well looked after by the RAF sports officer and a civil servant. With the help of their wives, I embarked on pre-marital shopping expeditions storing the items I bought in the spare parts compartment on board, making sure that a 100 piece set of Japanese china was well packed.

We made the best we could of Christmas Day when our thoughts were with our families thousands of miles away. In keeping with naval tradition, the wardroom and messdecks were decorated and the Admiral judged the Petty Officers mess as the best, awarding them a huge cake which they in turn donated to the junior ratings. The most junior rating, dressed in the

139

Captain's uniform, conducted rounds of the messdecks, a carol service was led by the padre and a large launch crowded with carollers came to wish us A Happy Christmas.

After the New Year we put to sea to carry out statutory drills, including gunnery bombardments and a full power trial which must be carried out once a year. We invited several Army and RAF officers to sea and took the opportunity of reciprocating their hospitality when we returned to harbour. The Army officers were treated to a presentation of their own large wooden signpost which we pinched from the entrance to their barracks on the previous night after an evening of heavy drinking at their mess. Ten officers were invited to fly with the RAF over Lodan and Mukeira, two towns in the Aden Protectorate very close to the Yemen border. Mukeira lies on top of a plateaux over 6700 feet high. They described the hair-raising ride on a Valetta aircraft over the winding Wali, East of Aden and between the jagged ridges of a volcanic rock, at 120 knots with the inner wing tip only a few feet from the sharp rocks. This method of providing supplies to our troops was used in preference to the difficult terrain by road transport, a slow and laborious process. Prolonged battles were fought regularly between local tribesmen and Yemeni tribes, a problem which faced the military in the protectorate.

On being asked by the Commander (the second in command) to organise more sports and a cheering party in association with the Dental Surgeon, the sports officer, I organised an Aquatic Gala inviting the Army and RAF to take part. One of the main objects was to involve as many members of the ship's company as possible and get them out of the ship. It proved to be a great success with keen competition between departments, with about sixty participants in the swimming events, as well as a fancy dress competition in the form of a mannequin parade. There were over 200 spectators from the ship and some from the other two services. The band of the Royal Marines added to the entertainment. The officers won the water polo competition with me as the captain, scoring all four goals against the junior seamen. The wife of the Electrical Engineering Commander, who had come to spend some time with her husband, presented the prizes. The occasion achieved its objective and helped in a small way to raise the morale of the ratings. The Captain and the Commander were pleased with the result and I was asked to organise more of the same. Although the officers and, to a certain extent, the senior ratings were entertained by their opposite numbers in the other two services, the lower ranks were not. They were, by this time getting bored with life in the Persian Gulf and Aden in the hot and humid atmosphere of the ship.

The idea of a long distance whaler expedition had been contemplated for some time. With the ship paying a short visit to Berbera on the way to Trincomalee, in Ceylon, this was an ideal opportunity. After a 6-inch gun shoot, two whalers manned by one officer and four ratings each, were lowered into the water, accompanied by cheers and jeers from the ship's decks. Sails were set and off they went on an 80-mile journey to Berbera, where Gambia was waiting to haul them back on board.

Berbera, a city in North Eastern Somaliland, the colonial capital of British Somaliland from 1870 to 1941, has a seaport which is the only deep sheltered harbour on the South side of the Gulf of Aden. It was the colonial capital of British Somaliland from 1870 to 1941. The landscape around the city is desert or semi-desert where temperatures in the summer could reach upwards of 50 Degrees C. Most of the residents are forced to migrate seasonally to cooler inland cities. The city has a long runway built by the Soviet Union in the 1970s. From 1980 it was designated as an emergency landing strip for the US space shuttle. Because of the unbearably hot weather, hardly anyone went ashore, but relief was at hand when we sailed away into a cool sea breeze on our way to Ceylon, (Sri Lanka), arriving at Trincomalee in late January. The purpose of the visit was to further enhance our ties with the island and its connections with the Royal Navy at a time when negotiations were in progress for the last steps in breaking the link with Britain.

Situated on the North East of the island, Trincomalee is one of the world's largest natural harbours with an abnormally high tide, capable of holding numerous ships. After a long trip on the liberty boat we landed close to the town in the confines of the dockyard where we took a rickshaw to the town centre to view the gems and precious stones in the jewellers shop windows for which the place was well known. There was a large sports arena and fine beaches providing us with the opportunity to relax. Apart from an open market dealing in fruit and vegetables, shopping was contained in one street. Strolling around the rocky headlands was quite a pleasure. I took advantage of an organised tour of Kandy, a hair-raising ride on an old bus, winding on track roads over the hills. The town, one of the largest in Ceylon, has several European buildings, white being the predominant colour, presenting a picture of cleanliness and beauty. The coach wound its way through the mountainous roads exposing a breath-taking spectacle with large plantations nestling in the valleys and huge cascading waterfalls thundering down the rock faces, dropping down hundreds of feet, our cameras clicking continuously to catch this unforgettable picture. In town we paid a visit to the famous Buddhist 'Temple of the Tooth', believed to hold one of Buddha's teeth, and quenched our thirst at the Queen's Hotel. During the journey we stopped for tea at rest houses. Five busloads of officers and men left for the leave camp at Diyatalawa. My turn was to come a month later when we visited Colombo for dry-docking. As we left Trincomalee, there was a feeling of sadness amongst the ship's crew and the British residents as this was to be the last time a British warship would leave to the cheers of the British Community. By the time we were due to return, about four months later, they would have gone. We set off for the beginning of our tour around the coast of India.

By this stage, I was gaining more experience as an Engineer Officer and was given major responsibilities, including the Engine Rooms, the most prestigious part of the Marine Engineering Department.

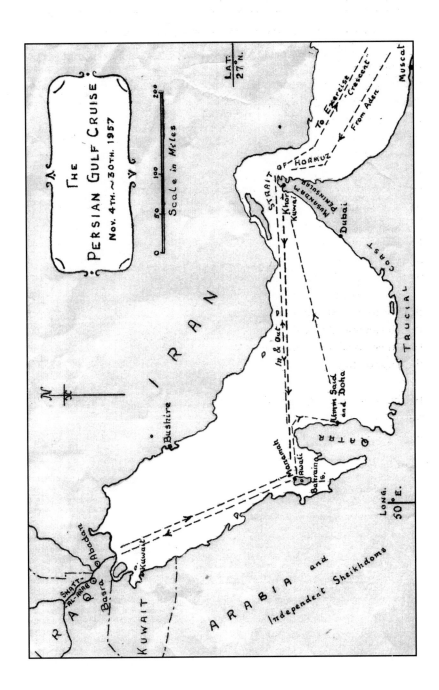

THE
PERSIAN GULF CRUISE
Nov. 4TH.~30TH. 1957

Scale in Miles

0   50   100   200

LAT.
27° N.

Muscat

To Exercise Crescent

From Aden

STRAIT OF HORMUZ

MUSANDAM PENINSULA

Khor Kuwai

Dubai

TRUCIAL COAST

IRAN

Bushire

N

In & Out

Umm Said and Doha

Q A T A R

Maraman

Awali

Bahrain Is.

Kuwait

Abadan

SHATT-AL-ARAB

Basra

I R A Q

KUWAIT

A R A B I A   and

Independent Sheikhdoms

LONG.
50° E.

143

CHAPTER 11

THE EAST INDIES

India, Ceylon and Pakistan
Crossing the Line Ceremony

For many of us, this was our first visit to India. We found Madras, the country's fourth largest city, with wide roads and bridges across the two rivers Coum and Adyar, to be a beautiful modern city with large buildings, clean and refreshing. Like Karachi in Pakistan, it was the ideal place for 'rabbits' (a naval expression meaning any goods bought and taken on board). There was an abundance of wood carvings, crocheted tablecloths and curios. Practically anything could be found at the Victoria Technical Institute, the official government store, but at slightly inflated prices. We had to take a chance between the two options, of being seen off in buying inferior goods on the streets, or paying 20% or 30% more at the institute. Bicycle rickshaws were an interesting feature of Madras, where taxis were in short supply. A tour of the city took us to the Temple of the Seven Pagodas, six of which were under the sea, while the other looked rather decrepit, some thirty miles south of the city. This was followed by a swim at one of the attractive beaches.

After a relaxed and pleasant stay we moved up the coast to Vizagapatam, a small town, but a port with growing importance and one of the main naval bases where the Indian Navy Boys Training Establishment was situated. In fact, the boys turned out a smart band to greet us. Unfortunately, while their band was playing, our Royal Marine Band was also playing, resulting in different tunes being played at the same time. The harbour was created as an outlet for a large area of fertile country, with considerable mining resources. Sight-seeing tours were laid on around the Caltex Oil Refinery and the Hindustani shipyard as well as daily visits to Lawson's Beach, a large stretch of sand, reputed to be the best in India. On arrival at the beach, we were surrounded by local children and adults who begged persistently throughout the whole afternoon. On leaving Vizagapatan for Calcutta we searched over a large area of the Indian Ocean for a ship which had sunk in mysterious circumstances. Miraculously, the crew had managed to get ashore with all their possessions including the parrot and cat, but there seemed, strangely, to be no time to rescue the ship's log or documents, probably with an insurance claim in mind. So we uncovered yet another mystery of the deep.

Calcutta, official name Kolkata, is the capital of West Bengal, also known as the Metropolis of India, the third largest city with a population at that time, of about 11,000,000. Lying on the river Hugli in the Ganges delta, it was founded by the East India Company as the capital of British India in 1773, and was the capital of India during the time of the British Raj until 1911. At one time it was the centre of modern education, science and politics. We witnessed scenes of dead animals and the occasional human among the flotsam and jetsam flowing down the river, not a pretty sight. The city gave a contrasting picture of affluence and poverty. I cannot forget the sight of numerous beggars who surrounded us wherever we went, and the skeleton-like deprived people sleeping on the pavements. When we visited the Army Officers' Messes we witnessed the contrasting side of the equation, entertained as we were by well fed and happy people who appeared to lack none of the luxuries of life. At a reception in one of the messes we met several dignitaries, among them the Maharaja and Maharani. India was at that time a dry country and so, while the dignitaries were around, we drank soft drinks. Their departure from the reception was the signal for alcohol of all kinds to surface, together with some exotic Indian food. The party lasted until the early hours.

There were the usual sight-seeing trips to such places as the Race Course and the Jain Temple or a visit to Firbo's night club. Except for the Hugli, the city did not live up to its reputation as the dirtiest on earth. It was relatively clean compared with other ports we'd been to. It lies about 90 miles up the Hugli in the cleaner land area, off Man-O-War jetty with open park-like spaces in the background. Here we experienced the last of the cool weather for a long time. The misty evenings were reminiscent of London in October. Those of us who had saved our money and not bought in Madras certainly had the last laugh at Calcutta, where woodwork was considerably cheaper than that at Walnut Willie's in Madras.

Leaving Calcutta, we sailed down the east coast of India to Colombo in Ceylon (now Sri Lanka), a contrasting picture to Trincomalee. Before we entered harbour there was no doubt of the importance of the place for along the approach channel was a queue of ships waiting to enter. Once inside the breakwater, the port was packed with hardly a berth unoccupied. A short walk out of the dock area was all that was needed to get into the main shopping area, with jewellers displaying an array of gems in beautiful settings and large department stores. The streets provided a wide variety of characters, from uniform-conscious policemen to baggy-trousered Afghans, mainly money lenders rendering themselves most unpopular in their search for repayment.

Soon after docking, I was among the second party to go to the recreation camp at Diyatalawa. As at Trincomalee, the green countryside and vegetation made a welcome change from the arid deserts of Aden and the Persian Gulf. As the five coaches sped along the narrow roads, the scenery changed rapidly. At times we might have been travelling through the English countryside. At Diyatalawa, at 4900 feet altitude, we could feel the cooler, quiet and serene atmosphere. On the first morning I was served with tea in bed. After breakfast, at the golf course, we had to contend with misguided missiles, straying cattle and a shower of cyclists gaily bedecked in dazzling shirts and safari hats. Waiters provided light refreshments as we went around the course.

The Royal Navy set up the recreation facilities at Diyatalawa during the Second World War as an area reserved for housing Italian prisoners-of-war. At the time of our visit, the village was not yet developed with several huts scattered all around. Local traders did some admirable business, selling what seemed to be an endless variety of garish shirts. Bandarawela, on the other hand, some five miles away, was larger and had a typical Buddist Temple and an unfinished Catholic Church. In the evening, the canteen was the main centre of attraction with games of whist and tombola in full swing every evening amongst the clinking of Tiger beer bottles. The officers were invited to tea at one of the tea plantations, where we observed the girls picking tea leaves which they carried in the traditional wicker baskets hung over their backs. Dress for this visit was Planters' Rig, consisting of a shirt

147

and tie and long trousers, dress which we were accustomed to wearing in tropical climates. The five days peaceful holiday, away from the hot and humid conditions and the monotonous routine on board served its purpose, after which we returned to the ship in Colombo to allow the next party to go on leave. The ship was still in dry dock when I arrived, just in time to inspect the underwater fittings before we undocked. The next few days were mainly taken up with hectic after-docking routines and preparing the machinery for raising steam and carrying out trials of equipment. As soon as the last of the leave parties returned, we set off on a diplomatic mission to Mali Island, capital of the Maldives. Before we left, there was some conjecture as to where it actually was, especially among us non-seamen. We had the Fleet Navigation Officer as well as our ship's navigator to advise the Captain on the safest routes to take as we sailed from one place to another. By the time we sailed, we had learnt that the Maldives were situated four degrees north of the equator. The main purpose of our visit was to take the new High Commissioner in Ceylon to pay his official calls on the Sultan and the Government of the Maldives.

The ship was undocked during the forenoon of the 3rd March, 1957, and what a relief it was to be afloat again and out of the steaming heat of Walker's Shipyard. In the afternoon, the High Commissioner, accompanied by his wife and first secretary, came on board and we were off, to the accompaniment of three rousing cheers from the Royal Ceylon Navy mustered on the breakwater. We arrived early the following morning and fired a National Salute which was returned by a most impressive muzzle-loading battery from an ancient Portuguese Fort. The High Commissioner and the Commander-in-Chief proceeded ashore to call on the Sultan. They were given a warm reception by the Maldivians who had decorated the large arch leading to the Palace Courtyard of the Sultan's Palace with a huge 'Welcome' sign. The Sultan returned the call, wearing his impressive blue and gold uniform, rowed in the state barge presented to him by Queen Victoria in 1897. He was received on board with the Guard and band of the Royal Marines playing the Maldivian National Anthem.

Male was a spotlessly clean place with white-washed walls, some made out of coral, burnished brass fittings on the houses and coral-sanded roads gleaming in the sun. The male inhabitants wore spotless white suits, their hair sleeked back with coconut oil which could easily have passed as Brylcream. At the time of our visit, the Maldivian economy relied heavily on fishing and marine products. They were in the process of developing their cottage industries such as mat-weaving, lacquer work, handicraft and coir rope making. The inhabited islands are highly populated and their birth rate is reputed to be the highest in the world. Every day we watched the numerous motorised dhonis overloaded with men and women travelling to and from islands for work. The islands' football team beat us 3-1 in our first game but we took revenge in the second, winning by 8-1. I refereed both games. After the first match our Royal Marines 'Beat Retreat' to thunderous applause by hundreds of spectators.

We were warned that in the deep water of the lagoon there was a danger from sharks, but where water was shallow it would be quite safe. Our bathing parties converted a most attractive beach on the nearest island into a swimming resort for the duration of our stay. From the waving palms on the edge of the beach, white sand led into the clear, blue water of the tropical sea. In the sea around the edge of the coral reef, where the depth fell almost vertically from 10 feet to 20 fathoms, a world of coral cities was inhabited by myriads of fish of every conceivable colour. You could lie in the water for hours watching the changing population below, all seemingly oblivious of the strangers in their midst. As I swam around the coral reef with clear silver sand beneath me I couldn't resist the temptation to dive and extract some coral (not protected at the time), as a souvenir from these paradise islands.

When the High Commissioner had had enough of his protracted negotiations, on Sunday 9th March, we reluctantly left this lovely haven of Tropicana. Our thoughts switched to the mail of nine days accumulated letters which were waiting for us in Colombo. After the High Commissioner disembarked and, when the mail was collected, and the ship refuelled and stored with fresh provisions, we were on our way to Cochin to continue with our journey around the Indian coast.

Cochin, is one of the country's principal seaports in the state of Karala. It is an attractive seaside city flanked by the Western Ghats on the East and the Arabian Sea on the West. Because of the diversity of its beauty it has become a popular tourist destination. We discovered some of this diversity when we visited the Cheeyappara waterfalls and the Church of St Francis, the oldest church built by Europeans, where the legendary Vasco Da Gama was originally buried, before his remains were shipped to Lisbon for burial in the Santa Cruz Basilica.

Our next port of call, Bombay, brought back memories of past friendships. For some of the ship's company it provided an opportunity to renew old acquaintances with Indian personnel who had trained in our ships and establishments at home. Most Indian ships were ex Royal Navy and, in fact, we were greeted by one of them, our old cruiser Nigeria, renamed Mysore, and the one time Achilles, renamed Delhi, renowned for her part in the battle against the German pocket battleship Graf Spee off the coast of Argentina. A number of the crew of Mysore, a sister ship of Gambia, came to Rosyth before we left to understudy their opposite numbers. Sadly, its previous commander, who we knew well during his stay in Gambia, was missing. In tragic circumstances he had killed his wife's lover and was serving a long prison sentence. Our senior officers went over to see him. In the busy and thriving port we were in full view of the Taj Mahal Hotel and the impressive Gateway to India, a huge arch built to commemorate the visit of King George the Fifth and Queen Mary in 1911.

Refreshments at the Taj Mahal were a must. This was a unique hotel built facing the wrong way round with the rear facing the sea, a mistake in planning which caused the architect to commit suicide. The sight of Sikhs, Bengalis, Parsees and Goans dressed in their picturesque costumes cannot escape the eye of the visitor. Gold rings can be bought for a few rupees in the streets, not far from the slopes of Malabar Hill and the attractive Hanging Gardens, with their exotic peacocks and fine examples of Eastern Gardens, and the Parsee Towers of Silence where people observe their religion by exposing their dead to birds of prey. We relaxed at the Breach Kandy Swimming Club with its well laid-out garden and a splendid restaurant, a one-time 'whites only club'. I was there when Prince Sadurin, the Aga Khan's son and heir walked in with his entourage. Nobody dared question his presence, and it was soon after that incident that the club was made open to all nationalities.

We found the city very interesting, the shopping centre in particular with a wide choice of goods at Crawford Market, the Victoria Gardens and the famous Maha Laxim Temple, where the Godess Laxim of wealth and plenty is worshipped. The adjoining streets offered a variety of goods from household wares to silk brocades and unusually patterned jewels with goldsmiths in one street, silversmiths in another, cloth and silk merchants in another. It seemed that no matter how long one stayed in Bombay there would always be something different to see. It is a city of a thousand changing faces and we in Gambia were privileged to have seen just a few of them.

We returned to Aden to take part in the military parade to inaugurate the new Command Structure, giving the combined local forces autonomous responsibility for the defence of Aden without answering to the Middle East Command and to deal directly with London. Gambia was represented by two platoons of seamen and Royal Marines, each of 42 men who marched past Field Marshal Sir Gerald Templar, the Chief of the Imperial General Staff, who had flown from London for the occasion. This stay in Aden lasted about a fortnight before we were off to Muscat and another stint in the Persian Gulf to remind the various Sultans and the British communities that we were still around, ready to help if need be.

It seemed as if we were going from one place to another looking for trouble and Muscat, the capital and largest city in the Sultanate of Oman, was one such place. In 1947, the Sultan, with the help of the British defeated the Imam and unified most of Oman, but internal strife continued. The British with an RAF and Army presence helped the Sultan to fight the insurgents. Our visit in April 1958 was a gesture to show solidarity with the Sultan. Unfortunately it wasn't long before we were off to deal with trouble in Aden.

I was one of thirteen officers who were invited to lunch with the Sultan at one of his palaces way out in the desert. We were collected by a fleet of limousines and escorted by armed guards at breakneck speed to be met by the Sultan. On arrival we were led to the throne room, a large spacious area surrounded by beautiful curtains and an array of Persian carpets. We sat talking to the staff of the British Consulate and some local dignitaries until we were led into the dining room and seated at a table full of large dishes laden with rice of a variety of colours, meats and vegetables. Waiters, with guns slung over their shoulders, piled the rice on to our plates as waiters on the opposite side of the table cut chunks of meat and tossed them on top of the piles with such accuracy that they landed right in the middle. As the dour-faced servers cut the meat with their long knives, their guns swinging from side to side as they moved from one plate to another, you couldn't help feeling that an accident might easily happen. After the fruit was served we were led back to the throne room for coffee served in little cups without handles. We sat in a long row of chairs as the waiters poured the coffee from tall silver pots. It tasted awful, and from the looks and grimaces on everyone's face it was obvious that we all felt the same way but we had to drink it. After all we were on a diplomatic mission! To our horror, the servants came round again to refill the cups. Eventually the Flag Lieutenant passed on a message telling us that if we didn't want more we were to tap the side of the cup with our finger tips. Within seconds, thirteen officers were tapping in unison as if we had rehearsed the gesture.

Coffee was interrupted when we were suddenly beckoned to get into the limousines to return to the ship as quickly as possible. The insurgents were on their way to attack us. After travelling at breakneck speed we breathed a sigh of relief as we walked up the ship's gangway. In the evening, the British High Commissioner held a reception in honour of the Commander-in-Chief at his residence, which resembled a fort with low stone bastions. We just had enough time left to have a quick look at the other palace of the Sultan, the surrounding barren mountains and two large forts, one housing the police and the other criminals. Although our hockey and tennis teams managed to go ashore and play against the British Community, Muscat, where drinking and smoking were forbidden, was not made for matelots. Rumour had it that, if found wandering about town after dark without a lantern, you were liable to be carted off to the mud fort to await the Sultan's displeasure. We sent a party to repaint the magic letters Gambia and the Admiral's flag on the rock face. This was not just a bright idea, but part of a campaign which had been going on since the men of HMS Perseus painted their ship's name on the brown rocks in 1857. As a result, the cliffs either side of Muscat form what is surely the world's biggest autograph album, covered with names of warships of several nationalities.

On the morning after the High Commissioner's party, at about 3am I was woken by the Commander, the second in command of the ship, inviting me to go on a banyan with him. It was a strange invitation. I had to explain to him that I was required to prepare the main machinery to take the ship to sea during the morning watch between 4 and 8 am. He told me not to worry because he had cleared it with the Engineer Commander who had granted me permission to join him. From the very beginning I thought that there was something very odd about the whole thing, especially when I was told to pack my civilian suit, just in case I needed it. At about 5am we were ordered to two army trucks which had appeared by the gangway. We were taken to a small RAF airfield way out in the desert and put on a Valetta aircraft to fly to an unknown destination. As soon as we took off, on a plane used for transporting parachutists without any passenger seats, the briefing started. We were on our way to Aden, where the ground forces were to carry out an incursion into Yemeni Territory to chase two Yemeni brothers who were causing most of the insurgency at Aden. In fact, our party consisted of the platoon commanders and their assistants, of whom I was one. These platoons were formed to land and deal with any trouble in the regions we visited. The plan was for us to take over from the army as soon as the ship, which was speeding towards Aden at full speed, arrived at Aden. The flight was a frightening experience. Sitting on a tool locker, with a harness around me, I held tight to it, as the plane tossed and turned all over in the air, at times dropping suddenly by as much as forty feet or more. As I listened to the briefing by the Commander I was more concerned with saying my prayers, preparing for eternity. I was saddened by the thought that I may be deprived of my last rites. What a relief it was when we landed at Tarxien airfield to be met by some of our RAF friends. We were instructed to wear only civilian clothes. I was assigned to an army major with an enormous moustache and in full uniform. I sat next to him as we circled around the streets of Aden in a jeep to be shown the main trouble spots, including a café which had been blown up by a hand grenade a few days before. The ship duly arrived at Aden. Apparently, throughout the journey from Muscat, the sailors had a great time preparing for action ashore, rehearsing hand-to-hand combat dressed as Arabs. The army left on their mission and we formed into platoons and took positions at strategic positions to defend Aden. The operation into Yemen proved successful, the Buffs (a British

Army regiment) returned and we went back to the ship to carry on with the normal ship's routine. We remained in Aden to wait for the military situation to return to normal.

Although Aden provided facilities for sports and swimming, living on board for long spells was taking its toll and morale among the ratings was at its lowest ebb. The task of the officers was to create activities ashore to get the sailors off the ship. The Sports Officer worked very hard at it, assisted by all the divisional officers, and I continued to arrange events against the other two services. With the help of the RAF sports officer, who was by now a close friend, I organised several inter-services swimming and water polo meetings, hoping that such meetings would develop into friendships between our ratings and their opposite numbers. Although the lack of air conditioning affected everyone, the officers were well looked after ashore, but the ratings were becoming bored due to the lack of entertainment. Unfortunately, we had a few who were hell-bent on causing trouble, some quite serious. It was at this time that parts of the anchor-cable capstan engine were found missing, tossed into the sea to be recovered by divers, prompting Admiralty detectives to be flown from UK to investigate a case of possible sabotage, leading to the conviction of two sailors. With civil unrest growing, we were required to stay in Aden for another five weeks. The situation was later aggravated by the news that our East African cruise, which was to be the highlight of the commission, had been cancelled. The only consolation was that the end of the commission and homecoming was in sight.

Aden has for centuries been recognised as a trading centre. It is also a refuelling base on the main shipping route to the East. In the dingy streets, one was surrounded by haggling shopkeepers, each attempting to sell you their shoddy goods. Past the taxi ranks along the causeway passing Ma'alla, native shipyards still produced their dhows which they had done for centuries past. At Crater City there is an extinct volcano which Muslims believe will erupt on the Day of Judgement. In the dark crowded streets, heavily-veiled women, camel-drawn water carts, ragged beggars asleep in the filth of the gutter, many goats and bright-eyed naked children, all mingled together. Past Crater City were the Tanks of Sheba, an ancient Persian construction capable of containing almost ten million gallons of water. Close by is

Sheikh Othman, the link between Aden and the villages from where loaded caravans depart across the deserts of Arabia and the magnificent gardens and where, at dusk, families of all nationalities gather to enjoy the cool of the evening amid flowering trees and lush vegetation. Because of these gardens, Aden has been described as the original Garden of Eden, although to most of us it never appeared in that light. We shall always remember it with mixed feelings, as a place offering amenities at a reasonable price, hot and humid, where some of us made many friends while others, especially most of the lower ranks, found the place boring. However, it was above all an introduction to the East. On leaving Aden we paid our second visit to Karachi, spending just enough time at the markets, and for me to continue buying items which would become useful when I eventually tied the knot.

Every 10 years, until 1958, the Eastern Commonwealth Navies met in the Indian Ocean for combined exercises covering a large area south of Ceylon between Sumatra and Kenya, the Arabian Sea and the Bay of Bengal to the North. The exercise was code-named JET (Joint Exercise Trincomalee). Naval units from India, Pakistan and Britain and the small Ceylonese Navy took part, with the British providing the major units, including an aircraft carrier and three support vessels. The Pakistani Air Force provided airplanes. This was the last time that a British Commander-in-Chief was to take over Command, his flag flown in HMS Gambia, the last Flagship of the East Indies Fleet. The base support was provided by the Ceylonese Navy. The usual battle operations were rehearsed. At a time when tension between India and Pakistan was nearing its peak, one of our tasks was to create an atmosphere of trust and friendship between the two navies, a task which proved difficult on the sports fields. As we anchored off Trincomalee several courtesy visits were exchanged between ships. At the end of the exercise the customary RPC (Request the Pleasure of your Company) flags were hoisted on the main mast inviting the officers of all ships. We met several officers we had known during their training in Britain. Good relations were maintained until the end of the exercise when we anchored for the Wash Up and sports competitions. As thousands of sailors witnessed the games, some of the contests between the Indians and Pakistanis degenerated into bitter skirmishes. Three players had their ankles broken at hockey, the Volley Ball match turned into a boxing contest and the Tug of War into chaos as the

155

spectators joined in the pulling. The referee, our First Lieutenant, was lost in the melee and trampled on until he was rescued by his fellow shipmates. So it was my turn to restore some order between the two nations. I was to referee the final of the Soccer competition between India and Pakistan, the climax of the whole meeting when the trophies were to be presented to the winners. The situation became so serious that the C-in-C felt it necessary to send for me, and over a drink in his quarters, advised me to be very strict with the players. I told him that I would not be refereeing the match unless I was confident that I could keep the game under control. The spectators stand was packed with sailors and members of the public, some standing just behind the touchlines. Naval patrols from all the navies could be seen in abundance. The situation was tense and I was well aware of the importance of this match. I was fortunate that I knew some of the players on both sides who I had met at the Royal Naval Engineering College at Plymouth. There were two brothers on opposite sides, evidence of the anomalies created by the partition of India. They all came to shake hands before I blew the whistle. I had no problem in controlling the game and as I blew the final whistle almost every player came to shake hands again, the two captains presenting me with the match ball. Overnight I had become something of a celebrity. The Admiral, through the Captain, sent his congratulations. He was particularly pleased that the last act he had to perform in presenting the prizes was achieved in harmony, goodwill and friendship. At the farewell cocktail party, under the ceremonial awning on the quarterdeck of Gambia, Indian and Pakistani officers came to congratulate me as if I had performed a miracle, when all I had done was to referee a football match as expected of any FA registered referee. I had the feeling that they were surprised that there wasn't a punch up.

We said good bye to every foreign ship as each one sailed past, saluting the Commander-in-Chief, while the Royal Marine band played 'Auld Lang Syne'. We said our farewells to Trincomalee with several blows from our steam sirens, as we disappeared over the horizon on our way to Mauritius, crossing the equator en route, with great anticipation of the start of the long-awaited East African Cruise. No ship crosses the line without the traditional greetings from 'King Neptune', his 'Queen', the 'courtiers' and the 'bears'. Although the king was pleased to see us, he did well and truly exact the penalties laid down for admittance to his realm. This was a break for the ship's company to indulge in some fun, with many wearing home made costumes as King Neptune's entourage. The usual punishments were exacted, offenders being ducked underwater and having their beards shaved off. The sailors were more than pleased to give the senior officers a ducking. In due course, we were all issued with Crossing-the-Line Certificates.

Diego Garcia, a small atoll 400 miles south of the equator, was our next stop where the only entertainment was provided by a soccer match followed by the 'Beat Retreat' ceremony by the Royal Marines. A laugh was raised by a newly qualified coxswain who, while trying to bring the ship's boat alongside, failed dismally against a beam wind and tide. Before his successful fourth attempt, a sailor shouted 'Jack, drop your anchor and we'll bring the jetty to you'. Diego Garcia is a British territory with most of the population made up of the American military, used as a strategic UK and US base. Discovered by the Portuguese in the 16th century, it remained uninhabited until the 18th century when it was ceded to Britain by the French.

Our next port of call was the volcanic island of Rodriguez, 1200 miles south of the equator where there was an important Cable and Wireless Station. Three soccer matches were played and the Marines performed again. They were a great asset to the ship on these occasions when we were showing the flag, never failing to attract thunderous applause wherever they performed. There seemed to be an inexhaustible supply of local beer and wines, which may have accounted for half the population being inebriated during the whole of our two day stay. In common with many of the other countries we visited in these regions, these two islands' histories highlighted the influence that Portuguese seafarers had had over the whole of the East Indies in the sixteenth century, from the Persian Gulf to India, Goa, Ceylon, Mauritius and the surrounding areas. Rodriguez was named after the Portuguese explorer Diego Rodriguez. Britain took possession of the island, which is now annexed to Mauritius.

Bad news was received from London which put paid to our dreams of mad moments in Mauritius, siestas in the Seychelles and the night-life in Nairobi. The social programme for Mauritius had already been arranged by the High

Commissioner's staff with the liaison officer who had flown to the island in advance of the ship, as was customary when we were showing the flag. It included several receptions and invitations from a number of groups, including teachers, nurses, expatriates and sports clubs with a number of functions to take place on board. It was to be the visit of the commission, just what was required to boost the morale of the sailors away from the hot and humid Persian Gulf. On the way to Mauritius, the Kilimanjaro Climbing team, led by the Surgeon Commander, started their vigorous physical training, looking forward to Mombasa and the journey to Nairobi to climb the mountain. As it turned out it was all in vain. There was no doubt that this cruise promised to be the highlight of our time on the East Indies Station, Mauritius followed by Seychelles, Zanzibar, Dar Es Salem and Mombasa. The cancellation of the cruise came as a great disappointment to all of us. As soon as we berthed at Mauritius we were ordered to proceed to the Gulf to go to the assistance of the Sultan of Oman, where trouble with the insurgents had re-emerged. After about six hours, on completion of refuelling and taking on fresh provisions, we left harbour at full speed. I just had time to pay a visit to the wife of my cousin Joe, who was at sea as the chief engineer on an ocean going cable ship, a matron at one of the hospitals. It was the first time I had met her just to say hello and good bye. The upshot of this change in our programme meant that we had to spend six weeks in the Persian Gulf, where the morale of the ship's company sank to its lowest ebb. The thought of living on board at anchor for such a long period was not something we looked forward to. On the way to the Gulf, we were diverted to Mombasa to load military stores and 400 men from the King's Own Royal Regiment and take them to Aden. There was just enough time for both watches, Red and White, to go ashore and savour whatever delights there were of East Africa. When they returned from shore some of the sailors couldn't find their hammocks. The soldiers had helped themselves from the hammock racks, thinking that they were up for grabs. One sailor was asked by a soldier to give him a hand slinging 'his hammock' which was clearly marked with the owner's name. When asked where he had got it from, the soldier replied 'Oh, from a rack down below, and if you want one you better hurry as they're going like hot cakes' This innocent act of misappropriation did not endear the soldiers to the sailors during the two days trip to Aden.

We spent three days in Aden, disembarking the troops and equipment, allowing the sailors to indulge in their last spending spree before a journey that was much in their minds as we approached the end of the commission. We arrived at Bahrain on the 29th July, 1958, and remained there until the 24th of August during which period we went to sea on three occasions with 300 Royal Fusiliers on board, practising beach landings on the barren island of Halul, nicknamed 'Hell Hole'. When these soldiers arrived on board, the sailors watched them like hawks, lest there was a repetition of the hijacking of their hammocks. The congestion of the living quarters and recreational areas on deck added to the discomfort and gloom which engulfed the whole ship after the cancellation of the cruise. This was not a pleasant experience especially for the Supply Department who had to cater for so many extra mouths.

The Royal Marines went out on their daily exercises on Halul Island, ideal for them with its hilly rocks but they overlooked the effect that the heat was going to have on them. Many of them succumbed to heat exhaustion and the few who became seriously ill were housed in the sick bay, the only air-conditioned compartment, the urgent cases being temporarily accommodated in the vegetable-cooling compartment. When practicable, the Captain anchored the ship as close as possible to Awali Island at Bahrain to enable the ship's company to take advantage of its facilities and the hospitality of the expatriate inhabitants. Some of us preferred to go to the Resident Naval Officer's house to read a book or write our letters in the cool air-conditioned lounge. The heat and humidity in the ship, compounded by the overcrowding, was unbearable. Light relief was provided by the concert parties in the first class air-conditioned theatre at Awali. These shows, the last of the commission, were each watched by an audience of 650, of whom 150 were members of the crew who were wined and dined for the evening by the residents. On the 23rd August the awaited news was piped on the Tannoy, 'HMS Newfoundland is now in sight on the Starboard Bow'. She was a welcome sight as our temporary relief at the station. She was due to be relieved by HMS Sheffield which was on her way from UK.

On the 24th August, 1958, we sailed for UK, flying the Paying-Off Pennant at the mainmast. As we sailed past Newfoundland her crew gave us three cheers which we heartily returned, while the Royal Marines played Auld

Lang Syne and Tipperary from the quarterdeck and, for the benefit of Newfoundland, a verse of Colonel Bogey. On the way out of the Gulf, we moved on to Muscat, where we gave a cocktail party under the ceremonial awning to return the hospitality of the High Commissioner and the Sultan for his lunch and the 'awful' coffee during our previous visits. In a more relaxed atmosphere, we were able to explore the alleyways. The gateways en route to the walled city and the bazaars were of particular interest. The walls, built into the mountains at each end of the old town and its harbour, were in a remarkable state of preservation. The great wooden doors of the gates had retained their intricate carving and iron work and it was here that we learned how the coastal Arab lives, his society being essentially simple, self sufficient and lacking in ambition. We had a last glance at the magic letters 'Gambia' and the Admiral's flag on the rock face as we said good bye on our way home.

One not so pleasant task facing the Captain was dealing with the large number of personnel who had contacted venereal diseases. They were all under stoppage of leave as part of their recuperation period and had to be cleared of these diseases before we got home. It was only at Rodriguez, amongst the half-drunk population, or Mombasa, that they were likely to have contacted these infections.

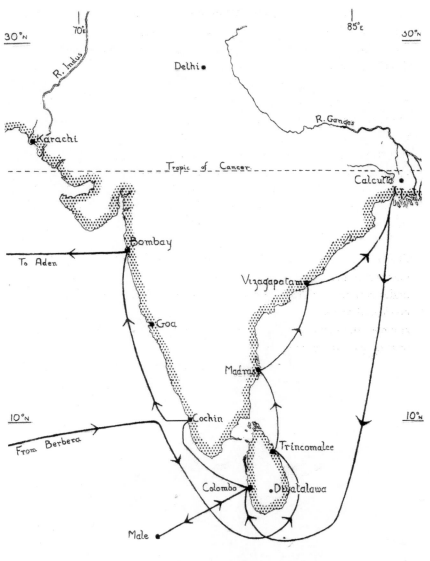

30°N   70°E

R. Indus

Delhi •

Karachi

R. Ganges

85°E   30°N

Tropic of Cancer

Calcutta •

Bombay

To Aden

Goa

Vizagapatam

10°N

From Berbera

Cochin

Madras

Trincomalee

Colombo

Diyatalawa

Male •

10°N

Indian Cruise. Jan.-March
70°E **1958**   85°E

HMS Gambia.

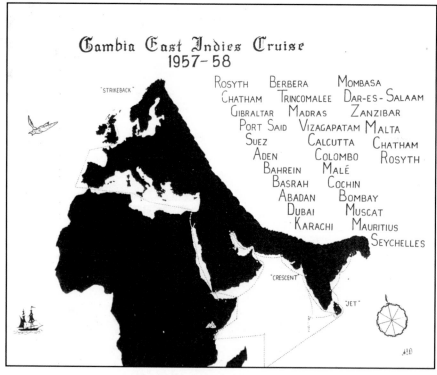

Gambia East Indies Cruise 1957 - 1958.

Royal Divisions in HMS Ocean.

Crossing the Line Ceremony.

163

Aquatic Gala Mannequin Parade.

Receiving the water polo trophy on behalf of the wardroom.

Gambia's team with the opposition made up of British, German and Dutch players at the Beach Kandy Swimming Club, Bombay (holding ball).

164

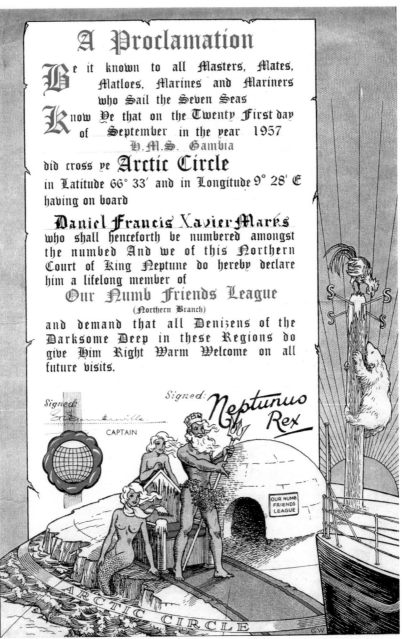

A Proclamation

Be it known to all Masters, Mates, Matloes, Marines and Mariners who Sail the Seven Seas

Know Ye that on the Twenty First day of September in the year 1957 H.M.S. Gambia

did cross ye **Arctic Circle**

in Latitude 66° 33′ and in Longitude 9° 28′ E having on board

Daniel Francis Xavier Marks
who shall henceforth be numbered amongst the numbed And we of this Northern Court of King Neptune do hereby declare him a lifelong member of

Our Numb Friends League
(Northern Branch)

and demand that all Denizens of the Darksome Deep in these Regions do give Him Right Warm Welcome on all future visits.

Signed: _____
CAPTAIN

Signed: *Neptunus Rex*

OUR NUMB FRIENDS LEAGUE

ARCTIC CIRCLE

My second Blue Nose Certificate.

165

CHAPTER 12

FROM SHIP TO SHORE

A Surprise Visit to Malta
Wedding Bells
HMS Caledonia

With the visits to Mauritius, Seychelles, Zanzibar, Dar-Es-Salam and Mombasa and the climbing of Kilimanjaro a distant dream, there was one place where we had to visit on our way home, Aden. We arrived there on the 30th August and stayed until the 2nd September, 1958. We paid our farewell visits to our friends and invited them to our final reception onboard. For the hospitality we received from the other two services we were most grateful. So farewell Aden, the Persian Gulf, the heat and humidity, the lost opportunities, King Neptune and his Kingdom and the barren deserts, but with happier memories of those countries that we had managed to explore. We left the East Indies Station on the day the 100th Commander-in-Chief hauled down his flag at Bahrain when the station ceased to exist. Another chapter in the history of the British Empire, when Britannia ruled the waves, was closed. Before we left Aden we disembarked the Somali seamen and stokers. Two of them were left behind in Trincomalee, caught smuggling jewellery. The Leading Stoker presented me with an ebony stick inlaid with an ivory pattern to remind me of the manner in which I drove his men in cleaning the machinery compartments' bilges!

As we sailed through the Red Sea, we rendezvoused with HMS Sheffield, transferring numerous hurricane fans to her. One of her crew was heard to say, 'We don't need these fans. We've been in the Mediterranean and we're used to the heat'. Little did he know what was to come! On the 7th September we sailed through the Suez Canal, causing what may well have turned into an international incident so soon after the Suez Canal War. As was customary in those days at Suez, we hauled up 'Jimmy Green' together with his boat, full of stuffed camels, camel stools, fake watches and all sorts of useless junk to sell on the way to Port Said. Throughout the journey he was caught buying watches from one end of the ship and selling them at a big profit at the other, leading to some nasty arguments between him and the sailors. When we arrived at Port Said the sailors took their revenge. They launched him and his boat unceremoniously over the side, stuffed camels and all. As if that wasn't enough, as he was swimming for his life, they pelted him with potatoes, cabbages, carrots and anything else they could get hold of from the upper deck vegetable locker. The pilot was disembarked hurriedly and the Captain made a speedy exit from Port Said. I happened to be on deck watching the whole farcical episode with amusement. With my connections and knowledge of Port Said, I was keen to see, with the aid of binoculars, what damage had been inflicted on the town during the attack by British forces during the Suez War.

On the way from Muscat to Aden the Captain had called me to his day cabin to tell me that he was not stopping at Malta on the way home, but had arranged for me to be flown from Aden on an RAF Shackleton aircraft so that I could see my family and, more importantly, to meet my prospective father-in-law for the first time. He arranged that, as the ship sailed past Malta, I would be dropped on board by a helicopter. When we arrived at Aden, he sent for me again to tell me that the Shackleton had broken down and he had decided to call at Malta after all. I knew that the Captain, and my boss, thought highly of me but not to the extent that he would alter the ship's programme. I was indeed grateful to him for this kind gesture.

We arrived in Malta on the 10th September, 1958, when Mr Alex Mc Rae came on board for our first meeting. It was a pleasure to meet someone who I came to know later as a fine gentleman. He was highly regarded by the Maltese workmen who worked under him at the Royal Naval Dockyard where I served my apprenticeship. He was a devout Catholic who went to church daily and was so kind and generous that his men thought of him as a saint. He was a great craftsman and an authority on ships' compasses and navigation equipment. The next time I saw him was just before my wedding to his daughter, Margaret. I spent two pleasant days in Malta with my family and Alex.

Malta was familiar to anyone who had served in the Royal Navy. Most members of the ship's company would have been stationed there at some time in their career. I understand that a few hundred bottles of Blue Label ale passed the lips of many sailors together with 'big eats' at the 'Gut', a narrow street once known as the Red Light area in the middle of Valletta, the capital of the island, reputed for its many restaurants, bars and night clubs. Tours of the Island were organised and the Services' lidos made available

We continued with our journey through the blue and calm Mediterranean, past Gibraltar and the unusually still waters of the Bay of Biscay, to Chatham where families and friends, including Margaret were waiting on the jetty to greet us. My 'relief' joined the ship to understudy me on the way to Rosyth. However much sailors enjoy travelling around the world, they always look forward to returning to their homes. To them there is nothing that beats the beauty of the green fields of England or the magic scenery of Scotland or the Welsh Valleys. As for myself, I could endure the bitter winter more than the muggy, hot and humid conditions of the countries that we had just visited. We looked forward to sitting by the fire and relaxing in a comfortable environment.

We arrived at Rosyth on the 22nd September, 1958, after almost a year away. During the commission we had travelled 43,000 miles, used 26,700 tons of fuel costing 160,500 pounds and 9,444,000 gallons of water. The Engine Room Department, working in the hotter conditions in the machinery spaces consumed 78,000 salt water tablets and, in the Persian Gulf, gave up 5,000 gallons of sweat. We used 10,263 electric bulbs and 16 miles of electrical cable, 12,500 jabs were given and 25,000 aspirin or codeine tablets were issued. We used eleven and a half miles of bandage, took 75 lbs and 200,000 tablets of salt and the doctors gave 135,000 treatments. We opened 155 barrels of rum and drank 173,946 tots. We used 65 tons of flour, baked 85,000 loaves and ate 250 tons of potatoes, 10 tons of bacon, 20 tons of baked beans and peas, drank 13,300 gallons of lime juice and 18,750 gallons of tea.

The new crew began to join the ship and we all looked forward to our next assignment with great anticipation. We gave a Farewell Cocktail Party in the wardroom and invited our families, friends and sweethearts, local dignitaries and senior officers from ships and establishments in the Rosyth area, including the Captain of HMS Caledonia who was introduced to me. He lost no time in asking me to introduce him to Margaret, my fiancée. I had hardly finished shaking his hand when he went off to talk to her. I left them to it. She told me later that he had asked her if she would be happy to take part in a pantomime, 'Sinbad the Sailor,' as the leading lady at the Artificer Training Establishment, HMS Caledonia, about a mile away from where we were berthed and where he was in command. Within a fortnight I was asked by my Engineer Commander if I would be willing to join HMS Caledonia. I'm still not certain whether the Captain of Caledonia wanted me or Margaret for her talents as an actress and singer. After taking my Foreign Service leave, I joined the Training Establishment as the Commander's Assistant and the Establishment Maintenance Officer. I was intrigued when the Captain's Secretary showed me the appointment list with my name 'DFX Marks' on it with scribbles all round it as officers tried to guess what the 'X' stood for during circulation before I joined.

When the first steam-driven ships were built the shipbuilders provided the engineers. They were civilians who had no official position on board and were not subject to any discipline. They were free to come and go as they pleased. They came from different backgrounds and were mostly men of little education. Very few stayed in the navy to be classified as naval engineers. They wore no uniform, carried no rank and were little more than engine drivers. The first steps to start training engineers were taken in the middle of the 19th century, training being carried out entirely at sea. The transition from sail to steam and the development of the Marine Engineering Branch in the Royal Navy took many years and has been the subject of a number of books, well described in one called *Up Funnel Down Screw* by Commander Geoffrey Penn RN. It took some time before the Admiralty, dominated by senior seamen officers, accepted the inevitable, that a system of training personnel to operate and maintain the equipment had to be introduced and the Engineering Branch established to the same level as any other department with its own officers selected from the Dartmouth Cadet entry and trained at the Naval Engineering College. A large proportion of Artificers from the Marine, Weapons (called Ordnance in my time) and the Fleet Air Arm trained at Caledonia and similar training Establishments, qualifying as officers, with a few reaching the rank of Rear Admiral. I was one of the few trained outside the Navy (Outside Entry) who qualified. In fact I don't know of any other. HMS Caledonia was one of the establishments instituted to provide training for the operators, educated to a high academic standard and skill. It took its name from the ex White Star liner Majestic which was renamed Caledonia and used as a training ship for artificers as well as boy seamen. It was the third ship to bear the name. The first was built in 1805, the year of the Battle of Trafalgar. The second was a Screw Ironclad with engines capable of 1000 Brake Horsepower. Until their training was established, ERAs were recruited from outside sources, mainly the Royal Dockyards. A small number continued to be recruited from these sources, including me, having been trained at the Royal Naval Dockyard at Malta. During the Second World War, the Navy was unable to turn out enough ERAs to man the many warships coming into service and relied on shipbuilders to provide the required numbers as HO ('Hostilities Only') artificers.

I soon realised why a new regime was taking control. HMS Caledonia was going through a critical period. The large, corrugated-iron huts which housed the apprentices, built during the war to last ten years, were over 18 years old. They lacked the facilities for accommodating the new generation of young men who were joining the Navy. Trainees came back from the sports fields covered in mud and freezing, to find that they couldn't have a hot shower. They had nowhere to plug in their HIFI systems, radios or electric shavers. The dormitory heating system broke down with regular monotony. Help from an old-fashioned Maintenance Officer was not forthcoming. He took the time-honoured view that the apprentices should be toughened up to face life at sea. In addition they were being fed with poor quality food and their night leave was restricted. These young men were becoming frustrated and began to take the law into their own hands. To get their electrical equipment to work they resorted to tampering with the wiring, overloading the system, causing their dormitories' main fuses to blow, prompting them to replace them with nails. The dockyard authorities would not sanction repairs after working hours, with dormitories, housing as many as 30 young men, kept in darkness for as long as a whole week-end. Regular complaints to the management by their Divisional Officers had to wait until the new regime solved the main problem of the unsatisfactory relations with the dockyard authorities. Just before I joined the establishment, the apprentices released their frustration when one of them was beaten by the Teddy Boys. Fighting flared up in the streets of Rosyth. The Teddy Boys resented the way the pretty girls from Rosyth, Dunfermline and the surrounding area were shunning them in favour of the naval recruits at the Snake Pit dance hall. Some of the Ordnance apprentices manufactured weapons and ammunition to use during the battles that took place. They were producing catapults which fired brass balls at the 'enemy'. Unfortunately the police had to intervene and a number of apprentices were arrested, giving the establishment bad publicity. On one occasion, after a night ashore, they attempted to launch the whaler used for training purposes from the Parade Ground over the edge of a cliff to the workshops area below. Despite all the trouble, it was believed that the local population and the police were grateful to the apprentices for teaching the Teddy Boys a lesson, because they were turning some parts of Rosyth into no-go areas.

The new Captain and Commander were appointed with the specific purpose of turning the situation round by improving the living conditions while at the same time maintaining discipline. It was my responsibility to carry out the improvements, in liaison with the dockyard authorities, which is exactly what I did. With full support from the Commander, I threatened the dockyard officers that if they did not carry out the necessary changes we would employ our own naval personnel to do the work. I won the argument. The Dockyard Authorities were allocated funds to spend on improvements, including attendance at weekends when necessary. Gradually, facilities and morale among the trainees started to improve. They realised that the new regime was on their side. I arranged for funds to buy them some musical instruments to form a band and reconstructed the main hall, making it more suitable to be used as a theatre and dance hall. Peace was restored. The academic results started to improve, the showers were working with an abundance of hot water, and the electricity system was modified to accept any amount of equipment unknown to my predecessor. The rewards came later when the Captain was promoted to Admiral, the Commander to Captain, and I, a humble Sub Lieutenant, to Lieutenant, in what was then record time. I did nothing special except that I adopted the motto of my life 'Hard work never killed anyone'. Even at the age of eighty four, I have kept to that motto. I'm often told to slow down.

Life at Caledonia was challenging but pleasant. With the Apprentices Divisional Officers in a more relaxed mood, and the living quarters for the trainees improving, a happier atmosphere prevailed. I got into my stride with sporting activities and was soon captaining the water polo team with ideal training facilities. The establishment boasted an Olympic size swimming pool, often used for training Olympic hopefuls from the surrounding districts. I represented Scotland Naval Command and was selected to play for one of the three main water polo teams in the Navy, the Nore Command, which included Scotland and naval establishments and ships attached to the Chatham Division. I played soccer and cricket for the wardroom in the departmental competitions and started a Referees' Training Class to train volunteers for qualification. I refereed all round Scotland for all three services at the highest level. With Margaret, I became heavily involved in stage and drama and helped to form the Caledonia Arts Theatre Society. I was eventually presented with the first 'CATS' crest for my outstanding contribution to the Society. Away from Caledonia, Margaret continued to perform as a leading lady and soprano at the Dunfermline Carnegie Hall.

Preparations for our wedding were by now well advanced. Alex McRae and my mother flew from Malta for the wedding set for the 4th April, 1959. It was a Saturday, when Divisions and the Captain's formal inspection of the apprentices and a March-Past were to take place on the parade ground. Because the Captain, Commander and several officers were to attend the wedding, the Captain cancelled Divisions and granted morning leave. On the day before the wedding, at St Margaret's Church in Dunfermline, bride and bridegroom, together with the best man and five bridesmaids attended a rehearsal. To our horror we found that the church was being redecorated and the altar area had been surrounded by scaffolding. Margaret was very upset so I had to do something to save the day. I arranged for the scaffolding to be removed and replaced after the wedding. This was accomplished by giving two of the scaffolders a fiver each. Years later I was telling this story to an RN Roman Catholic Chaplain when he started laughing, and revealed that he was a young curate at the church at that time and wondered why the scaffolding had been removed.

It was a crisp, bright, sunny day. With the scaffolding out of the way, Nuptial Mass was celebrated by the Naval Padre, Father Steve O'Conner, an Irishman with a good sense of humour. Most of the officers who attended had never been to a Catholic wedding. They were impressed by the Mass and its attendant ritual. The choir from the church of St John and St Columba, in Rosyth, where Margaret sang every Sunday, were at their best. Emerging from the church, we were greeted by a Guard of Honour with drawn swords. A piper from the Caledonia Pipe Band played us out, with friends, members of the public and the press clicking their cameras to record the day. The reception took place at the Woodside Hotel in Aberdour where I was seated at the table with my back to a large roaring fire, the heat made worse by the thick doeskin suit which I was wearing. But I had to stick it out. I had no option. As lunch proceeded and the fire started to recede, together with the happy atmosphere and witty speeches, I relaxed just in time to give my speech. Amidst the jolly atmosphere we were reluctant to leave for our first stop at the North British Hotel in Edinburgh on our way to Guernsey, via London where we spent our honeymoon at Le Chalet Hotel in Fermain Bay, a beautiful, quiet resort. There were just ourselves and another couple on their honeymoon, served by two Italian waiters on an exchange training course, and a French cook. We became very friendly with the waiters especially as they gave me the opportunity to practise my Italian. We even managed to talk one of them, a lapsed Catholic, into coming to Mass with us on Sunday. They gave us special treatment, even bringing breakfast to our room. With the other couple, we toured the island in a hired car and sailed to Jersey for a day's stay.

While in Guernsey, we received a letter from Margaret's brother. Our new car, which we had left in the hands of a 'reliable' friend from my Gambia days to ferry the guests to and from the reception to the Officers Club, had been involved in an accident and was a total loss. Reading the letter, I was more anxious to know what had happened to the driver rather than to the car. At the end of the letter, I learned that my friend, apart from slight shock had escaped unharmed. Apparently, travelling along a dual carriageway in the wrong lane, he had hit the kerb and overturned, landing upside down. We reckoned he'd been a very lucky man. I was determined not to let the news spoil our honeymoon so I ordered champagne and invited the waiters, the cook and the other couple to join us.

On our return from honeymoon, we moved into a dingy flat in Dunfermline, rented some six weeks earlier, as we were not entitled to a married quarter. However, after just one week, a small, well-furnished married quarter in HMS Cochrane at Donibristle, where I had lived as a bachelor while Gambia was under refit, became available. Now entitled, as husband and wife, we moved in, next door to my best man and his wife.

Living in married quarters was an experience which was repeated in my service life over and over again at different locations, including Malta. The closeness of living among fellow officers and their families, exchanging hospitality and helping each other made life very pleasant. In our absence at sea the wives and children got together and enjoyed each others company. Help was always at hand. We shared each other's celebrations. The wardroom, whether on a ship or a shore establishment, was the focus for big events, such as the winter and summer balls, the cocktail parties and Sunday cinemas with dinner provided. We certainly made up for the many days and months of separation. This is probably the one aspect of life that I missed most when I left the Service.

The social life at Caledonia was excellent. Every four months, when a class of trainees completed their course, there was the Passing-Out Dance to which many of us were invited. A reception was held in the Wardroom. There were frequent ladies' evenings and cocktail parties. The winter and summer balls were special occasions when officers from each department produced something particular towards the theme of the evening. It was the ideal start to our married life and a spur to the hard and responsible job that I was doing. There were regular sports meetings with other ships and establishments. Our Olympic-size swimming pool attracted well-known swimmers at training and aquatic events. It was also the venue for one of our Winter Balls. The pool was illuminated by coloured lighting under the water, and scenery was erected around it. A fishing boat loaded with lobster pots and fishing tackle floated on the surface surrounded by larger than life frogs sitting on lifebelts. The food was served at tables surrounding the swimming pool. The merriment was slightly overdone when three ladies jumped into the water, in full evening dress, and had to be pulled out by their husbands. On the following morning, one of the ladies rang me sounding rather the worse for wear, to tell me that she had lost her wedding and engagement rings in the swimming pool. Since the maintenance of the pool was my responsibility, I arranged a search by two shallow water divers and had all the strainers removed to see whether the rings had been sucked in by the pumps. After almost three hours, the lady rang again to tell me she had found the rings on her dressing table. I hesitate to describe what I thought of that lady.

Eighteen months after our marriage, on 18th September, 1960, our first child, Paul, was born. I was the duty officer when I received the news. A fellow officer, a bachelor who lived in the wardroom, volunteered to take over the duty and I drove to Dunfermline Maternity Hospital to see my wife and baby son. At about this time, the Captain sent for me to tell me that I had been nominated for selection to serve on the Royal Yacht Britannia. This was a great honour which caused me quite a dilemma. Having just married and settled down, and having spent eight out of the previous eleven years at sea, I was reluctant to move so soon. I asked the Captain whether, if I refused at this time, I would ever be asked again. He was very understanding. When he spoke to the Admiral of the Yacht and explained my situation, he was told that I needn't worry and that my decision would not prejudice my nomination at a later date. Unfortunately, I was never available at the right time and I was not asked again. A great opportunity was lost. Until this day I am not certain whether I made the right decision. Friends who served on the Royal Yacht all regard it as the most memorable two years of their naval career.

Living conditions for the apprentices continued to improve. The Captain spared no effort in concentrating on the main issue of boosting the morale of the establishment, caring very much as he did about the welfare of the boys under training. On one occasion, during the summer leave period, he came to my house to tell me that a sum of money was available which had to be spent before the end of the financial year, which was imminent. He asked me to allocate a preference for using it. There was no doubt in my mind that the living conditions had to be further improved by providing hot water when the demand was greatest. He had no hesitation in forwarding my proposal to Scotland Naval Headquarters. The Captain of HMS Caledonia had come to take the advice of a humble subordinate. Though strict, he was above all, understanding and humane, the characteristics required for someone who was later to become a Vice-Admiral.

I continued with my sporting activities, travelling to Ipswich and HMS Ganges to play water polo for the Nore Command. I refereed the Army Soccer Cup Final and other games all over Scotland. The Apprentices' Dance Band had built a good repertoire of dance music enabling them to play at regular intervals. The girls from the Snake Pit were now coming to join the boys on their own ground although they sometimes preferred the Kinema Dance Hall in Dunfermline. There were no more battles with the Teddy Boys. A truce had been declared. Perhaps one can begin to understand why so many apprentices married Scottish girls.

As my two years were coming to a close I began to speculate about where I would be going next. In time, I was told by the Captain that I had been appointed to the frigate HMS Pellew, stationed at Portland, as the Marine Engineer Officer and Head of Department, my first charge job. Before the appointment was made official in the Officers Appointment List, the promotion six-monthly signal was received from the Admiralty with my name on it. In his usual pleasant and charming manner the Captain sent for me to congratulate me and said 'I was wondering what they were doing sending a Sub-Lieutenant as Head of Department of a frigate'. Of course he was instrumental in recommending me for promotion with a glowing report.

There was one more hurdle to overcome. I was to be a guest at the mess dinner given in honour of officers leaving the establishment, where I had to make my first speech. Speaking to about fifty officers at an official function for the first time was a daunting experience. But I had prepared well for it. I avoided talking shop and concentrated on the humorous occasions that I had experienced throughout my two years. To my delight, they laughed heartily at my jokes, applauding loudly with the occasional, traditional banging on the table from time to time. This was a happy ending to a most satisfying, eventful and enjoyable period of my life.

Moving from Rosyth meant that we had to vacate our house. As I was now no longer stationed at Rosyth, I was not entitled to a quarter in that area. We were warned that getting service accommodation in Weymouth or Portland was very difficult and, indeed, finding somewhere to live there proved to be quite a problem.

CHAPTER 13

MY FIRST CHARGE JOB

The Search for Somewhere to Live
An Embarrassing Visit to Lisbon
The Commander gets a Black Eye

HMS Pellew was one of eight frigates attached to the Portland Training Squadron. She was one of a class known as the Blackwood Class Frigates, all named after Captains who had taken part in the Battle of Trafalgar. They were propelled by one main engine, a steam turbine of 35,000 Brake Horse Power and a new generation of boilers and steam driven equipment. Because of their many teething problems, they were notorious for breaking down, especially in the early stages. Fellow Marine Engineers commiserated with anyone appointed as the Marine Engineer Officer of any of them. They were particularly notorious for the unreliable control of the Boiler Water System. To keep supplying the boilers with water, engineers invented a Heath Robinson devise using a broomstick and a rope to force the water supply valve to open. But even this didn't prevent one of my boilers from burning out when it was starved of water. For a considerable period after they went to sea, they were not allowed to venture too far from the English coast. After several modifications they sailed on exercises with the fleet, and one sailed as far as Malta accompanied by other ships.

I joined the ship at Portland on Sunday 4th December, 1960, a newly promoted Lieutenant, relieving an experienced Lieutenant Commander, on my first charge job. She was alongside, on sailing orders for Portsmouth on the following day, where we stayed for the two weeks. My predecessor left after a week's handover, leaving me feeling very lonely. I soon discovered that I was also the Stores Officer and had to cope with a Stores Petty Officer, an alcoholic, who had just been court-martialled but was kept on board to sort out a chaotic stores inventory under the supervision of the Squadron Supply Officer. I had to watch this man carefully while he accounted for the missing stores and a chaotic book-keeping system, an unwelcome distraction from my primary job as the Marine Engineer of the ship. This period in harbour gave me the opportunity to come to know the forty five members of my department and form a working relationship with my two key men, the Chief ERA and the Chief Stoker. Half the ship's company went on the fortnight Christmas leave. The other half, including myself, took leave when we returned to Portland. I travelled to Rosyth in Scotland where Margaret was staying with her parents. At the end of my leave I drove her and the baby to Weymouth to stay in temporary accommodation at the White Ensign Club. The Admiralty had not built enough married quarters to house the many officers and ratings serving on the station. To make things worse, accommodation in Weymouth and the surrounding area was very much in demand by holidaymakers. After a long search we found accommodation with an elderly couple, with the proviso that we were to vacate the flat at Easter to make room for their regular guests. As we started the house chase for the second time, they were very sympathetic and tried their best to help us find alternative accommodation without success. The only hope was to be allocated a naval, rented, private hiring. The situation for many families was desperate. Rumours were rife about officers jumping the married quarters queue on the waiting list with financial inducements to the owners. At the last minute, we were offered a pleasant enough house but which, on inspection proved to be absolutely filthy. As we expected to be in the Portland area for no more than six months, and Margaret reckoned it would take that long to clean it, we refused it. So not for the first time, she had to pack up and return to her parents in Scotland. Eventually we were allocated a naval hiring in a little village called Preston, a 200 year old cottage, pretty but draughty! In the space of eighteen months we moved to seven different locations, not counting the times when Margaret's parents had to house us. This set the pattern for family life in the navy. We were constantly on the move, sometimes having to find our own accommodation, at other times settling for less than desirable places. We were finally able to buy our home just three years before I retired. It would seem that today, almost fifty years on, with the quality of service accommodation still being criticised, things haven't changed much.

For most of the time at Portland, we sailed daily, early in the morning returning to harbour any time after 5pm, engaged in a monotonous routine, training RN and foreign naval personnel in anti-submarine warfare. We also acted as decoys and the 'enemy' for ships working up after commissioning, under the strict supervision of the Flag Officer Sea Training. Despite the unreliability of these vessels, Pellew maintained a high performance, free from any serious defects for most of the time. From time to time we acted as Guard Ship dealing with emergencies in the English Channel. One of the most hazardous jobs was to go to the rescue of sailing boats and yachts in distress in heavy seas. During one heavy storm in the channel we had to attend to numerous boats which had drifted away on breaking loose from their moorings at San Malo and other French ports. As we got close to one of the yachts, the coxswain misunderstood the Captain's order of 'Five Degrees to Starboard' for 'Hard to Starboard'. The ship was caught by a huge wave and heeled heavily to one side. For a few moments she seemed unable to right herself, so much so that sea water entered through the funnel into the boiler furnaces, causing several minor explosions as the water hit the flames. I had to physically drag my office writer down one of the ladders as he panicked and attempted to open a watertight hatch shouting 'We're sinking'. When we returned to harbour we discovered that most of the gangway ladders, upper deck lockers and other storages secured to the deck had disappeared. As we risked the lives of sailors to go to the rescue of drifting boats we often found that there was nobody on board. They had broken their moorings without their crews. A break was at hand as Easter leave arrived.

The monotonous routine of training restarted as soon as the second watch returned from leave, going out daily except on most week ends, except that we had to go on board on Sundays to attend Captain's Divisions. There was never any guarantee that I would be going home as soon as we entered harbour. I had to make sure that the main machinery was properly shut down and that any snags that had occurred during the day, however small, were rectified. I also had to stay behind for the Captain's 'Requestmen and Defaulters' sessions if any of my ratings were involved. On the lighter side, we stayed behind to entertain visitors and to respond to any invitations to drinks by other ships or the occasional formal mess dinner or cocktail party. Every six weeks we stayed in harbour for self-maintenance, giving the men an opportunity to participate in sports competitions, which I organised in my capacity as the Sports Officer. We produced the best football team and won the squadron athletics meeting, a boost to the morale of the ship's company.

A change to the repetitive and boring routines at Portland came in March, 1961, when we joined the Home Fleet for exercises with our NATO Allies in the English Channel. We sailed for Brest and secured, with the aid of tug boats, alongside the Portuguese warship Diego De Cao. After preliminary meetings to plan the exercise, we sailed on a convoy screening exercise. The 'war' started with an order to take a severely damaged ship in tow and hand her over to a tug boat. Within the next few minutes we were steaming alongside a store ship for a light jackstay transfer while the 'enemy' unleashed a series of attacks of every description, drills which I encountered time after time on every ship I served in. But one of the most essential elements of the exercise was to improve communications with the various nationalities, practising standard NATO secret codes and terminology. The weather was dismal with nothing less than Wind Force 6, making life very uncomfortable. Movable objects were lashed with ropes and meals were taken, when action permitted, using table fiddles (square wooden frames) to protect the plates and crockery from slipping from the table. Life for the ship's cooks was even more hazardous, having to juggle with hot food containers, resorting to wartime rationing where cooking wasn't possible. But there was nothing much we could do to stop the inevitable shattering of crockery as the claim for rough weather breakages mounted. Fuelling alongside the tankers became almost impossible especially as we had to communicate with French crews. We had to postpone this manoeuvre several times. To avoid stretching the rubber supply hoses in rough weather, we searched for sheltered waters to maintain an even course with the tanker. After a week of being tossed about by the sea, it was a relief to return to harbour and do battle on the playing fields. The morning after returning from shore one evening, we discovered that our hats were missing from their hooks in the wardroom passageway. Although we couldn't prove it, we were fairly certain that our stewards, who had returned from shore half drunk, had probably tossed them over the side. We received a signal from the Norwegian destroyer Tromso, berthed about half a mile downstream which read 'Have recovered an officer's hat marked DFX Marks. Regret we cannot find the body'. It was just as well it was our working hats that were sent drifting out to sea.

A fortnight later we returned to Portland, back to the same routine. We embarked a class of Iranian Officers and six schoolboys and their teacher, adding to the regular stream of visitors for training or as spectators. Training was not confined to ASDIC (Anti Submarine Detection Investigating Committee) but also navigation, communications, logistics and other disciplines. As Navy Days approached, we started to smarten ship ready to entertain the public. The ship was dressed overall and floodlit at night for three days. But there was little respite as we went headlong into our annual inspection by the Squadron Captain and his Staff, at sea and in harbour. Our armament was tested and the ship inspected for cleanliness and preservation. Machinery was subjected to a series of breakdowns, and mock fires started to test our fire fighting and damage control capabilities. We steamed at full speed through the 'Nuclear Fallout' with the water pumps at full blast spraying the entire upper deck to shield us. As we fuelled, with the hoses connected to the tanker, we defended ourselves against attacks by surface ships, submarines and aircraft. As we have proved time and time again during combined exercises, no navy other than Her Majesty's trains its men to such high standards. The Squadron Captain's Staff created as much havoc as possible to test the ship's preparedness against possible conflict, but we passed the test with flying colours.

Their Lordships (The Navy Board) felt that we were due for a break from the long and repetitious routine. By request of the Town Council they sent us to Swanage, a pretty seaside resort not far from Portland. The navy was inundated with such requests. Our arrival was eagerly awaited, a fact made obvious by the reception and hospitality from the Civic Authorities and the community. We were overwhelmed with invitations. A Civic reception was held in our honour followed by hospitality at the homes of councillors and guests. The ship's company were given free access to the Sailing and Swimming Club, and the privilege to travel free on local transport. We returned their hospitality by opening the ship to visitors and giving a farewell reception. They were so pleased with us that they invited us back for their annual carnival week, a request that was granted. We were to see them again in August

After a fortnight of more of the same at Portland we were off again, this time to a foreign port and a temporary change from our training pattern. We were to operate as a squadron taking orders from the Squadron Leader. Our goodwill visit to Lisbon started well enough with sports meetings with local teams. It happened at a time when Britain was taking sides against Portugal at the United Nations over the Angola conflict. The national press soon became hostile, with one major newspaper showing a photograph of the squadron football team players stripped to the waist, sitting in the main square holding glasses of beer with the headline 'Would they behave like this in their own country?' I soon discovered how strongly they felt about Britain's stance with headlines like 'Britain stabs her longest ally in the back'. At that time Portugal was ruled by a virtual dictator, Antonio de Oliveira Salazar. I had to endure an evening with the Chief of Police during an unpleasant dinner with him spoiling what could have been a most enjoyable meal. I was on duty as the Provost Marshal to liaise with the police in the event of any trouble caused by our sailors and stationed at the Police Headquarters. The Chief of Police acted as my host, spending most of the evening bashing my ears, condemning the British. I was praying for some sailor to cause trouble and get me away from the dinner table. We were served with course after course of exotic food as he gobbled away relentlessly, wiping the excess from his mouth as he heatedly made his point. I anticipated severe indigestion on my return to the ship. I went straight to the Captain to relate the whole episode who, in turn, briefed the Squadron Captain. We arrived at Lisbon on Friday 16th June with the intention of staying until the 21st, but events were turning so ugly our diplomats decided that we should leave a day early, citing the breakdown of one of the ships as an excuse. We slipped out of harbour unceremoniously in the early hours of the morning at the end of the only embarrassing 'goodwill' visit I ever experienced to any country during my whole Service life. A visit which was designed to mend fences between our two countries had backfired badly. However, I did manage to see something of the city on an excursion which took us to the city centre of Baixa through a number of squares built after the earthquake of 1755, Lisbon Cathedral built on one of the seven hills and a ride on one of the three funiculars called 'Elvador da Bica' which took us to a hill overlooking a picturesque view of the city. The monument to Christ the King, resembling that at Rio de Janeiro, is unmissable. It was built after the Second World War as thanksgiving for Portugal having been spared the horror of that tragic conflict.

On the way back to Portland all ships carried out their annual full power trial at the same time, six ships steaming at full speed, as if we were trying to get away from that Portuguese Chief of Police as quickly as possible! The race was won by the leader, whose ship had more powerful engines than any of us. After another stint of much of the same we spent, the 10th of July, my birthday, preparing for a visit to Teignmouth. The reception we received at this pretty coastal resort equalled that of Swanage. We gave a reception in honour of the Mayor and local VIPs. The ship was open to visitors throughout the visit and floodlit every evening, attracting the girls to come to meet Jack. We were treated to a reception at the sailing club and invited to use its facilities. It was a welcome break which showed us once more how much the British public loved the Navy.

Back in Portland, we had what was thought to be a minor incident while we were refuelling from a tanker. As we approached, on a parallel course to receive the fuelling hose, the Captain went too close to the tanker and rubbed slightly against its side damaging two of its guardrails. The Captain of the tanker considered this a minor incident and advised our Captain that he needn't report it to higher authorities. So it was a shock to the Captain when he saw the Flag Officer Sea Training, a Rear Admiral, waiting on the jetty to inspect the ship's side and to demand an explanation of the incident. The Captain was completely bewildered when he was admonished for not reporting the accident by signal, especially since there were no visible signs of any damage to our ship. And yet on another occasion when a senior Captain drove his ship into our ship's side, there was not a word said or reported. The damage was repaired unofficially.

Our next port of call was Devonport for a maintenance period, and to give those members of the crew who lived in the area the opportunity to spend some time with their families. We returned to Portland for a long week-end before returning for our second visit to Swanage during Carnival Week, via Poole Bay and Sandown in the Isle of Wight, where we spent two days, arriving at Swanage just in time to receive the Carnival Queen on board at 11 am on Friday 1st August, 1961. We had a fantastic welcome and were again entertained officially and unofficially by the local population. We took part in the carnival procession and our Captain was invited on to the panel to select Miss Swanage at the beauty contest. We were challenged at water polo. I hadn't practised for eight months since I left HMS Caledonia, and had no idea what talent we had on board to form a team. I relied on volunteers and their stated experience. We soon found that their team was not of a high standard. It took them ages to rig the pitch in the sea. Once in the water, I found myself dictating the game, evading tackles with ease, and scoring goals at will against a goalkeeper who could hardly lift himself out of the water. On the following day, my photograph appeared in the local newspaper with the headline 'Veteran Danny scores all the goals'. What the paper didn't say was that I was completely exhausted, making me realise that my water polo days may be over. Water polo is a gruelling game and I certainly couldn't maintain my previous high standard without the training I was used to at Portsmouth and Rosyth. At the age of thirty six it would have been foolish to continue playing.

We returned their hospitality with a lunch party in the wardroom. As was the practice on such visits, we floodlit the ship at night and opened it to visitors during the afternoon. Hospitality received was returned in the wardroom and messdecks. Visits of this kind never seemed to end without some sailor getting into trouble. One of my stokers was arrested for being drunk and disorderly and we had to leave him behind to attend at the Magistrates' Court. I travelled from Portland to act as his Divisional Officer and give an account of his character. He was not a bad lad and I made the standard statement that 'his behaviour was completely out of character', which made no difference whatsoever to the sentence of a hefty fine. I took Margaret and the baby with me introducing her to the friends I had made during our visits. Thanks to my naughty stoker we had a good day out. Our visit to Swanage during a sunny and bright week-end was a welcome break. On the way back, encountering heavy seas, we sighted a dismasted yacht, the Ben Johnson, and the motor vessel Majorca towing the Yacht Valerie and searched for another two yachts which were reported missing. We boarded the Ben Johnson, a hazardous operation when two sailors tied to safety harnesses were lowered in an ugly storm to find that there was nobody on board. May the 24th was indeed an eventful day, one which I will never forget, when we thought that the ship was about to capsize in the incident described earlier in this chapter. After anchoring in Weymouth Bay for shelter we returned to Portland to count the cost.

On Thursday 31st August, while out at sea on guard duties, we received a signal requiring us to proceed to Lyme Bay in dense fog. As we steamed along cautiously, we sounded the bell at regular intervals and continued to do so at anchor. A Buccaneer aircraft had crashed into the sea while testing the launching catapult on the aircraft carrier HMS Hermes. We were required to act as the Salvage Headquarters for the next two days. Margaret had no idea why I hadn't returned home that evening. Having heard of the incident on the news she guessed that we may have been sent to the scene of the crash. When she rang the base authorities she was informed that they could only tell her that the ship would not be returning to harbour that evening. She was to ring again on the following day for more information. It was not until recently, when I visited the National Archives at Kew in London, that I discovered exactly what happened when I read the 'Secret' report on the incident released under the Government's Thirty Year Rule. I took a copy of the main conclusions of the Board of Inquiry. The aircraft, being launched from one of the catapults as part of a trials programme, nose-dived and stalled completely as it plunged into the water in eleven seconds, 500 yards away. The cockpit was jettisoned and the airplane remained floating for twenty seven seconds before submerging, but neither of the two occupants, the naval and civilian test pilots, succeeded in evacuating the aircraft. It was examined on the sea bed in the inverted position. The cockpit section had parted from the aircraft but was still held by a series of wires and cables. The pilots had detached themselves from the normal attachments but failed to clear the cockpit due to the impact damage. The board came to the conclusion that there was a mechanical and material failure which is of too complex a nature to include in this book. The On-Site Investigation was carried out by a Lieutenant Commander Watson, accommodated in Pellew, an Admiralty Salvage expert as well as an air pilot and diver. We were joined on site by a salvage ship and an RN Divers Launch. The plane was raised from the sea bed in the inverted position, using the fittings on the undercarriage as the slinging points, and after two days, we proceeded to Portland in the company of the salvage ship carrying the aircraft. It was transported to the dockside at Portland in this condition and righted by a dockyard crane where preliminary investigations were carried out. Further investigations were made at the Air Investigation Unit at Lee-on-Solent, the Fleet Air Arm base in Hampshire. Some parts were sent to Farnborough to be examined by the Structural

Department. The report was very detailed with numerous photographs of the relevant components and expert analysis. I found it quite absorbing. A Petty Officer Diver was afterwards commended for searching the ocean bed for three days running, and finding the offending part, a small pin, which may have been the cause of the accident.

We returned to Portland on Sunday 3rd September, 1961, for a short spell before sailing to Londonderry for a short stint at the Fishery Protection Patrol. The British trawlers were very appreciative of what we were doing and provided us with plenty of fresh fish, enough to feed the whole ship's company. In Londonderry, we berthed next to a flour mill, notorious for the huge rats seen at night. Rat guards were fitted to stop these beasts from climbing over the securing ropes into the ship. We had some fun picking them out with searchlights. Trouble from the IRA was then in its infancy. We were told to be careful as there were one or two troublemakers around. I did manage to go across the border to buy some fresh salmon from Buncrana, in the Northern tip of Ireland, which I kept in the ship's freezer until we returned to Portland.

The ship was by now getting close to a long scheduled refit when we had to de-store and de-ammunition. There was just one more duty to perform. We were sent to St Peter Port in Guernsey to take part in the annual commemorative ceremony in honour of the men who were washed ashore after two destroyers were sunk off the island during the Second World War. We embarked a Royal Marine detachment and band. I was detailed to act as the Second-in-Command of the guard and mourners to parade in the main streets and at the memorial ceremony. We attended at a number of receptions and reciprocated by inviting the civil authorities on board. I think I performed my seaman's duties, marching with drawn sword, admirably! The highlight of the visit was the football match against the island's first eleven, preceded by 'Beat Retreat' by the Royal Marines. Jobs of this nature and others, such as acting as Provost Marshal at Lisbon, were undertaken by Engineers to give the seamen officers a break from keeping duties. As a Head of Department I was excused duties in harbour, although I was always on call for any technical emergencies. I often had to remain on board to see through defects. In any case, I wasn't qualified to deal with any emergencies caused by storms, such as the strain on the securing hawsers and dragging of the anchors. The islanders treated the annual visit of a British warship for this ceremony as a special occasion. Thousands of spectators lined the streets and the ship was inundated with visitors. Fifty years after the war this ceremony was discontinued.

Just a few days before the ship paid off, a new First Lieutenant joined the ship. To give him some practice at handling the ship, the Captain kept us at sea after the day's exercises. A dumb buoy with a long pole in the middle was put in the water to give this new officer the opportunity to practise bringing the ship alongside it. Once he'd mastered this art of seamanship we were to head for harbour. Not used to manoeuvring a single propeller ship, and after several attempts, he couldn't bring the ship alongside the buoy. The Captain was well aware that the sailors were getting impatient and decided to head for home. I was beside him waiting for orders to go down to the engine room. He turned to me and said 'Come on Chief you have a go'. I took over control on the bridge and after just one attempt I brought the ship alongside the buoy. The seamen recovered it and the Captain ordered full speed ahead. The First Lieutenant was not amused at seeing a non-seaman perform this manoeuvre with such skill! When we arrived in harbour, and after a gin and tonic, he challenged me at chess. I was anxious to go home but he insisted. I beat him easily but he wasn't satisfied and insisted he try again, with the same result prompting him to say 'I'm sure there is something I could beat you at'. The next day he tried the submariners trick and invited me to eat glass, a trick that I had practised previously. After a few minutes, and a lacerated mouth, he gave up. Thank goodness I only had to contend with this man for a few weeks.

There was one more scare when we were recalled from leave to deal with a ship in distress in the English Channel. Luckily another frigate beat us to it. On Thursday 26th October, 1961 we gave a farewell party before sailing for Rosyth, anchoring at Crombie to de-ammunition, entering Rosyth dockyard at 6.15 pm. On Thursday 2nd November the Captain left the ship followed by most of the ship's company. A skeleton crew, including myself, were left behind to oversee the extended refit which was to last until October 1962. I went down to Portland to help Margaret pack and we travelled back to Rosyth in our Ford Prefect. Once again we found ourselves homeless, with Margaret's parents coming to the rescue, until a sub-standard married quarter was allocated to us at HMS Cochrane, Donibristle, where we had lived during my Caledonia days. On the 15th July, 1962 our daughter, Ruth was born. She was baptised, as our first born Paul had been, in the little chapel in HMS Cochrane, the ship's bell being used as the baptismal font. We were to be moved again within a few months, to a Commander's house in Rosyth, a spacious house but which cost us a fortune to heat. My brother Bob and his family, newly arrived from Malta to settle in England joined us for Christmas, during a bitter winter. Their first experience of snow brought the opportunity for the building of a life-like snowman in the garden!

The dockyard workmen descended on the ship and started removing the auxiliary machinery to take to the workshops for overhaul. Most compartments were gutted for preservation and painting. The ship's hull was completely stripped of old paint to bare metal in the dry dock. Regular progress meetings were held with dockyard officers as we haggled over getting the most out of them. Our offices were transferred to portable cabins ashore as we watched the ship dismantled and then gradually put together again. The inevitable last minute rush to achieve the planned date of completion led to chaos as dockyard workmen walked over each other to replace the equipment. Anything that looked like a pipe in the machinery compartment was bracketed. Some sophisticated equipment secured by mistake led to a major defect which delayed the completion date. The ship commenced basin trials followed by trials at sea. On the fourth day at sea, despite all the precautions I had ordered, especially on the boilers water supply system, doubling the watch and putting the Chief ERA to supervise the operations, one of the boilers dried out and burned. An empty glass water level gauge was mistaken for a full one by four people. The burst boiler had to be completely retubed, putting an end to the sea trials. We were stuck in the dockyard for another three weeks before trials recommenced. A Board of Inquiry was convened and the senior boiler room watch-keeper reprimanded.

The Commissioning Ceremony was held on Saturday 1st December with traditional pomp and ceremony. Prayers were held on the jetty alongside the ship. The First Lieutenant gave the order 'Roman Catholics fall out'. A few of us retired to a designated area where I, as the Senior Catholic, took prayers. This old routine has now been discarded and combined prayers have been held since the start of the Ecumenical Movement. After an extensive training programme the ship's company were sent on the fortnight's Christmas leave in two watches, Port and Starboard. We remained at Rosyth for six weeks preparing to resume active service with the Fleet, before we were off to Portland to continue where we left off with the previous crew. I remained on board to maintain continuity and train the new engine room personnel.

Once again we found ourselves without a home. I was told to vacate the quarter where we were living because the ship was no longer stationed at Rosyth. At the same time we were not entitled for a quarter in Portland because I was not expected to be there for more than six months. So once again Margaret's parents came to the rescue until I was appointed to my next assignment.

It wasn't long before a serious defect in the Asdic Dome, necessitating dry-docking at Plymouth dockyard to inspect it and remedy the defect, came to light. This is where I became conscious that, as well as being the Engineering and Stores Officer, I was also the Ordnance (now Weapons) Engineer, although I received precious little training for this responsibility. I relied on the Ordnance Artificer to advise me on weapons matters. While we were in dry dock, the Squadron Engineer Commander turned up unexpectedly on a Sunday evening when I was ashore. He expected me to be on board even though there was nothing I could do on a Sunday, when dockyard personnel were not working. This officer was well known for his lack of a sense of humour. It was rumoured that he had never been seen laughing, and was as miserable as sin. He told me to join him the next morning to go down the dock with him to examine the dome about which I knew very little. I asked the Ordnance Artificer to come down with us. The Commander came to look for me at about 7am, when I was still in my cabin getting ready for breakfast. As he started to change into his overalls I noticed that his vest was full of holes. I couldn't believe my eyes seeing a Commander wearing such a dilapidated vest. I left him to get on with getting changed and went for my breakfast. I hinted that I would have expected the Squadron Ordnance Engineer to deal with such a serious defect and, in any case, there was only one solution for a dented dome, it had to be replaced, which is exactly what happened. However, I did carry out extensive research on Asdic Domes, so I learned something new to broaden my education. The story about his vest soon spread like wild fire across the base at Portland.

We headed for base straight into a Force 8 storm, keeping a look-out for yachts or any ships in distress, and to prepare for another NATO exercise. We assembled, with our allies, at Brest for a short pre-exercise briefing and off we went as a convoy escort force while other ships acted as the 'enemy', repeating all the drills and mock disasters of past exercises. In a rough sea, we were getting short of fuel and were forced to move into a sheltered area to replenish from the French tanker La Seine. As a small ship, tossing about in the sea while trying to connect the supply hoses was difficult and dangerous enough. Communications failed dismally when the tanker passed the wine supply hose, used to provide the French ships, by mistake. When the fuel hose was finally passed over it had the wrong connection, without the standard NATO fitting. The situation became critical as we pitched and heeled while we adapted the fitting. Once secured in place, and as the Captain tried to keep a steady and parallel course with the tanker, the rubber hose kept stretching dangerously. Orders to evacuate the replenishing area were given when the Captain considered that there was a danger that the hose may snap. Despite all these obstacles, he persevered and was determined to prove his skills at manoeuvring the ship, ignoring the advice of the tanker Captain, who suggested that we should return to harbour to refuel. At the Wash-Up, it transpired that most ships did return to Brest to refuel. Our Captain was praised for persevering.

Back in harbour for the week-end, we embarked on a series of tussles against different nationalities on the playing field, with the rugby match between the British and the French as the highlight. As I walked towards the rugby ground with the Squadron Engineer Commander, we called at a wine shop for a glass of cheap local wine. When we went to a night club in the evening they sold us the same wine at an exorbitant price. The Commander complained to the manager, whereupon two bouncers got hold of him by the scruff of the neck, took him outside and beat him up. I followed him out to see him bleeding heavily from the nose and holding his head in his

192

hands. A tough character and an ex-navy rugby cap, he refused to go to hospital and we headed to the ship in a taxi. The next morning he was due to act as the president of an examination board in my office. By now he had developed an enormous black eye. One side of his face was so swollen that he could hardly open his mouth. He instructed me and the other member of the board to ask all the questions and do the talking. He hid most of his wounds by sitting next to the ship's side closest to his swollen face. A very clever man, much liked by all who knew him, he had a good sense of humour. On the morning after this incident he went to his immediate superior, the Squadron Captain, to report that he was filled in by two night club bouncers. Obviously this incident did not do him any harm as he went on to become a Vice Admiral. We went back to sea to continue with further rehearsals for a 'likely war', giving the Commander plenty of time to recover. By the time the 'war' ended, at the end of another week, he was ready for another run ashore.

On returning to harbour, I was faced with another major defect. In their eagerness to shut down the machinery to get ashore as early as possible, the boiler room crew had ignored the precautions necessary to prevent an explosion from taking place in the boiler furnace. A loud noise was heard across the ship. I rushed out of my cabin to confront a Chief ERA looking very pale. He informed me that there had been an explosion in one of the boiler furnaces but that nobody was hurt. The partition plate which separates the two uptakes from the boiler furnaces in the funnel was blown off and the boiler side furnace casing buckled. I immediately stopped leave for all the technical staff and, with the help of a French Repair Unit, got on with the necessary repairs. The partition plate was replaced and temporary repairs were carried out to the damaged furnace brickwork. There was nothing that we could do to repair the casing but hope for the best. Luckily trials proved successful. We were able to leave Brest with the rest of the fleet and head for Portland to carry out an official investigation into the circumstances which led to the explosion. The Petty Officer in charge of the boiler room at the time of the accident was found culpable, charged with negligence and punished. After three days we sailed for Chatham dockyard for further investigations and to carry out permanent repairs. Irrespective of the outcome of the investigation, I congratulated my staff for the hard work they had put in. It was an illustration of what could be achieved in an emergency. It was decided that it was not worth spending thousands of pounds to repair the boiler casing. The ship continued to operate successfully until it was scrapped several years later

There is one last story to tell of my time in Pellew. HMS Lynx was berthed ahead of us on the dockside at Chatham. Her Captain was related to our First Lieutenant. His secretary was Margaret's brother, James, then a young Sub Lieutenant. Life for a Captain on a ship refitting in a dockyard could be very lonely and boring. Living in isolation in his quarters he can't go to the wardroom for a drink without an invitation, so he used to detail James to invite him while most officers, who were living ashore, went home for their lunch. The wardroom was virtually deserted. So for the next four weeks he came to drink with our First Lieutenant in our wardroom, arriving daily just after 11am sitting alone until we joined him for the lunch break. He remained in the wardroom until about 3pm. On one occasion he drank thirty two Horse's Necks (naval name for a brandy and ginger) without batting an eyelid. I had the pleasure of renewing my acquaintance with Admiral Austin when we were both retired and members of the Sea Urchins at the RNR Officers Club at HMS Eaglet in Liverpool. His alcohol intake did not stop him living to a ripe old age. I attended his funeral about five years ago. While at Chatham, we gave the summer fortnight leave to each watch. On the 9th May, 1963 I sailed in the ship for the last time to Portland. On the 10th I left to join the family in Rosyth.

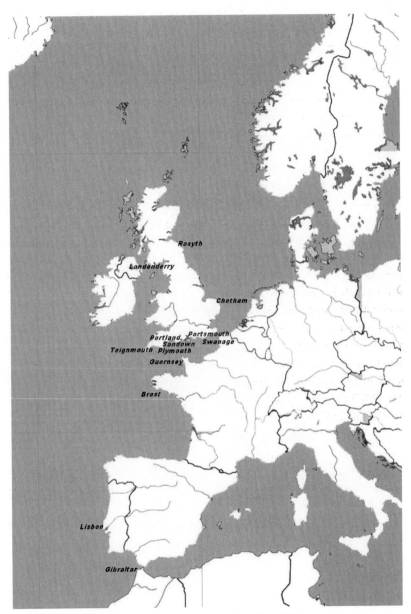

HMS Pellew December 1960 to May 1963

CHAPTER 14

APPOINTED TO SERVE IN MALTA

Independence Celebrations
The Legacy of Colonial Rule
The Task of Running-Down the Services

Before I left HMS Pellew I was asked whether I would take up an appointment as the Engineer Officer of the Port Auxiliary Service (PAS) in Malta Dockyard, serving under the Commodore of the Naval Base. I had to think hard about this offer. Although I was keen to go back to my native land, a Naval Officer's career depended mostly on his service at sea. I was assured by the Appointing Officer at Whitehall that it would make no difference to my future prospects. I decided to take on the job and prepared to move the family to Malta. On taking up the appointment in June, 1963, I discovered that I was responsible for a fleet of about forty propelled auxiliary vessels, including ocean going tug boats, water supply boats, tank cleaning vessels, storing craft, motor fishing vessels and a variety of other service craft and dumb barges. They were serviced and maintained under an old fashioned and expensive system. I took it as a challenge to modernise the planned service routines and inject new ideas similar to those applied to naval warships. To help me with this task, I had a sizeable workforce of Maltese skilled and unskilled workmen led by an outstanding Works Manager. I also felt that it would be in the interest of the Maltese that they were introduced to new techniques before the British left the island.

When Napoleon surrendered to Nelson in 1800, the British assumed the island's administration. In 1814 Malta officially became part of the British Empire as a crown colony, used as a shipping staging post and Royal Naval Fleet base. After the Second Word War, and after the then Prime Minister Mr Dom Mintoff made an unsuccessful attempt at integration with Britain with full representation in the British Parliament, the Maltese opted for Independence. By the time I arrived to take over my responsibilities, negotiations between the British and Maltese Governments were well under way to discuss the terms under which British forces could remain on the island, and the future of the NATO base. There was also the question of outstanding war reparations. Each Service had to negotiate the terms of redundancy payments and pensions with its employees. The Royal Dockyard had already been transferred to the Maltese Government and converted to a Ship Repair Yard with substantial financial assistance from the British Government. A small area was retained to accommodate the PAS and the Queen's Harbour Master's staff, including myself. One of my responsibilities was to prepare the fleet under my charge for transfer to UK or to sell to the highest bidder. The Maltese were given first preference at much reduced prices. After long and protracted negotiations agreement was reached. After one hundred and fifty years of British rule, Malta achieved its Independence on the 21st September, 1964. In December 1974 it became a Republic within the Commonwealth. The Defence Agreement with Britain and NATO ended in 1979 when the British Forces were withdrawn. In May 2004, Malta joined the European Union. While there is no doubt that Malta benefited much from the presence of the British Navy and the Military, there were times when relations were soured by the manner in which the Maltese were treated, as second-class citizens under Colonial Rule. There were periods of tense public unrest, culminating in disorder and riots leading to the fatal shooting of some demonstrators. Although granted British Nationality, the Maltese were never treated on equal terms with their masters. But that was in the past.

The rundown of the British Forces started in 1963. In November I attended the last Annual Taranto Dinner at the Fleet Air Arm base at HMS Falcon in the south of the island, on the anniversary of the attack by airplanes flown from HMS Illustrious when most of the Italian major warships were sunk or damaged at their main naval base at Taranto. A Fleet Air Arm airplane was sent to Taranto to collect oysters for the first course at the dinner, a gift from the Mayor of the city. All the prominent people on the island were invited, including the Governor, the Prime Minister and the Heads of the three services. When the first course was served I refused my oysters, remembering my first and last encounter with these shellfish, and passed them on to a Wren Officer sitting next to me. On the following day she, the VIPs and practically all those who ate the oysters were taken ill, some developing Typhoid Fever. The Italians had taken their revenge on the Fleet Air Arm!

On Independence Day, the three Services put on a spectacular performance of drills and ceremony with the combined bands of the Army and Royal Marines, assisted by the Maltese Army, playing and parading together. Naval warships gave a display of seamanship in the late evening, entering Grand Harbour in complete darkness. As they passed the breakwater they switched on their illuminations, showing the ships in profile. Shallow water divers were dropped from helicopters in the glare of searchlights swimming under water and emerging on shore. Fireworks, let off from ships, military bases and floating barges, lit up the sky. The Maltese, well known for producing a colourful variety of fireworks, released a barrage across the whole island. HMS St Angelo, the fortification used by Grand Master La Valette as his headquarters during the siege in 1565, was floodlit, as were other fortifications. All through the day church bells tolled and prayers were offered for the success of the island's future. On the parade ground, the Union Jack was solemnly lowered for the last time, and the red and white Maltese flag, bearing the George Cross, awarded for the bravery and suffering by its people during the Second World War, was proudly hoisted to signal the beginning of a new era.

Back at the dockyard I had to deal with the slow demise of the PAS, having to give redundancy notices to good men who had given a lifetime's service to the British Empire, only to face an uncertain future. A Chief Engineer would first be demoted to a second or third class, downgraded to a Chief Stoker, and then a Stoker, until he was beyond humiliation. As an Anglo-Maltese I found this task unpleasant, but I did my utmost to give my men the best possible terms of redundancy. It was a sad episode which exposed the injustice with which we treated fellow British Subjects in the old days of Colonial Rule. Similar treatment was given to those serving in the Royal Navy. They were only allowed to join as cooks and stewards, earning reduced rates alongside their British counterparts. The same applied to dockyard employees. Highly skilled and well educated technicians were only allowed to advance to the rank of 'local chargeman', and they were the exception. British chargemen, foremen, inspectors and civilian staff were appointed to take charge of the 'natives' at great expense in jobs which could easily have been filled by highly skilled Maltese personnel. Some of them were carried by Maltese craftsmen and engineers. To be a clerk or a draughtsman was considered to be a high position to be in because it meant that a suit and tie were worn and it was socially accepted by the local intelligentsia. When I joined the Navy, several friends and fellow apprentices, who qualified as I did at the Technical College, were not allowed to join simply because they were Maltese. I was, because I had an English grandfather, entitled to claim English Nationality. My two uncles were also allowed to join the Navy because their father was English. When, after the ordeal which the Maltese endured during the Second World War, the British acknowledged the injustice with which they had ruled the island, they relaxed the rules. By that time Malta was getting close to Independence and freedom from the shackles of a domineering power. At least this acknowledgement helped to create a reasonably friendly atmosphere to end one hundred and fifty years of Colonial Rule and now, the British are more popular and welcome as tourists. Independent Malta is flourishing, its economy is booming and the people are masters of their own destiny. The war years, and the common struggle against Hitler and Mussolini, brought the Maltese and British closer together and the handover of power was achieved with goodwill and friendship.

The running down of my Fleet, and the Services in general, produced some indiscriminate salesmanship. A small tug boat with a defective engine was sold for peanuts. A week later it sailed into the dockyard creek flying the Jolly Roger. One of the largest floating-docks in the world, which could accommodate battleships and giant tankers, was sold to a Maltese shipyard owner and then sold to an Italian shipyard with an enormous profit within months. It was sectioned into three parts and towed to Italy. Motor Fishing Vessels which were sold for three hundred pounds were being sold for seven thousand a year later. Large areas of land occupied by the military had to be converted to civilian use. Army barracks, naval bases and airfields were handed over completely demilitarised and compensation paid to convert them for civilian use, a process which was to go on until the British Forces left Malta long after Independence, giving the Maltese time to build their limited industrial capacity and tourism while at the same time finding alternative employment for thousands of workmen previously made redundant. Local firms and shipping companies started enlarging their businesses and tourism expanded rapidly as service land was transformed into holiday sites and hotels.

To complete my task of disposing of the craft under my charge, the Commodore asked me to stay for an extra year beyond my scheduled two, once again assuring me that, having spoken to the Appointing Officer at Whitehall, my future prospects would not be jeopardised. But by this time I had stopped worrying about promotion. As a family we were enjoying Malta, the many activities we were involved in and the many friends we'd made. I decided to accept the offer. As events turned out, one year wasn't enough to complete the job and another officer was sent to relieve me. In the meantime I got on with my many duties. One of these was to act as the Duty Harbour Master about once a week, when I had to spend the night at the Naval Headquarters overlooking the Grand Harbour, even though I was not qualified to deal with seamanship matters. In the event of an emergency I was to seek help from the Queen's Harbour Master. On one occasion a huge tanker, tied up to buoys fore and aft, started to drift towards Fort St Angelo. It was blowing its sirens at regular intervals. I was fast asleep when the Commodore rang me to tell me that the ship was in distress and calling for assistance. He ordered me to call the duty tug boat to help. I called its captain on the radio and ordered him to go to the tanker's assistance while I informed the Queen's Harbour Master. He and other members of his staff sailed with the tug. I discovered later why they had boarded the vessel. They were subsequently awarded a handsome share of the salvage money. The Commodore and I, who raised the alarm, didn't get a penny! From his house in HMS ST Angelo, the Commodore couldn't escape the booming noise of the siren while he watched the big hulk getting closer to the rocks. The tug arrived just in time to prevent a major disaster.

Margaret and I continued to enjoy life, involved in many activities, especially with MADC (Malta Arts and Dramatic Company) which boasted Noel Coward as one of its past members during his early years in the Royal Navy. Other actors included Patricia Roc who settled in Malta, and Stewart Wagstaff, mentioned earlier in this book. Margaret took part in the classic comedy Charlie's Aunt, and played the leading role in Bernard Miles musical

'Lock Up Your Daughters', performed for the first time outside the UK. She played the part of Moth in Shakespeare's Love's Labour's Lost, participated in concerts for the British Institute and sang for the Malta Choral Society. I stage-managed several plays. Contrary to my previous judgement that I was too old, I took up water polo again, playing only at ship level for HMS St Angelo. I played cricket and the occasional game of tennis. As well as being members of the wardroom we were also members of the Dockyard Officers Club, where I won the Billiards Competition in 1964. I renewed my acquaintance with many of my Maltese friends.

With all these activities and the busy social programme, life was hectic. It was not unusual for me to play a game of water polo at lunchtime and cricket in the afternoon, followed by a stage rehearsal and a cocktail party or a ball. On one occasion, after a ball, with a group of friends we went for a swim at a sandy bay. While I was changing I lost my bunch of keys. We decided not to attempt to find them in darkness to avoid burying them further into the sand and waited until daylight when, much to my relief, we found them. After a sleepless night we went home just in time to relieve the baby-sitter, my mother, and wake the children. Invitations to social functions were received at the rate of four or five a week. To add to my many commitments, I took on the job of wardroom social secretary. In this capacity I organised a wardroom ball on the bastions of Fort St Angelo. The architecture of this 16th century fortress, built by the Knights of St John, presented an ideal background for recreating the medieval age. I borrowed the runway emergency paraffin flare lights from the RAF and had them placed on the ramparts, producing a spectacular view of flickering lights, attracting hundreds of viewers across the Grand Harbour. The décor was augmented by coloured floodlit seating and dancing areas. The best dance band in Malta saw us through the early hours of the morning. The traditional Christmas Winter Ball was held inside a converted old bakery, also built by the Knights, presenting another opportunity to contrive another unusual effect. Life was a complete change from the arduous and tedious sea going routine of the previous two and a half years. Malta was not yet on the tourist trail. Its natural small sea inlets and fishing villages provided picturesque and peaceful surroundings. In the summer months my men converted one of the rigging cutters into a picnic boat with sun and shade decks. With family and friends, we started our picnic each weekend by calling at an ice factory to top up dust bins with ice to keep our beer and soft drinks cool. We sailed close to the rocky coast past numerous caves and small bays often anchoring at the Blue Lagoon, half way between Malta and her sister island Gozo, or one of the many quiet inlets, now spoiled by access roads, hotels, restaurants, bars and noise. The children loved every minute of it, spending much of their time in the water. What more could one ask than to serve Her Majesty in such ideal surroundings? There were times when we anchored for a whole week-end in one of the isolated bays completely undisturbed by intruders. Sometimes friends joined us with their speedboat, providing us with some amusement as beginners like me parted regularly from their water skis. As evening approached, we lit the barbecues, opened up the bottles of local wine and relaxed into the night. For safety reasons we kept in touch with HMS St Angelo by radio.

As part of the Independence Agreement with the Maltese Government, the armed forces were allocated a monthly ration of duty-free alcohol. With gin priced at six shillings a bottle this led to an explosion in the social life with everyone giving parties. We decided that it was time for a rest and booked a holiday in Italy, planning to visit Rome, Florence and Venice. By the time we were due to leave, Italy suffered one of the worst flooding disasters in its history. Communications between Rome and the rest of the country were cut off. Florence suffered badly and many of its precious treasures and works of art were lost or damaged. We decided to spend the whole fortnight in Rome and booked into a private hotel, the Woodcock Glavina, owned by a retired First World War British Army Major and his Italian wife, close to the Coliseum. At 11am sharp, for five minutes, the major played recordings of British Army regimental marches. We toured Rome's historic sites, buildings and monuments and were guided around the Vatican by a French priest, a friend of Margaret's family, who had arranged a place for us at a semi-private audience with Pope Paul VI after which he took us to Castel Gandolfo, where we ate the best Lasagna we'd ever tasted. What was eye-catching was a street where wine was sold at houses on either side of the road, each advertising the price on narrow wooden boards at their doorways. One of them showed the price with the words 'Senza Rubare' (Without Cheating). We found eating out in restaurants away from the centre of the city the best and cheapest way of sampling real Italian cuisine where Pizza was baked in ovens hewn out of the rock. After enjoying a performance at the Rome Opera House and a tour of the city by night, we returned to Malta more relaxed ready to withstand the demanding social life. On another occasion we had a break at the Services Lido in Tripoli. The Officer-in-Charge of this holiday resort was an old friend we'd known at HMS Caledonia. He was on a visit to Malta when he arranged for us to spend a week at the Piccolo Capri, a few kilometres from Tripoli in Libya. The Services had developed the Holiday Centre for the benefit of Service families in the Mediterranean area. It had a beautiful sandy beach, with restaurants and chalet accommodation in a quiet part of the country.

As an Anglo Maltese, my appointment may have been part of a diplomatic move to deal with the delicate situation of running down the workforce under my charge, a task which was accomplished smoothly. Outside my immediate task I was called upon to perform other ambassadorial duties. On one occasion, I was asked to act as an intermediary with the Tunisian Government when one of our frigates hit and sunk a fishing boat in Tunis harbour. A minister from the Tunisian Fishery and Agricultural Department was sent to Malta to negotiate a compensation package. The Commodore asked me to deal with this matter because I could speak Italian. When the minister arrived I found that he spoke French and Arabic and only a little Italian. I had to convince him to accept one of our Motor Fishing Vessels as a replacement to the boat we had sunk. He subjected the MFV to a thorough inspection and kept on insisting on being supplied with two spare engine starting batteries and a considerable number of spare parts. Since we were parting with these boats for peanuts, as part of the run-down, his request did not present me with much of a problem. I got on very well with the minister and invited him home to dinner. I managed to broker a deal in dodgy French, broken Arabic and a little Italian. He returned to Tunis a satisfied customer.

Margaret and I were both heavily involved in the Annual Inter Services Drama Festival. The talent available was of a very high standard. Each performance was judged by an adjudicator appointed by RADA. Soon after arriving in Malta, Margaret was asked to take the female lead in Unesco's

'Rhinoceros', a very demanding play. Unfortunately the male lead, couldn't remember his lines. On adjudication night the play degenerated into a farce. The adjudicator had a field day. The Festival was open to the public, so 'Rhinoceros' became the talk of theatre enthusiasts for months. Most of the players came from the Royal Naval Secondary School Staff, where some outstanding teachers were employed. Competition for appointments to serve abroad among teachers in the UK was at that time very strong. The selection panels had no problem in filling vacancies with the best. I formed a stage relationship with a well known painter and art master with outstanding creative talents who designed stage settings to exceptionally high standards. In a subsequent Drama Festival we cleared the board with 'The Noble Spaniard' when we won the best production, set design and stage effects prizes. In this production Margaret's opposite number managed to remember his lines! At MADC, which was dominated by British residents and the Services, we started handing over control to the Maltese by introducing more local actors. With the help of the three services, both financial and practical, I arranged for a complete overhaul of the club premises, rebuilding the stage, rewiring and updating the lighting and audio systems. We held a special opening night with three short plays, in addition to the three annual performances at the Manoel Theatre, an eighteenth century mini opera house, as well as the annual open air Shakespeare performance at San Anton Gardens, using the Presidential Palace as a background, the highlight of the Maltese Theatre Year. The natural setting, with its imposing large semi-circular stone stairway leading to a large flat floor area, stone walls and an iron gate at the entrance to the Palace Courtyard and an open balcony on one side of the palace, presented the ideal backdrop. Of major concern to the stage manager was making sure that the actors appeared on the stage at the right time. Some couples had the habit of getting lost among the trees in amorous exchanges. I employed a team of callers who were briefed on how to avoid the blushes on the faces of these young lovers. We looked forward to the last night and the party that followed until the early hours of the morning. On one occasion, one of Malta's leading actresses was taking part in a dress-rehearsal watched by hundreds of school children. In the middle of one of her longest speeches in one of Shakespeare's plays they started laughing and screaming. She couldn't understand what was going on and stopped mid-speech demanding the restoration of order from the producer. He had to explain that a big rat was climbing up a tree behind her. She joined in the laughter and got on with her performance.

The MADC committee, of which I was a member, was dominated by two elderly sisters who had connections with the professional theatre. One of them, Kate, was still producing plays with great skill. I stage-managed Arthur Miller's play 'The Aspern Papers' for her. She was a perfectionist who demanded a high standard from the cast and stage team. To help with the production, the Manoel Theatre provided an experienced professional stage crew who could construct a set in a matter of two to three days. They also operated the light and audio equipment and produced the sound effects. Ella, the older sister, almost blind, still managed to type and lay down the law. She treated me with great affection. During one of the rehearsals of a Shakespeare play she asked me to sit beside her on a bench. She said 'Come and sit beside me Danny. You have done quite well for a local boy, haven't you?' The sisters, daughters of a First World War Naval Captain, had settled on the island. They relied on the Services and British residents to provide most of the actors. Only the best Maltese performers were invited to audition. They were, however, held in great esteem and affection and were both awarded the MBE for their service to the Theatre. They were always name-dropping, regularly boasting about their friendship with Noel Coward. Before I left Malta, I presented a memento to the Director of Agriculture and Fisheries in the form of a brass plaque showing the opening and closing time of San Anton Gardens, in appreciation for allowing us to use the gardens without charge.

After over three years, the Appointing Officer rang the Commodore from Whitehall to tell him that I was urgently required to take up an appointment as the Engineer Officer of an old destroyer which was in serious trouble. The Captain and the Engineer Officer were dismissed from the ship, which was declared unfit to go to sea for several weeks due to mechanical failures, and replaced. He also spoke to me on the telephone to tell me that it was time that I went to sea to get back on the promotion ladder. He probably wasn't aware of his predecessor's assurances that my service in Malta would not affect my future prospects. But by this time I had already decided that I was not going to let the promotion bug bother me unduly. In any case, I didn't need any incentive to do my job to the best of my ability. I accepted the appointment and started preparing to fly to UK. In the meantime a temporary engineer was appointed to the stricken destroyer and the condition of the ship was sufficiently improved to proceed to Singapore, stopping at Malta on the way. I was made aware of her problems and started preparing to give technical assistance, using my civilian work force. I also arranged a social programme for the ship's officers. When the ship arrived in Malta, the Captain sent for me and told me that the new temporary engineer was doing well. He felt that it would be unfair to ask him to leave the ship, having worked so hard to make it seaworthy. He told me that the Appointing Officer would be contacting me to advise me of another appointment.

I was appointed to HMS Sirius, the newest ship in the Navy, which had just completed trials after building in Portsmouth Dockyard. So, from being offered the oldest ship, I was to take over the newest. The ship was due to sail for the Far East calling at Malta on the way. When she did, I took the opportunity to meet the Captain, who I'd known as a young Lieutenant when I served in HMS Saintes, and to transfer some of my kit to await my arrival at Singapore. I was sad to leave Malta but felt it was time we led a more normal life, away from the hectic social activities of the past three and a half years, as normal that is as service life dictates. I hadn't realised how many friends we had made during our time in Malta, until we started to make the list of guests to invite for our farewell party in the wardroom of HMS St Angelo, friends from MADC, St Angelo, the Dockyard Officer's Club, the Malta Choral Society, the British Institute, the staff of the Naval School, the RN hospital and our many Maltese friends and relatives. It was just as well that the drinks were duty free! We flew from Malta in December, 1967. We had nowhere to go except to stay with Margaret's parents in Rosyth, where we spent our Foreign Service leave. I attended a pre-commissioning course at the Royal Naval Engineering Training Establishment in Gosport, Hampshire, where I was briefed on the teething problems that the ship was experiencing. I flew to join her at Singapore in April, 1967, leaving the family in a married quarter in Portsmouth.

Leaving St Margaret's Church Dunfermline.

HMS Pellew.

At the Commissioning Ceremony, right wearing medal.

The Bastions near the entrance to Grand Harbour. Ships in background getting ready to enter to take part in the celebrations.

Fort (HMS) St Angelo, floodlit during Independence Celebrations.

With guests at the Farewell party with Margaret on my right, my sister Ethel and husband on extreme right.

The cast of 'The Noble Spaniard' - Margaret third from left.

CHAPTER 15

MY LAST SEA ASSIGNMENT

A New Ship with Serious Problems
The South West Pacific
The Coronation of the King of Tonga

HMS Sirius completed its building at Portsmouth Dockyard eighteen months before I joined her. I had a brief look at her when she called at Malta on her way to the Far East and I was looking forward to being the Head of Department of a bigger ship than in my previous charge job. She was fitted with two steam turbines of 40,000 Brake Horse Power each, with a maximum speed of 32 knots. For the first time in my naval career I was to serve in an air-conditioned environment, on a ship equipped with stabilizers, adding to the comfort of my new home for the next two and a half years. In the hot and humid conditions of the Far East and the Tropics, and the heavy seas in which any ship has to operate, these were vast improvements in the living conditions of a naval warship. She had a complement of two hundred and sixty officers and ratings and I was directly responsible for sixty of them. During her trials, she had encountered several teething problems, some not resolved before she left Portsmouth.

During my pre-commissioning course I was briefed about the major problems and given guidance on how to solve them. I joined her on the 26th of April, 1967 at Singapore Dockyard during a self-maintenance period, discovering that water had been rationed and that the two main propulsion turbine engines had been vibrating violently under certain conditions. Other problems kept appearing. The main propeller shafts were not resting properly on their bearings between the gear boxes and the propellers, and the stabilizers were breaking down at regular intervals. The spare parts system was in a chaotic state. In the last minute rush to take the ship to sea, spare parts were bundled on board without proper storage identification. For a new ship these were serious lapses. My dreams of assuming the responsibility of the newest ship in the navy with modern and reliable equipment were soon dashed. I had no time to relax as I set about solving these problems. In addition, the machinery compartments' preservation and cleanliness were not up to the standard one expects of a new ship. I was faced with a big challenge which I relished.

The ship was Portsmouth based, making me eligible for a married quarter in the area. Unlike my experience in Portland, where I and my family found ourselves homeless on two occasions, I was soon allocated a large flat in Eastney on the Southsea front overlooking the sea. I had time to settle the family, to read my pre-commissioning notes and scan the makers' handbooks of the machinery which I was about to inherit before flying to Singapore. As is the case in most married quarters, there is usually a friend or two to be found when moving in. There were some who I had known from previous ships, so Margaret had friends to rely on in my absence. After I joined the ship I discovered that the Weapons Engineer Officer occupied a flat next to ours.

The ship was ready for sea on the 3rd of May. As we slipped away from the jetty, I began to experience some of the expected problems as the main engines started to vibrate, causing me concern about the effect this was having on the watch-keepers. I reported the problem to the highest authorities by signal. None of the advice I received was having any effect. I saw to it that the water distilling plants were properly serviced and were now producing plenty of water but I was not aware that an order had been issued rationing consumption. On returning to harbour, I was having a bath when a fellow officer told me that bathing was forbidden. I told him that there was no shortage of water. He was delighted and advised me to inform the First Lieutenant and the Captain. Within minutes a pipe was made to inform the ship's company that water was no longer rationed. A loud cheer was heard coming from the direction of the messdecks. One by one, the defects were rectified and the machinery spaces started to look smarter. By the end of October their appearance was transformed, so much so that the Flotilla Captain sent a signal 'The ship presented a clean and smart appearance and I was particularly impressed by the Boiler and Engine Rooms'. But the main engines defect would not go away. When we eventually located the cause of the problem, the turbines were found distorted beyond repair. The only way to rectify the defect was to rebalance or replace the turbine rotors at a cost of hundreds of thousands of pounds. In the meantime, I advised the Captain not to order full speed ahead or astern unless it was absolutely necessary in the event of an emergency. I continued to make representations at the highest levels. The outcome of these exchanges was to unfold later. The stabilizer systems continued to give trouble as reinforced rubber hoses kept bursting, causing hundreds of gallons of oil to be discharged into the bilges. This defect had to wait until we returned to UK. In the meantime, my men kept on changing the hoses as they burst. At the end of the exercises off Singapore we anchored at Changi, a beautiful seaside resort, the notorious Japanese prisoner-of-war camp during the Second World War transformed into a residential area for the RAF, where I paid a visit to a distant relative married to a Surgeon Squadron Leader. We returned to Singapore to refuel and take on provisions before sailing for Hong Kong.

It took us three days to get to Hong Kong, my first visit to that fascinating island. Jenny's side party was waiting on the jetty, a force of female workers well known to the naval fraternity as the best painters and bilge cleaners in the game. The First Lieutenant commandeered a number for painting the ship's side. I was allocated a fair number to clean and preserve the bilges in all the machinery spaces, much to the delight of my stokers who hated the job. The Chinese Maintenance Manager called on me to discuss a small defect list but there were other priorities such as stepping ashore at the earliest opportunity. It was customary for officers to start a 'run ashore' by calling at the Honk Kong British Club, well known as a meeting place for diplomats, judges, businessmen and distinguished visitors to the island, where we could order food and drink and have the cost debited to our wardroom account. The place was decorated in the old Victorian style with shiny red leather upholstery and carpets, surrounded by oak panelled walls, reminiscent of the old Imperial grandeur. The service was provided in silence by a multitude of Chinese waiters. We felt almost obliged to talk in whispers. The Mandarin Hotel was just around the corner where an orchestra, which included about twenty violinists, played light classical music mixed with songs from the movies of the day. But Hong Kong had other attractions. At night, before the tunnels were dug out to join the main island with Kowloon, the harbour presented a spectacle of moving lights as about sixty ferries were afloat at any one time crossing between the two locations. From the Peak, which was reached by a tram moved by steel wires, an impressive panoramic view of Victoria Harbour and Kowloon could be seen, while from the Crow's Nest at the top of the Hilton Hotel, at the Sunday special curry lunch, the island could be viewed from a different angle. Repulse Bay, the best of the beaches, provided ideal conditions for swimming and relaxation. Western style night life was found among the bars and restaurants and club area of Lang Kwai Fong. Eating out on a floating restaurant at Aberdeen Harbour provided yet another unusual experience. But I couldn't resist the famous Hong Kong hair cut, when two or three Chinese girls moisten your face with hot towels and massage your head with their delicate hands. As you relax, one of them manicures your hand and toe nails. For me, not having much of it, the hair cut was of secondary importance. Shopping provided a challenge, especially if you decided to buy jewellery, as I did. I was advised to shop only at reputable shops, even if the cost was higher. I took a chance and bought Margaret a pearl necklace which turned out to be genuine. With the ship repainted and the machinery spaces bilges cleaned and preserved, we said good bye to Jenny and her side party and disappeared over the horizon on our way back to Singapore where, with great excitement and anticipation, we began preparations for our departure to one of the most pleasant and interesting journeys of my whole naval career.

A week later, we sailed for our first destination on the South West Pacific Cruise, arriving at Darwin six days later. We fuelled and stored with fresh provisions and stayed long enough to enjoy a barbeque as guests of an Australian Naval Officer where I tasted kangaroo steak for the first time. We were well prepared to lose a few sailors on this trip as Australia was well known as an attraction for deserters who wished to fulfil their dreams of emigrating to the New World. True to form, three seamen and one stoker started on the trek through the desert, heading for the nearest big town to start a new life in their dream land. We continued on our journey to Sydney, stopping at Townsville on the North East coast, steaming through the hot sun and calm waters of the Coral Sea, past the Great Barrier Reef, exploring the beauty of the Marine Park stretching from Cape York as far as Townshend Island north of Rockhampton. We cut through the reef to reach Townsville, where we anchored in the blue waters to wait for permission to enter harbour on the Queen's birthday, the 10th of June, 1967. As we berthed alongside, we dressed ship in her honour. On finishing fuelling we undressed ship and slipped away on our last lap to Sydney. As I was required to be at my station in the engine room, I missed sailing through the beautiful Sydney Harbour. We berthed at Darling Island, the main Australian naval base. I had no idea where we had entered from the Pacific Ocean until I visited the city many years later, and had the route pointed out to me by a guide during an excursion. I have since returned to Sydney to see my younger son and his family on a number of occasions.

The British High Commissioner, the Lord Mayor and the Premier of New South Wales called to be greeted by the Captain, the Officer of the Day and a piping party. I was looking forward to meeting my friends, ex-naval Officers who had transferred to the Australian Navy, and the many relatives who had emigrated from Port Said during the turbulent years of the Suez Crisis. I invited some of them to our reception in the evening. At lunch time many of my friends called for a drink and later in the afternoon two of my male cousins came to see me. I hadn't seen them since they were evacuated in a landing craft during the Suez War. I was inundated with invitations, but with eleven official functions in a week, at most of which I was expected, I had difficulty in coping. When my relatives realised that I couldn't possibly visit all of them at Maroubra and Paramatta in the time available, they put a chauffeured car at my disposal. At one of the official functions, we presented a silver-plated bell belonging to a previous warship bearing the same name to commemorate the participation of the first HMS Sirius in the foundation of the state to the Premier of New South Wales. Unfortunately, I couldn't find enough time to see much of Sydney, although I have made up for it since. I managed to visit many relatives and was driven by an ex-RN friend to his home to dinner, at Hunters' Valley. The wardroom served me well in reciprocating some of the hospitality. Our sports teams were kept busy, playing all kinds of sports against the Australian Navy. The ship was open to the public throughout the visit and we were grateful to our cooks and stewards who coped admirably with a stream of guests to the wardroom.

Operating alone as a ship for such a long period without the rigours of a continuous programme of exercises was a new experience. Perhaps we were chosen for this PR exercise across the South Pacific because we had an outstanding ship's Captain and a diplomat, one who was destined to go far in his career. He eventually became a full admiral and retired as the Governor of Gibraltar. Although we were still required to carry out the statutory drills and firing exercises as we travelled from one place to another, this was a cruise to remember. The best was yet to come as we headed for Wellington in New Zealand. As we approached Oriental Bay, our helicopter pilot invited me to fly with him in his Wasp for a view of Wellington and the approach to the capital of New Zealand. The Wasp towed a large White Ensign flag, as if to announce that the Royal Navy was on its way. The detour took us to within range of a magnificent view of the Green Mountains on the North and South islands where they meet near Cook Strait, and Mounts Cook and Victoria. Unlike Sydney, where I missed sailing through its beautiful harbour, I could see how we were to approach, enter and berth at Wellington. The weather was fine with perfect visibility as we flew over a calm sea and landed back on the ship's flight deck. We sailed through Cook Strait and berthed alongside in full view of the green hillside. As in Australia, we received a rapturous welcome as hundreds of British settlers, eager to meet their compatriots, came to see us berthed and, throughout the visit, many of them were greeted on board. Hospitality couldn't have been more generous as a pile of invitations were brought on board by the postman. His Excellency, the Governor General of New Zealand, came on board as did a hospitality committee to discuss the social events, entertainment programme and invitations to local clubs. On the second day, we gave our traditional cocktail party to the local VIPs and other guests recommended by the British Embassy. After the party, we were invited to drinks at the Sailing Club. I went on a sight-seeing tour of the city and surrounding countryside in perfect weather which contrasted with the reputation of Wellington known as the Windy City. Judging by the crowds who queued up to visit the ship, we made a good job of showing the flag.

After five days, we sailed for Suva in the Fiji Islands, our main fuelling base during our period in the South West Pacific. At the usual wardroom reception some ex-patriots invited us to an exclusive Beach Club at an attractive sandy bay where we were made honorary members. By coincidence, a cousin who was the Chief Engineer of the Cable and Wireless cable laying ship 'Edward Wilshaw', and who I hadn't seen for many years, happened to be in harbour. We exchanged invitations to dinner on our respective ships before moving on to our next destination, and the highlight of our cruise, Tonga, in the Friendly Islands.

The main purpose of the South Pacific cruise was to represent the United Kingdom at the Coronation of His Majesty King Taufa' Ahau Tupou IV of The Kingdom of Tonga. We were the first warship to arrive at 0900 on the 1st July, 1967. An Australian frigate was due later. The Captain called on the Premier as soon as we secured alongside Vuna wharf. An 11-gun salute was fired in honour of the British High Commissioner and Council. At 1830, guests started arriving for a reception on board. The heir to the throne, a 29-stone huge figure with members of his staff and council and their spouses, some of them just as heavy, came over the gangway and were greeted by the Duke and Duchess of Kent and the Captain, Commander Derek Refell. The ship immediately developed a small list, until we escorted the guests to the Helicopter Deck under the ceremonial awning, ensuring that they were evenly spread to port and starboard to stabilise the ship. As is the case at such receptions, we circulated amongst the guests, who included representatives of the Governments of Australia and New Zealand, among whom conversation was more relaxed than was the case with the local dignitaries. Most of us found talking to the Duke of Kent hard-going in contrast to conversation with the Duchess. Two hours later, the would-be king and his entourage disembarked, as the ship took a lurch towards the jetty.

Among the guests at the Coronation were a number of rich New Zealanders, Australians and Americans who were staying at the only hotel on the island 'The Dateline'. A few very attractive women were unaccompanied and were obviously keen to meet the Officers of the Royal Navy. On the first day, after the reception, in honour of the heir to the throne, they invited us to a dance. We soon developed a friendship with them which for some, was to last long after we left Tonga. We danced the evening out and walked back to the ship with some of our hosts in the early hours of the morning, in what seemed to be a paradise island surrounded by banana trees and thousands of fox bats hanging upside down from the trees like a scene from Disneyland. We invited our new friends on board for a night cap which proved longer than we expected, leaving us with very little time to sleep before breakfast. On the next day, our hosts turned up alongside on a hired cabin cruiser to take us on a picnic. They provided the food and we loaded the booze. We sailed around some of the 169 Friendly Islands, so called because of the friendly welcome the inhabitants gave Captain Cook in 1773 when he discovered them, leaving the rest of the world behind us as we admired the silver sand through the clear and tranquil waters of the South Pacific. At Blowhole Bay we gasped with amazement as hundreds of columns of water shot out of the rocks as much as 40 feet into the air, producing the effect of a Mexican Wave as the sea struck the rocks on one side and moved across the bay, an unforgettable scene. We anchored at a peaceful little island where we could dive and swim to the beach and relax on the silver sand as we stared at the magic of the blue lagoons with our gorgeous female hosts swimming around us like those sea nymphs whose seductive singing was believed to drive sailors to destruction on the rocks they inhabited. The waiters brought the food in the small dingy as we sunbathed and admired the natural beauty which surrounded us, no high rise buildings, no hotels, no tourists or loud music to distract us. This was a purely private party. Back alongside the ship we unloaded the empty bottles and what was left over, and our hosts. They were drawn back to the ship whose name was Sirius, the brightest star in the sky. They liked it and we couldn't keep them away as they followed us throughout the rest of the South Pacific Cruise and Simon's Town in South Africa. Some of the husbands returned to their respective countries to earn for the upkeep of their wives who were booking accommodation in the most expensive hotels wherever they went.

On the 3rd July we moved away from the jetty and anchored off-shore. HMAS Anzac arrived and took station a cable to our stern and in the evening both ships were floodlit in full view of the islanders. On the 4th we embarked members of the press, including Alan Whicker, the renowned television presenter, with a female companion who was reputed to be worth millions. At 2000 the Duke and Duchess of Kent were piped on board to dine with the Captain and Officers in the wardroom and were treated to one of the best Chinese meals that I have ever tasted. Our Chinese cooks had really gone to town. After the Duchess had expressed her words of praise, the First Lieutenant, who traditionally presides at wardroom functions, called the chief cook to the table for a glass of sherry. The Duke and Duchess, the British High Commissioner and senior members of his staff left the ship at midnight while some of us stayed on board to rest before attending the Coronation and reception on the following day.

The heir to the throne was the son of Queen Salote, who had attended the Coronation of our Queen in 1953. On her death, her body was flown from New Zealand where she had died, and driven over a two-mile long carpet which her subjects had made from banana leaves, stretching from the airport to the Royal Palace. A two-year official mourning period was declared before her son was to succeed her. The people had loved her dearly. The coronation ceremony, the procession and the lunch lasted over ten hours. By the end of the evening, wearing the formal summer uniform with a stiff jacket collar right up to the chin, and sitting cross legged on a mat for about three hours, I felt quite exhausted. A succession of dancers from the Polynesian and Pacific islands and Maoris danced throughout lunch and beyond, the men performing ritual drills with hunting spears to almost identical routines. After a time, the drumbeats and intricate hand twisting and turning by the woman dancers became repetitive and boring. We were gasping for a stiff gin and tonic well before it all ended. Despite all this, I felt honoured to have witnessed the unique and unusual nature of a most spectacular occasion. Coronation Day ended with an impressive torch ceremony on the island and a fireworks display from HMAS Anzac. At the end of a memorable day, we returned to the ship to a much needed shower before our friends from the Dateline joined us in the wardroom for a final drink. I retired to bed in time to get a good rest and to make sure that I was fully alert as we prepared the main machinery for leaving harbour on the following morning, on our way to Suva.

The news of this visit and the splendour of this momentous occasion reached home via the media long before my letters. I received a dressing down from my wife for failing to tell her that I was in Tonga for the Coronation. She and the children learned of it from the programme 'Blue Peter', when Valerie Singleton appeared modelling the robes (made in London) that were to be worn. Unknown to them, I had been sitting facing an array of suckling pigs, exotic fish and other delicacies which I had never seen or tasted before. Next to me was the daughter of the Finance Minister, a New Zealander. Throughout our stay in Tonga our sailors entertained the local inhabitants, including children, with parties escorting them around the ship wearing pirate costumes, some with black eye patches, waving wooden cutlasses in the air. In return, the people of Tonga showed their appreciation at their homes.

Leaving Tonga on the day following the Coronation, we berthed alongside the fuelling jetty at Suva on the 7th and left on the following day for an island which I had never heard of, Savu Savu, one of the few remaining colonies left from the Great British Empire. Arriving in mid-afternoon, we had time to prepare for a film show on the jetty while the Captain went ashore to meet the Chief and the British Consul. On the following morning we were invited to meet the Chief who gave a mock demonstration of the old ritual of cannibalism. We returned to the ship in time for a lunchtime reception on the forecastle. The island is the second largest of the Fiji Group and is, like the other islands, full of thick vegetation, coconut and palm trees with an attractive marina and ideal conditions for swimming. It is known locally as the 'hidden paradise' as we discovered on a short walk along the mountain road. On my birthday, we returned to Suva. The Captain had forgotten our agreement that he was not to order 'full speed' unless it was absolutely necessary. He wanted to show-off by leaving from the jetty stern first, at full speed. I promptly rang the bridge to query the Full Astern order when it was immediately changed to Slow Astern. On return to harbour, the Captain, conscious that he had made a mistake, called me to his cabin where a double gin and tonic was waiting for me, a traditional naval custom for a Captain to say sorry to the Engineer Officer. Although the engines were driven at full astern for a very short period, they produced the worst possible effect by vibrating and shaking everything around them.

On the way to Suva we sailed past Lambasa and a number of little islands in the Fiji Group, close enough to see the natives waving as we fired the occasional gun salute. The Captain and First Lieutenant took it in turn to fly by helicopter to pay their respects to the Chiefs as the ship continued on its way. I understand that at each island they were entertained to the same ritual of cannibalism, not knowing whether it was a mock exercise, or whether it was the arm, leg or some other part of the anatomy of a human being that they were eating! I do remember them coming on board covered in garlands smelling heavily of the scent of the flowers. Our last visit to Suva lasted long enough to spend two afternoons at the Beach Club. When an English lady sailed her boat into the rocks and damaged its rudder, in a gesture to return some hospitality, I arranged for my shipwright to make her a new one. As we went round the world showing the flag there was nothing more important than helping our ex-patriots in distress! She sent him a nice letter to thank him. After three days we set off for New Caledonia, a group of islands under French Rule, arriving at Noumea, a beautiful island and a French Naval Base, two days later, firing a 13-gun salute as we entered harbour. This was yet another part of the world which was completely unknown to me and as beautiful as all the other islands around the South West Pacific. The French Navy looked after us well and organised tours, sports events and receptions for the whole ship's company. At the invitation of the French Officers, we spent an afternoon with them and their families at a barbeque on a private beach. A Scout Group was entertained on board by the sailors, and the Captain invited some local dignitaries and French Senior Officers to lunch. As was the case everywhere, we kept meeting ex-patriots. It seemed that the British were everywhere, a sign of their adventurous spirit, perhaps.

I continued to learn more about this part of the world and to realise how lucky I was in achieving what I had set out to do when I joined up as a young artificer, to see the world. There was more to come as we set off for yet another British Colony, Ugi, where we anchored for twelve hours, just enough time for the Captain to pay his respects to the Chief and for some members of the crew to go walking among the coconut trees and the forest inland. This was a beautiful and peaceful island like all the others, a contrast from the crowded, affluent society in which we live in the West. I stayed on board to deal with some minor engineering problems.

After leaving Ugi we sailed through the Condominium of the United Kingdom and France, the New Hebrides, past several islands visited by Captain Cook and other British and French explorers in the 18th century.

We sailed past Espiritu Santo and Santa Cruise until we reached Honiara in the Solomon Islands, where we stopped for two days to fuel and provision ship. Here we saw some of the relics left over by the Japanese after the fierce battles that took place in the Second World War at Guadalcanal, a sister island, including guns, suicide fighter aircraft and a variety of other weapons. A few half sunken ships could be seen beached along the coast.

From Honiara we proceeded to Papua New Guinea and berthed alongside at Port Moresby, where my stokers polluted the beautiful harbour with thick furnace fuel oil supplied by gravity from a hill overlooking the harbour. Communications with the natives by flagging broke down as thick black oil shot out into the air from the perforated air vents as the tanks overflowed, creating a spectacular umbrella effect, causing damage costing thousands of pounds. It was an embarrassing moment for me and my department. The First Lieutenant was not happy to see his immaculately clean ship and the shining upper deck, including the ceremonial awning rigged in readiness for the official reception, covered in thick oil. We spent hours covering the sea with Gamlin, an agent which turned the oil into heavy particles which sank to the bottom of the sea. We exhausted our whole stock and that of the island. I employed my stokers to help the seamen to clean the upper deck. Normal service resumed just in time for the formal reception under the ceremonial awning. New Guinea was a fascinating place with many of the natives living in huts. It was here that I heard Pidgin English spoken for the first time. I found it quite extraordinary hearing how the English Language was transformed by the natives. As always the white population were delighted to see an influx of new white faces and, as everywhere we went during the cruise, they entertained us lavishly. On a tour of the island I finished up carrying away two fish hunting spears and two canoe paddles, which I have kept ever since.

We sailed for Darwin on Saturday the 29th July, 1967 on the last lap of a memorable and eventful experience. For much of the time, we traced the routes which Captain Cook had followed on his voyage around the South Pacific between 1777 and 1779, visiting several places which he discovered and named, but we avoided Hawaii where he was so cruelly killed on his last journey while his ship 'The Resolution' was at anchor. We stayed at

Darwin for two days acting as hosts to the local VIPs and visitors from the general public. The deserters who had disappeared at the start of our visit to Australia, having given themselves up to the police, were delivered to the ship and placed under close arrest. They were dishevelled, penniless and haggard looking, having lost weight as they almost starved during their trek across the desert. In the process of dreaming of a new life, they had missed the opportunity of a lifetime, travelling around some of the most beautiful islands in the world. Warrants were read on the way to Singapore where the culprits were escorted to the shore establishment HMS Terror to await their punishment and a long period in the detention quarters. We were due for a self-maintenance period and stayed at the dockyard in Singapore until the 28th of August. During this period Commander Refell inspected a guard of honour for the last time before he handed over command to Commander Humphrey Baker. A newly promoted Engineer Sub-Lieutenant joined the ship to act as my assistant. He was extremely capable and proved to be a great help to me, allowing me to relax after a worrying spell dealing with serious defects and giving me a better opportunity to look after Margaret who was due to join me for three weeks. However, I thought that it wouldn't be fair to let him take the responsibility of supervising the rectification of some serious defects at such an early stage. I was about to cancel an arranged holiday to Malaya when the Engineer Commander on the Admiral's Staff virtually ordered me to go on leave, while he undertook to oversee the work. It was a very kind gesture by a true gentleman.

The plan was to take Margaret to Kuala Lumpur and Pennang. When we arrived at the hotel in the Malaysian capital we discovered that the toilets consisted of two cement footprints and a hole in the ground. Margaret couldn't face this arrangement, so we cancelled our booking and motored to Port Dickson, a seaside resort with a good reputation. We travelled through rubber plantations and some magnificent scenery, lodging at a sandy beach hotel in an air conditioned chalet in quiet and peaceful surroundings with only a few residents, adding to the privacy of the beach. It was a relaxing holiday which helped me forget the problems I had left behind in Singapore. As we sat to dinner on the first evening, Margaret was horrified to see numerous lizards crawling over the ceiling, wondering when one of them was going to drop on her plate as we ate. The waiters assured her that they were harmless but I sensed her unease as she watched these small creatures whizzing about in all directions. I was quite used to seeing lizards and playing with them in my childhood in Malta.

For most of Margaret's visit, we stayed in Singapore with close naval friends who we'd known during my service in Malta. They took us shopping, helping us choose the camphorwood chest which now stands in our hall. Singapore presented a contrast to the European way of life, especially to Margaret who had never travelled to that part of the world. Although it has a very humid climate it doesn't get particularly hot. During the Monsoon Season it could rain continuously for weeks on end. Luckily, Margaret was there during the dry season. With the ship working tropical routine, we were able to spend most afternoons relaxing at the Singapore Swimming Club or the Services Lido not far from the dockyard. Evening entertainment was provided by attending receptions in the company of our hosts, on the ship, and the various clubs. We were invited to the wedding of our ship's tailor, known to the sailors as 'Sew Sew', who married the Commander-in-Chief's Chief Steward's daughter. The Admiral was also invited and it was here that our new Captain met him for the first time. Before he had time to present his credentials, wearing sword and medals, he was introduced to his Supreme Commander by Sew Sew! The wedding and the reception which followed were quite an experience with the best Chinese food provided in abundance. As the celebrations progressed so did the noise, as the traditional drinking competition proceeded, until the participants collapsed in a heap around the bride and groom. On the following morning the Captain, in full ceremonial dress, left the ship to present his credentials to the Admiral, having already been introduced to him by the ship's tailor.

The time had come for Margaret to return home and she left a few days before we were due for sea trials and exercises. With the help of my assistant, I found more time to relax, as he attended to problems in the machinery spaces, allowing me to concentrate more on planning and administration as well as dealing with my ratings' problems. Keeping up the morale of the men in my charge was of vital importance. I was responsible for resolving some delicate and private domestic affairs happening thousands of miles away. The longer the ship stayed away the more problems were likely to arise. If the Captain sent someone on compassionate leave I had to find a replacement. I spent much of my time dealing with these divisional matters.

The sea trials went well but the main engines continued to vibrate every time we left harbour. Most of the other problems had been solved. I had to give the same advice to the new Captain to use the engines with great caution. So far the ship was not subjected to heavy manoeuvring, but we were due to join the fleet at exercises and the Captain had to follow the Admiral's orders. Luckily, we were not put under great pressure. In the meantime, the C-in-C Far East recommended that the turbines should be lifted for examination as soon as we returned to UK. As described later this advice was not heeded, with serious consequences. As if to spare us becoming involved in heavy manoeuvring, we were ordered to return to Hong Kong unaccompanied, my second visit to that fascinating island. Jenny and her side party were again waiting on the jetty to the relief of my stokers. The local contract manager came to discuss a short defect list which included the panelling of my cabin with fire resistant wood. I had to live at the shore base while this job was in progress. As the Weapons Engineer Officer (over six feet tall) who lived in the adjoining cabin was resting on his bunk, with his legs propped up against the bulkhead, a Chinese workman, drilling through the bulkhead, started drilling into his foot, fortunately not deep enough to cause permanent damage. Apparently he jumped out of his bunk screaming all the way to the Sick Bay. With his feet bandaged and limping, I apologised to him over a drink.

During this visit, one of my Petty Officers arrived drunk on board and punched the Officer of the Day on the nose. This was a serious offence which could have led to a court martial. It was my duty to act in his defence when he appeared at the Captain's Defaulters table. On the following evening, at the Hong Kong Club, I came across the famous barrister Bennett QC, who had flown from UK to defend two murderers. I asked him to give me some tips on how to defend my Petty Officer. He said 'In this case it is not what you say, but the way you say it that will convince your Captain of any mitigating circumstances'. On the next morning at the Captain's table, with great passion, I tried to convince the Captain of the integrity and out-of-character behaviour of the accused. After the hearing the captain sent for me in his day cabin and, over a drink remarked 'That was a load of bullshit you came out with at the table'. He wasn't far wrong. The Petty Officer was punished by a Warrant, just short of a court martial which was approved by the Commander-in-Chief and read to the whole ship's company mustered on the forecastle. He was given a long sentence in the local detention quarters and demoted to a leading rank followed by a long period under stoppage of leave, and dismissed from the ship.

Before we left Hong Kong, we were given the news that our commission was to be cut short, as the Government had decided to start running down the Far East Fleet. We were to return to UK in early October. Our Sew Sew, who lived on board when we were away from Singapore, got into a panic. He had done some tailoring for the sailors, to be paid in instalments over the next year. He started lobbying all the Divisional Officers in an effort to retrieve the money he was owed before we left the station. By the time we arrived at Singapore, he had made little headway. As this was a private arrangement between him and the sailors, we couldn't force them to pay, although we arranged for some of them to pay by lending them the money and then having it docked from their pay packets. We succeeded to a great extent, except that there were some who wouldn't pay because their clothes didn't fit. One of them was a stoker nicknamed 'Mild and Bitter", the words tattooed over his chest when he'd got drunk in Boogie Street, the red light area of Singapore. The First Lieutenant arranged an unofficial defaulters table to review the cases of the dissenters. They were asked to bring their clothes with them. 'Mild and Bitter', all of five foot four inches, put his jacket on. It was obviously not made for him. The sleeves overhung his finger tips by several inches and the shoulders were far too big. As he put it on, the First Lieutenant and all those around him burst out laughing. The case was dismissed and Sew Sew was left with a suit for an unknown sailor, although we managed to help him retrieve most of the money. We had to. After all he was married to the Commander-in-Chief's Chief Steward's daughter! We arrived at Singapore on the 1st of October, 1967, and immediately started preparing to leave the station. We said good bye to Sew Sew and his sewing machine and to the cobbler with his last. The Chinese cooks, stewards and laundry crew we retained until we arrived at Portsmouth.

On the 5th of October we flew the 'Paying Off 'pennant and gave our

226

farewell party, sailing for Mombasa four days later. On the way we stopped briefly at Fua Mulalu, but long enough to play football and hockey against the little island, and for a swim. Two days later we crossed the Equator. The traditional 'Crossing the Line Ceremony' was held on the flight deck with officers and ratings joining in the fun. We spent five days at Mombasa on shopping expeditions and playing at a variety of sports against the army. I spent most of my time ashore in the company of a close friend who was seconded to the Royal Kenyan Navy as the Supply Officer. Sadly, his wife was just recovering from a traumatic experience when she was attacked by a native at a swimming beach. Despite this, she and her husband went well out of their way to offer me their kind hospitality. With the aid of binoculars I was treated to an unusual sight from their house, as wild animals ran around in the forest beyond. While we were anchored in the middle of the harbour, we refuelled the ship and took on provisions, getting rid of a number of empty oil drums by selling them to a local tradesman and using the money to boost our Welfare Fund. On the 21st of October we held the traditional Trafalgar Night dinner.

Our next stop was Simon's Town, where we exchanged hospitality with the South African Navy and British ex-patriots. Our sports teams played at a variety of games against our hosts. On this occasion I confined my sporting activities to acting as a scorer at cricket. I joined the Captain at dinner when I was reminded of his expensive tastes. I was appalled at the manner in which the Black Africans were treated as second class citizens. I was to witness more of the cruel policy of Apartheid when I returned to South Africa on another occasion. I renewed my acquaintance with two ex-RN officers who had transferred to the South African Navy and the British Naval Attache, a Commander Engineer with whom I had served at HMS Caledonia. He had a very energetic wife who organised most of the entertainment, providing female partners for members of the ship's company at social functions. Travelling round the world, unexpected things are often encountered. At one of the functions, a colleague told me that he was off to 'break the beam'. I soon realised what he meant. As I stood in front of one of those long wall type urinals, water started flowing over the wall. It was activated by a laser beam which I broke as I stood facing the wall. Another piece of useless information was added to my education. By this time the ship was getting too close to home, and some officers had to deter the beautiful ladies they had met in Tonga from flying to Gibraltar. At the jetty, as they dried their eyes and waved their handkerchiefs, we disappeared over the horizon. After a week at Simon's Town we left on our last lap home to Gibraltar, stopping at Freetown in Sierra Leone for a few hours to refuel. Steaming at the economical speed of 14 knots for a fortnight, we reached our next destination. En route, I concocted and produced my first Ship's Concert Party.

Gibraltar was a good place to go shopping for the last time. We exchanged hospitality with invitations to drinks from units of the Home Fleet and one evening, at the Rock Hotel, we indulged in playing for small stakes at the casino. Throughout our stay I busied myself preparing for the short refit at Portsmouth Dockyard. I received the news that, despite the recommendations of the Commander-in-Chief at Singapore, the main engines were not to be examined. Serious consequences were to follow. On the 23rd November, 1967, we arrived in Portsmouth in time for Christmas, to be greeted by families and friends who were waiting on the jetty, including Margaret with Paul and Ruth. There is no place like home.

CHAPTER 16

BACK HOME FROM THE FAR EAST

A Tragic Fatality as we Sail through a Hurricane
The West Indies
A New Crew is put to the Test

On arrival at Portsmouth we became attached to the Home Fleet. The usual protocol started with the visit by the Admiral Portsmouth Command calling on the Captain, followed by the Lord Mayor to see his adopted ship, the last to be built at the city's dockyard. I was busy planning a two-month refit to overhaul equipment which had worn out after two years since the ship went to sea and steaming over 70,000 miles. It was my responsibility to co-ordinate the defects of all departments into one list. Preliminary, departmental meetings were held on board with the Commander-in-Chief's Technical Staff, prior to the Conference with the Dockyard Authorities. We had to justify the merits of each major item to be repaired or overhauled at the cost of several thousands of pounds. There were no major disagreements, except that I expressed my disappointment that the main engines were not to be examined to establish the cause of their excessive vibration. The post refit trials proved successful, and we started preparing for a 6-week Work-Up at Portland, with a new crew and Captain, under the watchful eyes of the Flag Officer Sea Training. The Stabilizer Systems were modified and were now trouble free.

On the 20th February, 1968, we arrived in Portland to begin a gruelling programme and to train several new members of the ship's company to operate the ship's equipment and armament under simulated wartime conditions. By the end of six weeks we were ready for the final inspection. The Admiral and his staff embarked early in the morning while we were preparing the engines for sea. I received a call from the engine room to inform me that the port engine wouldn't turn under steam. Divers were sent down to examine the shaft under water for any obstructions, but none were found. It was evident that the engine had seized as a result of the vibration reported on numerous occasions. I gave the order to lock the shaft. Although I had been expecting serious consequences for a long time, I was devastated, especially when the breakdown occurred at such a critical moment. The Captain and Admiral tried their best to cheer me up, and so did my fellow officers. It was a big setback for my department who had worked so hard during the Work-Up. The only consolation was that I had warned the authorities at the highest level of this possible outcome. As stated earlier in this chapter, the authorities at Portsmouth ignored the recommendations of the C-in-C Far East, and my Captain, to examine the turbines. The inspection was cancelled and we sailed for Portsmouth with one engine. A tug boat came to assist us berthing alongside at Portsmouth Dockyard. On reporting to the Admiral, the Captain requested that a Board of Inquiry should be convened to investigate why the engine had seized. His request was turned down for obvious reasons. Heads at the highest level would have rolled for ignoring the alarm bells over a long period. Both the Captain and I insisted, against stiff resistance from on high, that both engines should be checked, a point made to the Admiral. We spent two months in dockyard hands while both engines were lifted and replaced at a cost of hundreds of thousands of pounds. They were found to be severely distorted.

There are periods when an engineer's life can be miserable. Although the main engines trials proved successful, more trouble was in store. The two boilers were filling with water to such an extent that we couldn't see the water levels, an alarming situation. We had to shut down both boilers, making it impossible for steam to be provided for the main engines. The ship couldn't move and we were forced to drop anchor. A tug boat was sent to tow us into harbour, a humiliating experience for both the Captain and myself. Two pieces of steel were found lodged in two valves, preventing them from closing. It was quite common that pieces of metal or other debris were discovered in pipe systems after dockyard refits.

Occasionally captains of ships are given the opportunity to visit a port of their choice, especially after a series of setbacks. Our First Lieutenant was married to a Danish girl who came from Aarhus, the second largest city in Denmark, on the Jutland Peninsula, with a population of about 300,000, an industrial city with a large recreational marina and a hilly landscape. He assured the Captain that his wife could arrange a good programme of events and entertainment with her many contacts, over a six-day period, and so it turned out. On the first day we held a private reception in the wardroom, inviting many friends of the First Lieutenant and his wife. On the following day we held the official reception, inviting the same guests as well as local civic dignitaries. We were overwhelmed with hospitality, including a reception at the Town Hall. The wardroom was kept busy with a stream of guests. There were a few occasions when the bar was kept open until the early hours of the morning until the guests made a move. But work had to go on.

It was the duty of the officers to ensure that the ratings were given every opportunity to take part in the activities that were organised for them, especially at sports meetings against local teams, and the Welfare Committee dealt with the many invitations and excursions for sight-seeing tours. I met some of my senior ratings at a restaurant, giving me the opportunity of meeting them socially and to treat them to a drink. Unfortunately, on this visit I couldn't find much time for sight-seeing. I was too busy dealing with the aftermath of the engineering problems of the previous few weeks, reporting the behaviour of the replacement turbines to the Fleet Engineering Admiral and tidying up the mess left by the dockyard workmen. After a worrying three months, the visit to Aarhus served as a tonic to raise spirits. However it may appear, sailing the ocean is not one long holiday, and the cost of the entertaining had to be borne by the officers. Only official receptions are subsidised.

We returned to Portsmouth for a few days before setting off for a heavy programme of exercises off the Isle of Wight, anchoring daily at Sandown Bay, then northwards to Rothesay and Brodick Bay in Scotland and back to Portsmouth. We were soon heading north again to Harwich and Rosyth, where I was able to call on Margaret's parents and see some old friends, then back to base again. After a month in Portsmouth for summer leave, we were off for weapons training anchoring at Falmouth Bay. The ship was dragging anchor and all seamen officers were required to stay on board to keep watches on the bridge. The Captain had nobody to play golf with so he asked me, as a non watch-keeping officer, to join him. My experience of golf was minimal and I didn't have any clubs or golf shoes on board, but I had no option. I borrowed both from another officer and off we went by motorboat. I struggled around Falmouth golf course, slicing the ball into the bushes at regular intervals. I couldn't wait to get back to the clubhouse. After a warm shower we retired to the bar where we were met by the Club Captain who, after treating us to a drink, kindly informed us that it was customary that personnel from visiting RN ships were guests of the club, and were not charged a course fee. I was quite ready for that drink after the ordeal of the previous few hours. We returned to the ship and headed for the Atlantic on the way to Florida.

The main purpose of our next assignment was to take part in combined anti-submarine exercises with the American Navy, around Andros Island to the south of Florida. We embarked a second helicopter and crew and immediately commenced on a series of flying drills with alternate flights and mock anti-submarine chases. We stopped at Ponta Delgada in the Azores to refuel, and headed westwards to Bermuda in the company of the frigate HMS Rhyl. On the 18th of September, 1968, Paul's 8th birthday, we found ourselves steaming into a hurricane in weather that I had not previously experienced. The ship had to slow down as we headed into enormous waves, at a speed which resulted in burning our fuel at an uneconomical rate. At the same time the Captain had to steer the ship off course into the oncoming waves to keep it as stable as possible. Fuel consumption became critical and it was my responsibility to keep it down. Whereas in this situation, for safety reasons, I would double up machinery, I had no option but to single out to economise, augmenting the number of watch keepers on stand-by to double the machinery in case of emergency. Standing close to the Captain on the bridge, slide rule at the ready, and from information transmitted to me by the Chief of the Engine Room Watch every hour, I worked out how much fuel remained. In the meantime the Captain, at quarter hour intervals, broadcast on the loudspeaker system, warning the ship's company that nobody was to venture on the upper deck, and that if anyone was to fall overboard the ship could not be turned round to rescue him. It was impossible to launch the sea boat or the helicopter. From the bridge I could see the enormous waves coming at us from well above upper deck level as the ship ploughed straight into them. It is incredible what punishment ships can endure in such conditions, a tribute to their designers. For about forty eight hours life was almost unbearable as we pitched and tossed furiously in the storm. Cooking in the galleys was suspended and emergency wartime rations issued for those who had any appetite left.

An emergency was soon to hit us when the message 'man overboard' was sent from the quarterdeck to inform the Captain that a man had fallen over the side. I immediately ordered all machinery to be doubled up. The Quarterdeck Duty Petty Officer of the Watch soon after drinking his tot of rum, without a safety harness, and despite the regular broadcasts by the Captain, had attempted to go out to the helicopter deck to cut off the rope attached to a sinker which had broken loose. As he was about to reach the rope, the ship pooped and a huge wave came at him from the stern taking him away. The Leading Seaman who was assisting him, tied to a harness, escaped with both his legs and arms broken. Under normal circumstances, an emergency broadcast would be made to activate the standard rescue operation. On this occasion there was complete silence. Two twenty-man life rafts were released in the unlikely hope that Petty Officer Lindsay might have survived, and we pressed on with the journey. As it turned out, my emergency order to the engine room was to no avail. After about half an hour the Captain went on the broadcasting system to explain to the crew why he was unable to turn the ship around to attempt a rescue. We became concerned about Rhyl, which was not fitted with stabilizers, as she tossed and dipped, disappearing from sight for minutes on end. We received a signal from her to say that her Engineer Officer had worked out that her fuel wouldn't last until we reached Bermuda. As she wasn't fitted with the latest means of extracting every gallon of oil from her tanks he asked me for advice. I recommended that he lowered a submersible pump into the tanks to transfer the fuel from one tank to another which he did. We both signalled the RN Officer Bermuda to arrange for fuel to be transferred to us at sea as we approached the island.

In the meantime, the Captain informed their Lordships of our fatal accident. They ordered him to turn back to try to find PO Lindsay as soon as we'd reached calmer waters. He replied by telling them that we were running out of fuel and that, if we turned back, we wouldn't make Bermuda. We were informed that they had diverted a tanker to rendezvous with us. Four hours later the tanker signalled to say that it was caught in a storm and couldn't meet us as arranged. Without waiting for any orders from their Lordships, the Captain immediately turned the ship round in the direction of our destination. I ordered some of the Diesel fuel, used for running the electric generators, the Avcat used for the helicopter and any spare cooking oil to be added to and mixed with the furnace fuel oil producing an 'Engineer's Cocktail'. On our way back on course we retrieved one of the life rafts but, sadly, PO Lindsay was not in it. We sailed into Bermuda with another frigate steaming alongside loaded with drums of oil ready to transfer them if they were required. Within minutes of berthing, the oil pumps lost suction, the boilers were shut down, the steam-driven generators stopped running and the ship was plunged into total darkness. The fuel tanks were completely dried out. HMS Rhyl was already alongside with her top paintwork gone, presenting a sorry sight. Being a new ship, built with zincified steel, our paintwork remained intact. On the next day a Board of Inquiry was convened to establish the cause of death of Petty Officer Lindsay. It was concluded that he wouldn't have survived for more than a few seconds with a sea spray in a wind of 150 miles per hour.

Exhausted as most of us were, having had hardly any sleep for three nights, there was only one thing to do. We headed for the wardroom where the wine steward mixed a White Lady cocktail which we consumed without much effort. An official car came to take us to the Resident Naval Officer's residence to celebrate his daughter's 21st birthday. It didn't take long before the effect of the White Lady and tiredness caught up with me. Early in the morning I felt someone kicking me on the side. I had fallen asleep on the luscious lawn of the Admiral's garden. It was the Captain telling me that the official car was waiting to take us back to the ship. We remained alongside at Ireland Island, admiring the beauty of the bay and entertained by the naval community and British ex-patriots in the evenings.

On the 25th September, 1968, we secured alongside at Fort Lauderdale in Florida in full view of the old passenger liner Queen Mary, used as a floating hotel with its restaurants, swimming pools and casino. As well as local VIPs, we had some lunchtime visitors from the sailing club. One of them invited us to visit his submarine. We couldn't believe what he was saying. He did indeed own a midget submarine with side glass panels from where he could explore the sea bed and the creatures living as far down as about thirty feet. This was the first taste of American hospitality. They clearly loved the British, as we discovered during visits to other cities in Florida.

From Fort Lauderdale we proceeded to the Autec Range around Andros and Nassau for five days of extensive anti-submarine warfare training with our American friends, working around the clock on a 24-hour day basis. On completion of the exercise we headed for Freetown in the Bahamas. On the way, we were directed by a US Coastguard aircraft to a motor yacht drifting in the Providence Channel, having run out of fuel. We replenished her tanks and set her on her way. We spent three days at Freetown, long enough to go ashore for a swim before sailing for Miami. My recollection of this city was that of a promenade with a chain of hotels occupying a large section of the beach. I was more impressed by a visit to Salmon Island, watching the porpoise jumping in the artificial lake. We embarked the new Governor of the Bahamas and his wife, Sir Francis and Lady Cunning Bruce, for passage to Nassau where I attended the official reception at Government House.

On the following morning we sailed for St Petersburg in Tampa Bay, the fourth largest city in Florida with a population of about 200,000, nicknamed 'The Sunshine City'. It boasts 360 days of sunshine a year. This proved to be the highlight of our visit to Florida. The local reception committee came on board soon after we berthed to discuss an extensive programme of hospitality, excursions and sports meetings. One of the events was to be a dance for the crew. We were given a list with the names of all the ladies acting as hosts, giving their height, looks, hobbies and occupation and asked to match a sailor to each one of them. Overwhelmed by the reception we received we couldn't cope with all the invitations. Hundreds of visitors were greeted on board. Members of the Yacht club, the rich and the famous acted as hosts to the officers. We were invited to a private dinner and dance at a palatial house with two swimming pools, one warm and the other cold, pool and table tennis rooms, a huge garden, a grand hall and a multitude of other facilities including four or five rooms equipped with bars for self-service. The house belonged to a retired army colonel who had obviously amassed a fortune through his business dealings. At this place we met what

235

seemed to be the elite of the city, among them retired Hollywood actors, high ranking retired and serving officers and their families, confirming that St Petersburg was a sanctuary for the retired well-off. We were taken on a tour of the National Park as far as the Everglades, staying at a hotel overnight. They couldn't have been more generous. The only way we could return their hospitality, was to open the wardroom to them at any time. They loved coming on board, staying till the early hours of the morning. A dinner was given in our honour at the Yacht Club when the Commodore spoke warmly and glowingly about the friendship and the bonds between Britain and America, but he also indulged in some light hearted remarks. He told us that the best thing he had ever done was to remarry his wife. 'Captain Bligh' invited us to report to HMS Bounty, the replica used for the film 'Mutiny on the Bounty' the 1962 MGM version with Marlon Brando. I had to act for the Captain and was received by Captain Bligh dressed in the full uniform of the period of the late 19th century. Before I walked over the gangway, two girls dressed in Hula costumes, placed garlands around my neck. I received the salute from the Captain and retired with him and my fellow officers to his cabin for drinks. All this was happening at 'Tahiti Village' which surrounded the ship with its bamboo huts and South West Pacific flavour, where the Hula 'natives' acted as guides to the tourists.

We were scheduled to stay in St Petersburgh for a week but had to leave a day earlier. On the day before we were due to leave, we received a warning from the American Coastguards that Hurricane Gladys was on her way, meaning that we had to leave at once. A broadcast was immediately made on local radio and television recalling all liberty men. I was ordered to prepare the main engines for sea at immediate notice. Just before we were due to cast off, the last two remaining sailors arrived, each with a girl. They asked the Captain to marry them, invoking an old naval custom which has long been discarded. When he told them he was not authorised to conduct a ceremony, the two girls burst into tears as the dejected sailors held them close. The girls wouldn't move away from the jetty remaining there in tears as the two sailors alternated between preparing the ship for sea, and glancing over the guardrails to wave and blow kisses to their heart-broken lovers. The ship cast off leaving two sailors and their prospective partners with all but a memory of a dream that might have been. There are many parallels to this story and tales of romances that misfired, but a few did materialise to survive the test of time. Before we arrived at St Petersburg, the ship's company were reminded of previous cases of intrusion into sailors' romantic exploits by the city's press, and were advised to avoid being photographed. After we sailed, I received a letter from Margaret with a cutting from the Portsmouth Evening News showing a picture of me and fellow officers with a Hula girl and Captain Bligh on the Bounty! Just before we left, I received the news that Margaret was expecting our third child, a cause for celebration with drinks all round, in the wardroom.

We successfully avoided Hurricane Gladys and moved on to Bermuda, securing alongside at Ireland Island and anchoring in Hamilton Bay on the following day, surrounded by a deep blue sea and a splendid view of the landscape, with just enough time to take up an invitation to the Royal Bermuda Yacht Club. In contrast to the stormy journey from the Azores, we returned to Ponta Delgada on a flat calm sea, making full use of the two helicopters for four days of intensive training in anti submarine warfare. On completion of refuelling, we headed for Gibraltar, where we docked to examine the port shaft and propeller which were showing signs of obstruction. We found a nylon rope wrapped around the propeller but the discovery was not significant. We concluded that one main engine was running more efficiently than its counterpart.

I was looking forward to our next destination, and seeing my mother and the rest of the family in Malta, during the combined Home and Mediterranean Fleets exercise named Eden Apple. We tied up to buoys in a prominent position in Grand Harbour. Many of my friends made during my previous assignment in Malta were still there. In liaison with them I arranged a social programme for the wardroom. Half way through the second phase, with units of the combined fleet, we sailed into Naples for my third visit to Italy's second city, revisiting the Amalfi Coast and Pompeii. I never tire of that beautiful country and its ancient history. There is always something new to discover. I learned that many of the precious treasures previously in Pompeii had been transferred to the Museum at Naples. After four days we returned to Malta and tied up at the same berth overlooking Valletta, surrounded by the bastions built by the Knights of St John. The Grand Harbour reminded me of the old days when it used to be packed with ships. There were enough of them in harbour on this visit to produce a spectacular sight, especially at night when they were all floodlit, with HMS Sirius proudly exhibiting the Dog Star over the forward gun turret. Unfortunately, the Commander-in-Chief didn't like it and asked the Captain to remove it because, he said, it spoiled the unified effect produced by the whole fleet. However, we did manage to look different when we hoisted the 'Paying Off' pennant at colours on Tuesday 26th November, 1968, a signal to the Fleet that our commission was to end on reaching UK. At 0900 we slipped from our moorings as the pennant stretched across the whole length of the ship, looking like a snake crawling in the air. In keeping with tradition, as we passed each ship, they gave us three loud cheers. On the penultimate day at Malta I bade good bye to my mum and the rest of the family.

Throughout the previous weeks I had been busy organising the Farewell Concert Party. The Captain and most of the officers and ratings were due to leave the ship to make room for the new commission. Preparations were almost complete, but I had problems with some of the scripts which I felt went beyond the limits even for an audience of sailors, considering them to be too vulgar. The Gunnery Department threatened to boycott the show, only to change their mind when the Captain intervened. Their Divisional Officer removed the crude and vulgar lines. Due to rough weather, and as we were in the company of other ships for most of the time, the concert had to be abandoned on a number of occasions. The only opportunity to put the show on was after we had left Malta as time was running out before we were due to pay off. In rough weather we had to find somewhere sheltered to anchor. After trying several remote inlets on the Tunisian coast we anchored in a small bay. The helicopter deck was turned into an auditorium and a stage erected in the hangar. I acted as the producer, stage manager, prompt and stage hand, assisted by an unrehearsed stage team who did what they were told. The wardroom officers performed 'The Black Witch and the Wardrobe', and my stokers 'Glory Glory Halleluiah'. In secret they dressed up in Engineer Officers white overalls with the Maltese cross on their chests. It was a hilarious performance ending at almost midnight followed by hot dogs and, as a special treat, a can of beer to each rating. After the fun, we weighed anchor and headed for Gibraltar for a three-day stay before continuing with our journey to Portsmouth, where we arrived three days later.

The Lord Mayor came to greet his adopted ship and to pay his respects to the Captain, Commander John Humphrey Baker, before he left the ship. Two days later John, by now a close friend of mine, was relieved by Commander John De Leittes, my third Captain since I joined the ship at Singapore. Except for me and my deputy, all the other officers were replaced, as were the vast majority of the ship's company as the new commission was slowly assembled under a new Command. At my request, I stayed as the continuity man, prepared to go through the gruelling six weeks Work-Up at Portland again in order to leave the ship just before the birth of our third child during my Easter leave and between appointments. Friends thought I was mad. I also put it to the Commander-in-Chief's staff that it would be a good idea if my relief joined in the last week of the Work-Up, to see the machinery and the fire-fighting organisation working at the most demanding pressure under simulated wartime conditions. With my previous experience, which ended with the seizing up of one of the main engines, I was determined to complete a full inspection and to see my department achieve a good result.

We stayed in Portsmouth until the end of January, 1969, where the new officers and ratings attended several short courses to learn about the equipment which they were about to handle. Everyone was sent on a one-day course at the Fire Fighting School, and familiarisation training started in earnest. The new crew were put through a training programme at sea around the Isle of Wight, Portland and Poole. I made sure that my department was fully trained to tackle everything that was thrown at them during the inspection. My previous experience stood me in good stead, and by the time we got to Portland I was quite relaxed. In fact, things were going so well that I was able to adjust my programme to allow other departments to use time allocated to my department.

A few days before the final inspection, we gave a cocktail party for the Admiral and his staff and my 'relief' joined the ship. I was so confident that, on the Saturday, I let my deputy, by now a very competent and reliable engineer officer, guide him around the department while I went to the shore base wardroom to watch the cup final on television.

239

On the final day of the inspection, all hell was let loose when the Admiral arrived with his staff, all dressed for action stations with anti-flash headgear and action clothing. As soon as we passed the breakwater, we were 'attacked' by aircraft, submarines and surface ships. I took charge of the Damage Control Headquarters to co-ordinate damage control and fire-fighting, tackling mock fires and explosions planted by the inspecting staff. After an exhausting day, we returned to harbour with a sigh of relief. A supposedly damaged ship, still floating, returned to harbour to the peace and quiet of a silent berth. The Admiral spoke to the ship's company to congratulate them on a satisfactory Work Up and singled out my department with the highest assessment of 'very satisfactory'. I was taken aside by the Staff Engineer Officer who told me that he would be writing a very good report. Unfortunately, as my days on the ship were numbered, I was not to see the report. However, I couldn't have left the ship in a happier mood, with the satisfaction that I was turning over a well organised and efficient department to my successor. I was looking forward to a good rest, a few home comforts and the birth of our baby. As soon as the Admiral had left the ship, the First Lieutenant handed me an invitation card. The Captain and Officers were to treat me to a farewell lunch on the following day, my penultimate before leaving the ship, the last in which I was to serve. On the next day I left, with some sadness, for a spell of leave.

A few days after my leaving the ship, the Captain of HMS Sultan, the Royal Naval Marine Engineering School, asked me and Margaret to dinner at his official residence in Gosport, Hampshire. Captain Barton had been my boss when I acted as his assistant during his time as the Commander of HMS Caledonia in Rosyth in Scotland. He asked me whether I would like to join HMS Sultan, and told me that, if I accepted, he would find a job for me. After a few days I received confirmation of my appointment.

HMS Sirius Commission April 1967—April 1969

Aarhus

Hong Kong

Singapore 26.4.6?

Papua New

Bougainville

Fiji

Noumea

Townsville

Darwin

Sydney

Wellington

Fua Mulalu

Mombasa

Malta

Naples

Simon's Town

Portsmouth
23.11.67

Azores

Gibraltar

Freetown

Bermuda

Miami

Andros

Bahamas

Fort Lauderdale

St. Petersburg

Tonga (7.7.67)

Ugi

Savu Savu

241

HMS Sirius in Sydney Harbour.

Reception on arrival at Suva.

242

Royal Suva Yacht Club

The Commodore and Committee
have pleasure in inviting

LIEUTENANT . D.F.X. MARKS.

to be an Honorary Member

for .... month(s) from June 28th '67

Introduced by ....

.... Secretary.

THE FORM AND ORDER OF
THE SERVICE THAT IS TO BE PERFORMED
AND THE CEREMONIES
THAT ARE TO BE OBSERVED IN

THE CORONATION
of
His Majesty King
TAUFA'AHAU TUPOU IV
in
The Chapel Royal Nuku'alofa

ON TUESDAY THE FOURTH DAY OF JULY 1967
AT 10 A.M.

At the Coronation Lunch.

243

Sirius sailing past a little island in the Fiji group.

Ugi-Fiji Group.

244

Left behind by the Japanese at Honiara-Solomon Island after the Second World War.

On board the MGM replica of the Bounty with fellow officers and a member of the crew, with me left of 'Captain Bligh'.

My second Crossing the Equator Certificate.

CHAPTER 17

A NORMAL FAMILY LIFE

The Royal Naval Marine Engineering School

After my last hectic few weeks in HMS Sirius I began to settle down to a normal family life, able to give Margaret the support she needed during the short time before the baby was due. My days at sea were over and I was destined to serve my last few years in shore establishments. Simon Dominic John was born in Portsmouth on 15th May, 1969, shortly before I was due to start my new job. I applied for a married quarter over the water from Portsmouth in the Gosport area, near the shore establishment HMS Sultan, the Royal Naval Marine Engineering School, where I was to be stationed. I had already served in two shore establishments where, as a bachelor, I had missed the excitement of travelling from place to place, visiting countries in all five continents, but now family life had become a priority and I had something far more important to look forward to. After all, I was lucky to have seen so much of the world during my career.

I was to join HMS Sultan at a crucial stage in the history of Marine Engineering, in May 1969, when the transition from Steam to Gas was gaining momentum. As far as I knew I had served as the Marine Engineer Officer of the last Steam-Driven Warship to be built, HMS Sirius. The change to Gas Turbine Propulsion spelled the end of boilers, used to supply Steam-Driven Turbine Engines and the supporting auxiliary machinery, subject to frequent maintenance. The space required to house the new propulsion systems was reduced considerably as was the size of the Engine Room Complement. Machinery spaces became unmanned, their operation controlled from one Electronic Control System Compartment. Extra space became available to improve accommodation as bunks replaced hammocks. No such transformation had taken place since sail gave way to the Steam Engine-Driven Propeller. By the time of the Falklands War most ships operating in the War Zone were Gas Turbine driven. HMS Hermes, which took part in that war, the last surviving steam-driven aircraft carrier, was due to be scrapped three months after the war started.

247

HMS Sultan, previously a Fleet Air Arm Base, is one of the largest Shore Establishments in the Royal Navy. In 1969 it was expanding rapidly to absorb the training of Technicians and Stokers from other smaller Training Establishments across the United Kingdom to conform to Admiralty Policy to concentrate all Marine Engineering training in one location, and to economise in the cost of training. In overall charge was Captain Steve Barton, supported by a Commander as Second-Command responsible for Discipline, Sporting Activities, Parade Training and Establishment Maintenance. A Training Commander was responsible for the training of Theoretical and Practical Marine Engineering, the Nuclear School and Workshop Practice. The Instructor Commander was responsible for the Academic, Educational and Cultural activities and the Supply and Secretariat Commander for the Secretariat, Stores, Catering, Salaries and Accommodation. The Medical Branch was controlled by a Surgeon Commander. Under the Training Commander I was appointed as the Senior Engineer of the Maintenance School, a large hangar converted to house Steam and Diesel Engine driven machinery. A specially built compartment housed a Gas Turbine Propulsion Unit used in the first generation of Combined Steam and Gas Turbine driven ships about which I knew very little. Before assuming my responsibilities I attended various courses on this new technology, including the prototype Pre-Commissioning Training Course for the new All Gas Turbine Driven ships due to join the Fleet. I visited Gas Turbine Assembly Manufacturers and attended an Instructional Technique Course to prepare for lecturing officers and senior ratings. After a week's hand-over from my predecessor, I discovered that I was to be responsible for some forty instructors and a turn-over of about six hundred trainees a year. The establishment was buzzing with activities and there was a constant stream of VIPs and personnel from all branches of the Royal and Foreign Navies, Naval Dockyards, Civic and Government Authorities visiting my department

The changing technology, the advent of new means of propulsion and the progressive teaching methods, necessitated the regular updating of courses syllabi. Changing the Teaching Plans became a perpetual problem. As soon as we changed the format to that agreed internally, at an inspection by the Administrative Authority, we were made to change it to suit Command Instructions. With reluctance, I had to instruct my staff to rewrite the

Teaching Plans in a different format. It was a new experience, totally different to the exciting life sailing around the world. Millions of pounds were spent to provide training equipment and on modernising the buildings to house new machinery. Frustration set in as delays in completion programmes were such that most equipment was already in service before we set up training courses to teach trainees how to use it. In hindsight, I feel that, whilst most resources were used wisely, there was some justification in the criticism levelled at the Ministry of Defence that public money was being wasted. A large laundry was erected with expensive equipment, costing hundreds of thousands of pounds, equipment which any technician could maintain by just looking at handbooks. Apparently it was built to save the Welfare Fund money used to send the sports gear to the local laundry. An enormous hangar was modified to install numerous machines which provided hardly any scope for teaching purposes. I include this criticism to highlight the wastage in the Defence Budget which is often the subject of adverse comments in the press. It was a case of setting inappropriate priorities and a lack of detailed scrutiny of the cost to the tax-paying public. But I wish to make it clear that HMS Sultan provided training of the highest possible standard, envied by navies across the world, chosen by them to send their personnel to be trained by the Royal Navy. We trained officers and ratings from the Commonwealth, Argentina, Chile, Libya, Iran and other countries which had ships similar to ours. Unfortunately, we experienced a few problems with some of the foreign trainees. There were regular complaints from ratings of the Islamic Faith that food was cooked in fat previously used to cook meats banned by their religion. After protracted diplomatic consultations with Consulates, a number of foreign trainees were sent home after becoming involved in unpleasant affairs with local girls or arrested by the police for criminal offences.

I was now subject to a regular routine, going to work in the morning and returning home at the end of the working day, except when I was on duty. Variety was provided by the many extra-curricular activities, the social, cultural and sporting prospects proving exciting. I soon found myself involved with sporting activities, taking part in inter-department soccer and cricket and refereeing at football matches for the three services in Hampshire. A friend told me that, before our arrival on the scene, the rumour went round that Danny and Margaret Marks were about to join and liven up the place. Encouraged by the Captain, aware of our experience in the theatre, when I was his assistant, when he was the Commander at HMS Caledonia, Margaret and I joined the Theatre Group. Within days I was involved in decorating the wardroom in preparation for the Summer Ball. In my second year I masterminded the next Annual Summer Ball, 'Il Ballo Italiano'. Each department was given a task. The courtyard by the entrance to the Wardroom was transformed into 'Piazza San Marco' with lampposts in the Venetian style and a fountain forming an impressive sight as water sprayed into the air. The large dining room became 'Venice' with numerous gondolas of different colours hanging from a large fishing net, another room became 'Naples', with 'Vesuvius' in one corner, timed to erupt at a given moment as we danced to a band playing popular Italian songs. Scenes from 'Pompeii' were painted on hessian cloth and hung from the walls. The murals included men and women pictured naked. One of the officers on the organising committee objected to the showing of the male genitals so we painted fig leaves over them. When the Commander walked in he was furious and told us to remove the fig leaves. A marquee was turned into 'Il Ristorante Bologna' and the passageways into the 'Amalfi Coast' with seagulls hanging from the ceiling and lobster and fishing nets at 'Positano'. Maltese naval cooks were brought in from Portland to cook Italian food and to set up an Italian 'Restaurant'. Paraffin runway emergency lanterns were borrowed from the Fleet Air Arm and placed at the various entrances. As the flames flickered in a clear summer evening's breeze, musicians serenaded the guests as they arrived. At midnight, the cast of a play being performed at the Chichester Festival Theatre, including Nigel Patrick and his wife, arrived as guests. From 4 am onwards breakfast was served for those who wanted it. All this was done at the expense of the officers out of the wardroom mess funds.

We became heavily involved in Drama and Theatre activities. When I arrived, rehearsals for the next play were in progress, but getting nowhere. The Instructor Commander asked me to raise some enthusiasm amongst the cast and production team. I attended a rehearsal at the appointed time but there wasn't a soul in sight. Everybody arrived an hour later from a pub nearby. Over time standards started to improve and I managed to talk the wife of a friend of mine serving in Sultan, a professional actress, into taking the lead in a black comedy, 'The Anniversary'. The news that the leading part was to be played by a professional actress encouraged others to attend the auditions. We managed to build an excellent cast including Margaret and the Training Commander, and entered the play in the Royal Naval Drama Festival. The adjudicator, Mr Walter Lucas, appointed by RADA, who I had met before in Malta when he came to adjudicate plays in which I was involved, gave his verdict on the last night. We could tell the play was a success from the reaction of the audiences. We had won the competition, the best performance out of eleven establishments across Britain. From then on the Theatre Club flourished with one success after another.

My turn as a producer came when I organised the Christmas Concert with each department taking part in traditional naval sketches, music and dancing with the theme of 'Full Ahead Together'. As we were getting close to the dress rehearsal, the Electricians Unions decided to go on strike, presenting me with the dilemma of whether to cancel the event or find alternative ways to provide electric power. The Commander and Second-in-Command wanted to cancel the show for safety reasons only to be overruled by the Captain, who felt that an Engineering Establishment should be able to provide alternative power and adequate safety precautions. To provide DC lighting, we connected electrical cables from one of my Diesel-Driven generators to the electricity main power points, no doubt breaking the Electricity Board rules in the process. For AC power for our sound effects, we hired an ice cream van equipped with an AC Generator. Fire Parties were positioned back stage and around the theatre. Thus, we beat the strike. The show was hilarious and a roaring success. While producing and directing this show, I asked the director of a West End play, which was running at The King's Theatre in Southsea, for his opinion about the manner in which I was producing 'Full Ahead Together' and showed him my script and stage directions. I was surprised when he told me that the stage directions were very similar to those that he was used to on the professional stage. Other productions followed on a three monthly basis. When I came to produce the next Christmas Show I was faced with another dilemma. The Assembly Hall, used as a theatre, was due to be demolished as part of the reconstruction programme. We had to make use of the Town Hall in Gosport, which was not available until the day of the dress rehearsal. We built the set to a model which I made to scale to suit the Town Hall stage, transporting it in sections in the afternoon to be used on the same evening. With a frantic effort, last minute problems and hard work by our shipwrights, we had the set in place with minutes to spare. A cast of about fifty sailors, wrens and naval wives entertained packed audiences for three nights with typical naval humour. Margaret took the part of Little Blue Riding Hood, in the pantomime written by one of the Instructor Officers. This was a fitting finale to my stage activities, the last time that I was involved in theatrical productions. However, I did organise two mini Gang Shows, after retiring from the Navy, in my capacity as Chairman of my Parish Scouts and Guides Group.

Life in married quarters was like one big family, enjoyable, with frequent get-togethers, a pattern which we found missing in civilian life. Compared with the adventurous travels and the challenges presented in serving in a warship, life was now more relaxed. The pleasures of seeing the world were substituted by family life and enjoying watching the children growing. As I was getting close to completing my two years serving at HMS Sultan, the new Captain asked me to stay for an extended period. I preferred his offer to an appointment at Gareloch in Scotland, which involved another family upheaval, so I decided to stay. At this stage, I was not yet aware that, in my next and final appointment, I was once again to come in close contact with ships, when I was to fly far and wide to inspect them, a reversal of the role I'd been accustomed to over many years.

With only a few years left to serve I had to come to terms with the fact that we had no home of our own. In the early 1970s the housing market was thriving, with house prices escalating by the day. We rushed into a frantic effort to buy a house before prices became prohibitive, gazumped time after time in the process. Eventually we found what we thought was the ideal house in a pleasant locality and were just about to sign the contract when we were informed, by a man who had come to repair our washing machine, that the house foundations were sinking as the ground beneath, over a natural spring, was giving way. The owner confirmed the story but assured us that the problem had been solved when the foundations were re-enforced but we were not happy and so decided not to buy. It was a four-bedroom house worth five thousand pounds sold for forty five three years later. We eventually settled for a house which we had rejected as being too small during its building. We paid the first owner six thousand pounds more than the original asking price. At last we were the proud owners of our first home.

On leaving HMS Sultan I was appointed to serve on the Commander-in-Chief Technical Staff at Portsmouth, so I didn't have to move house, travelling daily by ferry across Portsmouth Harbour with a short walk to my new office in the Royal Naval Dockyard. At this stage in my career I was more concerned with leading a stable married life, enjoying being with the children and avoiding disruption to their education. I had missed enough of their early childhood and was looking forward to sharing the responsibilities for their upbringing.

CHAPTER 18

MY FINAL ASSIGNMENT

Role Reversal

Having been subjected to almost continuous inspections and supervision during my previous twenty four years in the Navy, I now found myself in the reverse situation inspecting other Engineer Officers during their ships' refits, building or at sea. I was appointed as the Technical Routine Officer with the Technical Staff of the Commander-in-Chief Fleet. The various Fleets in the Mediterranean, the Far East, East and West Indies and elsewhere around the world were being wound down and combined into one Fleet with a worldwide role, concentrated mainly around the United Kingdom as one of the main NATO Alliance Naval Forces. The number of ships was drastically reduced. Assisted by two Senior Artificers from the Weapons and Marine Engineering Departments, I was to inspect Ships' Technical Administration Systems and advise officers how to keep publications and regulations regularly updated with modifications issued by the Admiralty. I was to ensure that their Planned Maintenance Routines were fully implemented and their spare parts systems controlled to such an extent that, in the event of a breakdown at sea, equipment would be repaired by replacement whenever possible. In my monthly bulletins, I advised the Fleet of imminent changes to the standard documentation systems and the remedial actions necessary to deal with recurring defects and other technical and logistics problems.

The transition from the time when the Marine Engineering Branch was the dominant technical authority, through the demise of the Electrical Branch, to the introduction of sophisticated, computerised and electronic weapons control equipment, resulted in the emergence of the Weapons Engineering Branch. As this new department gained momentum, its senior officers demanded equal status. They became part of a combined Technical Authority. Many of the responsibilities of the Gunnery Department had become defunct and most of its personnel transferred to the ever-expanding Weapons Branch. Guns, missiles and anti-submarine weapons and detection equipment were now controlled by computerised systems and other electronic devices. Even the Propulsion Systems for the new generation of warships were to be electronically controlled. The rivalry between the two Engineering Branches was still in evidence when I took over my new job. Because I was in the Marine Branch, I had to tread carefully when issuing my reports. Indeed, some Weapons Engineer Officers objected to any adverse comments, however constructive, a problem which I reported to the Admiral of the Fleet Technical Authority, when he asked for my comments on the day I left the service. However, most of them appreciated my helpful and impartial reporting and sought my advice.

As time went on, I became disillusioned by the new generation of Technical Officers, who were repeating the same mistakes of the past. While I was making every effort to reduce their paper work and documents which they had to keep updating, they seemed to want to pile them on. There were times when officers rang to obtain information which was contained in the monthly Fleet Technical Orders which they hadn't bothered to read. As I neared the end of my time, frustration set in, and I started looking forward to my retirement. With two years to go, I was given the option of a number of EVT (Educational and Vocational Training) Courses in preparation for civilian life. I chose the toughest course, an HNC in Business Studies by correspondence, with only eight weeks residential tuition at South West London Education College. I travelled to London for a two-week introductory period. It was hard work, with most of my studying and essay-writing done on aircraft, as I travelled around the world to meet ships to inspect them at Hong Kong, Simon's Town, Singapore and, on numerous occasions, to Gibraltar. I also travelled frequently to the other main naval ports at Devonport, Rosyth and Chatham and to the shipbuilding yards at Cammell Laird in Birkenhead and Vickers in Barrow-in-Furness. While most of the time I inspected ships in harbour or went out to sea with them, there were occasions when I was transferred by jackstay, or winched by helicopter from ship to ship at sea. I found the several hours flying, preparing my course essays on Economics, Human and Industrial Relations, Commercial Law and the Principles of Business Administration, a refreshing change.

Although life wasn't as exciting as living on a warship, showing the flag, I was still lucky enough to be travelling, adding to my many foreign experiences. I travelled to Cape Town with British Airways. Stopping at Johannesburg, gave me the opportunity to meet Margaret's uncle, Father Dominic Campbell, a Redemptorist priest working in Rustenburg. He came over to meet me at the airport and took me to the province where he lived, among the poorest people in South Africa. He was known as a saintly person who devoted over thirty years of his life looking after them. As chaplain of a prison, he looked after the spiritual and welfare needs of hundreds of inmates who were jailed for their resistance to the Apartheid laws, or for the most minor of offences. He risked imprisonment by breaking the curfew restrictions almost every night to attend to the sick and the poor. This was the second time that I was to witness the oppressive regime of that beautiful country. Wherever I went, I couldn't escape the sight of hideous segregation signs, 'Whites' or 'Blacks' everywhere. Everyone pushing a broom or attending to the toilets was black while those sitting in offices were white. It all looked so blatant and cruel. I was to see more of this during my week's stay in the Cape Town region. As I travelled by train between Cape Town and Simon's Town, I wondered what would happen if I dared to sit on a bench at the station or in a coach marked 'Blacks Only'. Compounds surrounded by high walls and barbed wire, where the black population was confined during the hours of curfew, were to be seen at regular intervals. When I went to a Catholic church, as I was about to walk through the door, a young black boy approached me and said 'Good Morning Master'. I told him that I wasn't his Master, but his friend. Once inside the church I was pleased to see black worshippers defying the laws of Apartheid and being welcomed by the congregation.

I travelled to Cape Town on an internal flight. At Kimberly, the plane landed on its nose in an upright position, righting itself almost instantly. It was enough to set a number of passengers screaming. It stayed at the airport a little longer than the scheduled half an hour to give a chance for everyone to recover from the shock. Passengers were given the choice of staying on board or disembarking for a few minutes. On arrival at Cape Town I heard the rumour that the landing at Kimberly was the first the co-pilot had made with a plane full of passengers. From there we travelled by train to a hotel in Wynberg, a few kilometres away from Simon's Town. There was time to settle down for the evening and relax in a pleasant hotel by the seaside. In my room I found one of those breakfast order forms, to be hung on the outside of the door handle, offering an unusual choice of food. On the following morning I enjoyed beefsteak for breakfast for the first time.

I was looking forward to meeting my old friend, Dick Fry. Dick had been like a brother to me when I lived at his parents' home in Portsmouth. He left the Navy after fifteen years. Although qualified educationally and professionally, he failed to be selected for promotion to officer rank and emigrated to South Africa, where he worked for an Engineering Company providing services to the South African Navy and visiting ships. On the following day I had the pleasure of meeting him and his wife, Maureen, who I had known well during their courtship. They lived in a lovely district, not far from the hotel where I was staying at Somerset West, where they invited me to dine with them at a restaurant together with their two lovely daughters. The last time we had met was when we were stationed in Malta in 1965. At the restaurant, I was introduced to what was common practice in South Africa, BYO (Bring Your Own) wine. I invited them to a reception on board HMS Hampshire, the Guided Missile Destroyer which I was inspecting. During the reception a fire broke out on a South African Frigate. Hampshire's fire parties, wearing their protective clothing, were ordered to assist. They loaded their motor cutters with fire extinguishers, portable water pumps and first aid equipment. With the Frigate's staff, and assisted by Tug Boats, they soon had the fire under control. This event gave the Inspecting Team the opportunity to see the ship's fire-fighting organisation in action for real. That was the last time I saw Dick and Maureen both of whom have since died. I also met other ex-RN friends who had transferred to the South African Navy.

I flew to Singapore with the rest of the Inspection Team to inspect HMS Tiger, one of the oldest cruisers in the Navy. Although we no longer had a Far East Fleet, our ships still used Singapore as a base. Much had changed since I was stationed there. We stayed at the Officers' Club, now run by the Australian Navy. The old base and dockyard had been converted into a private Ship Repair Yard. The country had been expanding its commercial activities and flourishing under the leadership of Lee Kuan Yew. HMS Tiger was a similar ship to HMS Gambia in which I'd served. On this occasion,

I was to inspect the Marine Engineering operational performance as well as the Documentation System of the two Engineering Departments. The evenings ashore were confined to the Officers' Club and a nostalgic visit to the Singapore Swimming Club in the city. I visited other ships which needed my advice at sea in the Indian Ocean, transferred from ship to ship by jackstay or winched by helicopters. HMS Tiger was despatched to rescue the crew of a merchant ship which sank when its cargo of fertilizer products caught fire. From the conversation I had with the rescued Captain and Officers, it appeared that their crew had made little effort to fight the fire. They all took to the lifeboats and were rescued.

During my time attached to the Commander-in-Chief's Technical Staff, bearing in mind my experiences on the other side of the fence, I viewed the problems confronting Engineer Officers with great sympathy. They expected support and understanding from their senior officers when things went wrong. As an Inspecting Officer you can soon judge the state of morale in a department, especially where there is lack of leadership. Although my reports were impartial, I was always careful not to be too hard on junior officers experiencing problems.

As I'm relying on my memory while writing most of this chapter, I may well be confusing ships' names. As far as I can recollect, the ship I inspected in Hong Kong was HMS London. Soon after we arrived, a Typhoon warning was issued, and the ship had to leave harbour in a hurry. We were left behind, living at our hotel in Happy Valley until the ship returned. In the ship's absence we had to attend the many social events that had been organised for the ship's officers, an unexpected duty which we fulfilled without much pain. Unfortunately, there were not enough of us to fulfil all the engagements. A visit to the Hong Kong Club was mandatory, as was a drink at the Mandarin Hotel, and I was dragged off to watch the horse racing at Happy Valley Race Course. One evening was spent dining at one of the floating restaurants in Aberdeen Harbour. From here I was able to see the spectacular night's scene witnessed on previous visits.

I made several visits to Gibraltar at a time when the Spanish Government was still preventing our airplanes from flying over its territory. I had to get used to the sharp hair-raising turn which our airplanes had to make while landing on the short landing strip jutting out into the sea. A number of friends extended their hospitality, including the Flag Officer Gibraltar, an Admiral, who married a friend of ours, a Surgeon Lieutenant Commander who we knew well when she served in Malta. But for most of the time, I caught up with my studies, working on the essays which I had to send to my tutors at South West London College, with the occasional visit to the Rock Hotel.

I found the Correspondence Course most interesting. I learned how to read the Stock Market Reports, and the financial jargon used by politicians became clearer, or more confused, as I listened to the so-called economic experts with their contradictory views. Equally interesting was the reading of past cases of judgement on Common Law as related to Commerce and the Sale of Goods Act. I was delighted when my Commercial Law Tutor, on returning one of my essays, which he marked ten out of ten, remarked that I should study to become a lawyer. I had to read books on Psychology and Sociology and the complexities of Industrial Relations. In fact the course became a hobby which I relished as I grew more confident about the outcome. As my job was coming to an end, I travelled to London for the final six weeks residential intensive revision course. The class was made up of different ranks from all the three Services. There was a Colonel from the Army, a Group Captain from the RAF and other senior ranks, some older than myself, working under obvious pressure, some on medication to relieve the stress. There was much to learn in a short space of time, before sitting the exam at the end of the course. At week-ends, when I went home, I did nothing but study. At the end of the course, I took the exam and returned to Alverstoke, relaxed and relieved that it was all over. I was advised to telephone the college for the result on a specific date. Although I was quite confident of the outcome, it was a relief to hear that I had passed well in all subjects, and that my certificate was to follow. I was by then almost fifty years old and thought I'd had enough of exams. However that was not to be.

My 'relief' arrived about two months before I was due to leave the Service. After a week's turn-over I was employed on a project requiring me to produce a report on an aspect of ships' fire-fighting capabilities. My last job was complete, and that was it! With a colleague, who was retiring about the same time as me, we made arrangements to give our farewell drinks party in the wardroom. In the meantime I applied for my last DOMCOL leave, given to serving personnel who were domiciled in the Dominions or Colonies, to go and see my mother in Malta. The free flight date clashed with the day of the party, so Margaret had to act as my stand-in. On returning from Malta I was invited to the traditional Farewell Dinner for officers leaving, with my colleague and a Commander. My speech went well as I described some of the humorous escapades of my naval life. On the next day the Admiral sent for me to say thank you and good bye. He asked me to tell him, bluntly, what I could draw from my experiences over the past two and a half years. I expressed some of my misgivings while he took notes, and he handed me my flimsy, a short statement which an officer receives from his Captain (in this case an Admiral). It was a gratifying report of my performance under his charge. We shook hands, my last act before leaving the Royal Navy after twenty nine years. In due course the Admiral sent me a formal letter of thanks. I also received letters of thanks from the Chief of Naval Personnel, the Second Sea Lord and the Secretary of State for Defence (see appendices) to tell me that I had been placed on the retired list and thanking me for my 'long and valuable service'.

A few months before I retired, I started looking for a job in Civvy Street. In 1975 there were plenty of jobs to choose from, especially for Chartered Engineers. Some of the jobs offers included an element of Trade Union negotiations and sitting on Industrial Relations Committees. I chose not to be involved in anything that led to any stress or disputes. During my HNC Course in London, one of the students showed me an advertisement in the Daily Telegraph for surveyors with Lloyds Register of Shipping. With Lloyds' reputation, I thought that I'd have security until I reached state pension age. On my way down from Rosyth in Scotland, where I was inspecting a ship, I called for an interview at Lloyds Headquarters in Fenchurch Street in London, a most impressive building. Within about ten minutes I was told that I would be offered a job. When the official letter arrived I discovered I'd been offered the choice of a job in Hull or Newcastle. I opted for the latter, but when the appointment letter arrived, I was advised to report to the Liverpool Office with an extra thousand pounds added to the salary.

Margaret and I were doubtful about moving to Liverpool, until I spoke to my boss, the Marine Engineer Captain on the staff. He told me that he and his wife spent three very happy years living in the Wirral when he served as an overseer at Cammell Laird in Birkenhead. We promptly arranged to stay with a naval friend with whom we'd always kept in touch and, with her help, bought a house in Bromborough. We have been living here for over thirty years and have never regretted it. We also fell in love with Liverpool to the east and Chester to the west, only twenty minutes drive to either city. My Golf Club is just around the corner, so I achieved my ambition of living on the outskirts of beautiful countryside, but only a few miles away from the big cities. I timed the start of my first civilian job to start on my 50th birthday at the end of a fortnight's retirement leave, making sure that I didn't spend a minute on the dole.

CHAPTER 19

A NEW LIFE

Adjusting to Civilian Life
A Second Retirement

Lloyds Register of Shipping is a publication listing the Classification grades of ships and details of their characteristics. It is the Underwriters Register first published in 1760. It is also the name of the Classification Authority. As in the case of Lloyds Insurance and Lloyds List, the oldest London newspaper, it originated in Edward Lloyd's Coffee House in Tower Street in the City of London, where shipowners, builders and shipmasters used to congregate to discuss shipping matters during the age of the sail. Alarmed at the rate at which ships were being lost at sea, they decided to create an organisation to produce strict ship-design rules to improve stability and reliability. A1 at Lloyds refers to the top grade, indicating that a ship is in first-class condition. At one time Lloyds Register of Shipping dominated the Classification World but has, in recent years, been threatened by competition from other major countries which have formed their own Classification Authorities. However, the Register contains the names of all ships irrespective of the Authority. Historically it is specifically a maritime organisation. In the late 20th century Lloyds expanded its business with the classification of Off-Shore Oil and Gas Rigs and Installations and the survey of Industrial Products. It has also branched out into Management System Certification through its subsidiary Lloyds Register Quality Assurance Limited. It is non-profit making, and for Marine Classification is registered in the UK as a charity, providing safety at sea, and through Lloyd's Register Group, funds to charities supporting safety of life, property and the environment. Through its Educational Trust it assists colleges and universities. It is strictly audited by the Charity Commission.

There are three grades of surveyors, Engineer, Hull and Electrical, supported by Designers, Draughtsmen, Metallurgists, Administration Staff and a Training Division. As a Marine Engineer I was graded as 'Engineer Surveyor'. In the appointment letter, I was instructed to report to the

Liverpool Office Manager at 10 am on my birthday, the 10th of July, 1975 at the Water Street Office. When I arrived he wasn't there. The office was almost deserted except for the Administration Staff and one surveyor. All the other surveyors were away on ships or with manufacturers across Merseyside, Lancashire and North Wales. The surveyor, who wasn't aware of my imminent arrival, apologised on behalf of the Manager. I sat at a desk browsing through Lloyds Rules and looking at the surveyors' desks completely submerged in paperwork and design plans, piled up in bundles. When the Manager eventually turned up he informed me that I was expected to undertake ship surveys by myself but would, from time to time, be seconded to the Hull resident surveyor at Cammel Lairds in Birkenhead to understudy him in aspects of shipbuilding and repair work. What nobody told me was that I needed a car to travel to the docks at Liverpool and Bootle. By mid-afternoon the surveyors started returning from their assignments and I was introduced to them and the Principal Engineer Surveyor. At 5pm sharp everyone downed tools and headed to Ma Boyle's, a well-known and long-established old pub just outside the office. I began to notice a distinct working pattern different to that with which I was accustomed over many years, a contrast to the clear-desk routine and the managerial responsibilities of a Head of Department. I was now just a member of the staff.

For the first six weeks I stayed in digs at Oxton in Birkenhead, travelling back home to Alverstoke in Gosport, Hampshire, at week-ends. After the first week-end, I returned to Liverpool by the much needed car. Offering some extra money, we had agreed with the owners of the house we were to purchase that they would vacate the house before the beginning of the Academic Year. I timed the sale of my house accordingly. In the meantime, I took the opportunity to have another look at the house we were buying when the owners informed me that they would be unable to vacate in time. With our plans disrupted, Margaret came to join me to start looking for another house. When the Estate Agent informed the owners that we were about to buy another house they relented, and moved a few days after the agreed date. By the beginning of September we were settled at our new residence.

I continued to notice the difference in the inspection techniques which I had been used to and the pressures surveyors were subjected to by some masters and shipowners to influence their decisions. On one occasion I condemned a large main engine bearing as defective. I was told that, unlike the Royal Navy, where expense was no object, when dealing with the Merchant Navy I had to be careful not to make costly decisions. A few months later the Principal Engineer Surveyor asked to see my journal where I logged the incident. I did not bother to ask why. In due course I realised that most surveyors were very conscientious, and inspected ships to the strictest standards. They worked to a Planned Maintenance System with mandatory periodic surveys.

I soon started coming across some interesting experiences. I was sent to survey equipment under repair on a cargo ship manned by an Indian crew. On leaving the ship while walking down the gangway, a hoard of Customs Officers descended on me and took me to a waiting van. They asked to see the contents of my bag where I kept my overalls, working shoes and testing equipment, and proceeded to search my clothes. When they discovered who I was, they apologised and told me that they'd mistaken me for a member of the Indian crew. They had reason to believe that some of the crew were landing stocks of illegal drugs to sell ashore. It was not the first time that my nationality was mistakenly identified! In summer my skin tans quickly and I can easily be mistaken for a native of the Indian Sub-Continent. On another occasion I was asked to go on a ship after working hours to survey the modification of a Compressed Air System to conform to Lloyds Rules. The ship couldn't leave harbour without my acceptance certificate, paying thousands of pounds in port duties. I wasn't satisfied and declined to issue a certificate. The Greek Master took me to his cabin and offered me a drink and pointed to a crate of whisky. His bribe didn't work. Another ship failed the leak test of its holds. They called the welders to repair the securing arrangements to no avail. As heat was applied the hold covers securing fittings were further distorted. The vessel had to stay in harbour at considerable cost. The Master reported the situation to the owners in London and told them that a Lloyds Surveyor would not issue a Load-Line Certificate. They in turn rang the Office Manager who rang me in the middle of the night, giving me his total support. I successfully performed my first Hull Survey. There were several instances where undue pressure was put on Surveyors to relax the rules.

It wasn't long before I was transferred to Industrial and Offshore work to replace a surveyor who was to be moved to another office. This was an opportunity to expand my Engineering knowledge and learn something about Industry. The job involved a considerable amount of welding of heavy and light structures and pipe fabrications. The hand over was made difficult by my predecessor who was not happy with his move away from Liverpool and his change of job. He told me bluntly that he was not going to teach me, and that it was up to Lloyds to send me for training. When he departed, I was left to fend for myself, relying on the manufacturers' technical staff to teach me how to read and interpret radiographic, ultrasonic and other methods of fault detection reports or witness crack detection applications in the welding of materials. I embarked on an intensive self-learning course, reading material which I borrowed from the office library and manufacturers. What I had learned about Metallurgy was in the distant past. By the time I was sent to the Training Centre at Crawley in Sussex I was sufficiently trained to tackle most welding inspection with confidence. When the results were received, the Office Manager congratulated me, informing me that I had obtained 100% in Radiography and 90% in Ultrasonics. Other courses followed in Metallurgy, Welding, General Engineering and Quality Assurance. I was to attend refresher courses in Welding Fault Detection every five years to keep up with new technology. I also specialised in the survey of the building and testing of Saturation Diving Systems.

As I gained in experience, the Manager informed me that I had been selected to attend a six-month course in America, to qualify as an inspector of the fabrication of pressure vessels to ASME (American Standard of Mechanical Engineering). I pointed out that I was fifty nine years of age. By the time I returned from America, Lloyds would only benefit from my qualification for about three years before I retired at the age of sixty five. He confessed that he hadn't checked my age before asking me and assumed that I was about fifty. He made my day! He agreed that it wasn't a cost-effective exercise. A few months later Lloyds lowered the retiring age to sixty two. By this time, I had accumulated a considerable amount of experience in industry. The transformation from a Marine Engineer Officer in the Royal Navy was complete. I inspected all manner of equipment involving the heavy welding and construction of sections of oil and gas off-shore structures, assembly and testing of saturation diving systems to Rolls Royce gas turbine driven machinery. On each occasion I had to read and study the contract requirements and the product standards and specifications stipulated by the client, before I inspected the product.

From time to time surveyors were required to relieve others working on Off-Shore Rigs. I was asked to go to Abu Dhabi for three months to work on a Zakum Field Gas Rig. I agreed to go, subject to the results of medical tests which I was undergoing at the time. To prevent any delays, the Society sent me to their Harley Street Specialist in London where I was diagnosed with a gall bladder problem. I told my boss that I was willing to postpone my operation until I returned from Abu Dhabi. I duly flew to my destination to find that I couldn't obtain a visa to go on the rig. Efforts to expedite the issue of my visa fell on deaf ears. I spent six weeks waiting, helping out at the Lloyds local office sorting out a chaotic situation of hundreds of obsolete plans lying on the surveyors' desks, and searching for the latest revised drawings. The complexities of the construction of an off-shore installation the size of the Zakum Field were enormous. Thousands of obsolete plans which should have been destroyed were sitting on the surveyors' desks. It was evident that there were some problems, which were soon resolved, and action taken to preclude a recurrence. Over the course of 250 years Lloyds Register of Shipping has gone through several re-organisations in order to keep up with the times and maintain its position as the leading classification and certification body.

I was fortunate that my best man at my wedding was serving as the Commissioning Engineer of a Shell Chemical Plant. He and his wife offered me their hospitality at their home and at some of the Oil Company social events. At my hotel I couldn't help being amused seeing the locals, wearing their long white national robes, and holding pint beer glasses. The hotel was one of the few places where they were allowed to drink and they flocked to it by the dozen. After forty years since I first visited Abu Dhabi, when it was just a desolate stretch of desert, I was amazed at the transformation which had taken place.

After six weeks I received my visa and was flown by helicopter to the accommodation barge of a Gas Rig under construction. I was appalled at what I witnessed. The British and Americans were comfortably living in single cabins while the Indians, Pakistanis and Filipinos were accommodated in portable cabins while, contrary to Safety Regulations, large heavy loads were lifted by cranes over their living quarters. Drinking of alcohol was supposed to be prohibited but was taking place in a big way, leading to regular fights among the Americans. Divers working off the accommodation barge told me that hundreds of empty alcohol bottles were lying under the barge. With no police on board, the barge skipper was responsible for discipline, unless he was also drunk. In fact, the police were called on one occasion when the situation got out of hand. Used to the strictest hygiene and cleanliness standards on RN ships, I wasn't satisfied with the standard of cleanliness in my cabin. I called the skipper to show him where I needed improvements. He obliged by appointing his best Filipino cabin boy to look after me. When they learned who I was they nicknamed me 'The Commander' whereupon I received special treatment. I was even offered a liqueur which I promptly refused. The chief cook told me that he kept some for cooking purposes! With little work to keep me busy I was, for most of the time, on stand-by waiting for work to be completed before I could inspect it. For exercise, I walked round and round the helipad for ten to twenty minutes at a time. As I switched on the television I was confronted with pornographic films which went on for twenty four hours a day to satisfy all the watches. After I complained I was given my own television set. There was an abundance of food with an extensive menu, served at all times of the day to cater for all watches and the different nationalities. A library was provided with a predominance of books of doubtful material. When I left the rig I couldn't help feeling that I hadn't achieved much, and that the money it had cost the client to fly me to Abu Dhabi and the Gas Rig was not justified. As far as working on off-shore rigs, those working on them deserved all the money they got for living in such an artificial setting. I would like to think that conditions on the North Sea Oil Fields are more civilised. After three months I returned to Liverpool to tell the tale, hoping that I would never be asked to work off-shore again.

At the office, the social life to which I was accustomed was non-existent. Unlike naval communities living together in married quarters, and the social life in ships and shore establishments, the office staff lived over a scattered area in Liverpool, Wirral, Formby Southport, Fleetwood, and as far as Manchester. There were a few who were quite happy to party, but the main social event consisted of a few pints at Ma Boyle's during the 'Happy Hour' after leaving the office. As time went on we grew very fond of Liverpool and the Scousers' sense of humour and hospitality with their distinct identity, in contrast with the cosmopolitan nature of a naval city like Portsmouth. Quite by co-incidence, several of our neighbours in the Close belonged to our parish. I soon reverted to naval tradition, organising dinners and barbecues at our respective houses. Every year, while our children were young, I organised a barbecue in my large garden, flood-lighting the trees and rigging coloured lighting by the brook. One neighbour who saw to the bonfire acted as a stoker, another acted as the purser, and the chief cook attended to the barbeque, and so on. They were all given a naval rank with me as 'No1' in-charge of the whole operation. The programme showing the responsibilities for the various tasks was promulgated in 'The First Lieutenant's Standing Order'. The parish had a very active social programme. Margaret joined the Parish Scouts and Guides Council, but she was missing her singing. She auditioned to join the Royal Liverpool Philarmonic Choir and has been singing with them for the past thirty four years. She was awarded a degree from the University of Liverpool in English Language and Literature. I became a member of Bromborough Golf Club, about a quarter of a mile down the road and joined the Royal Naval Reserve Officers Club at HMS Eaglet in Liverpool, the 'Sea Urchins', with membership open to retired and serving RNR and RN officers. Traditionally, a serving Admiral is invited as Guest Speaker at our Annual Dinner to keep us updated with developments in the modern navy.

I joined the Historic Warships Fund Raising Committee to support the maintenance and preservation of the old HMS Plymouth, the submarine Onyx, a landing craft and a recovered Second World War German submarine. The frigate and the submarine both took part in the Falklands War. Wearing my Mess Undress uniform I organised dinners in the wardroom of 'Plymouth' in accordance with naval custom. After piping them on board, the guests were escorted on a tour of the frigate and submarine, followed by a video of the Falklands War, showing Plymouth in action. We then mustered on the bridge for pre-dinner cocktails followed by dinner in the wardroom where we passed the port in naval tradition and toasted Her Majesty the Queen. This was followed by a toast to the 'Immortal Memory of Lord Horatio Nelson'. In the wardroom of Plymouth was a large picture of the Argentinian Naval Officer signing the South Georgia Surrender Document. When the Tall Ships visited Liverpool, members of the crew of the Argentinian vessel came on board HMS Plymouth and saw the picture. They went back to tell their shipmates, and on the following day they came on board to see it, but it wasn't there. The Ship Manager, thinking that it was an embarrassment to the Argentenians, had it removed. They complained to him and he obliged by putting it back in the original position to the accompaniment of a dozen clicking cameras.

In 1998, as President of the Sea Urchins, I invited Lieutenant Commander Ian Fraser VC as a guest. The principal guest was Rear Admiral R. Stevens, Flag Officer Submarines. I dedicated the evening to the combined wartime effort of the Royal and Merchant Navies and the Submarine Service. I joined the Catenian Association, a Catholic Lay Organisation becoming the president of one of the circles. At about the same period, the Parish Scouts and Guides Groups were going through a bad patch and were short of funds, the Guides and Ventures groups were disbanded and they couldn't get any volunteers to act as leaders. I was asked to take over as chairman. Within a few months the Guides and Venture Scouts were reformed, numbers in all groups increased dramatically with long waiting lists for Cubs and Brownies and our funds were bulging. Our camping equipment was augmented with new and additional facilities provided. With surplus money in the bank we were able to build a new store as an annex to the parish hall. Despite the hard work, I found the task of being involved with a Youth Movement rewarding. I had not had any contact with the stage for some time but I saw an opportunity to put on a show in which the boys and girls and their leaders could participate. I organised a 'Mini Gang Show' in two consecutive years with limited back stage and lighting facilities. It was a pleasure to see so many youngsters taking part. In the second performance I was not aware that behind the scenes, the leaders, with the help of my wife, were plotting to get me on stage with their version of 'This is Your Life'.

Fourteen years ago I joined Rotary, becoming President of The Rotary Club of Bebington. In the meantime, my golf improved to such an extent that I accumulated a number of prizes playing for the Seniors and other societies. My successes came to an end when I became more ambitious and started taking lessons. My game collapsed and, although I still play the occasional good game, my low handicap evaporated. At eighty five years of age I am now past recovery. I still take part in some competitions and try to play three times a week with friends in a foursome to enjoy the walk and their company, or playing with the Seniors to meet old and new friends.

My dreams of a reliable future with Lloyds Register of Shipping were shattered when, out of the blue, they reduced the retirement age from sixty five to sixty two. Having planned all my future to co-inside with my 65th birthday, this was a big setback. Lloyds was going through a bad patch as competition from emerging Classification Authorities was forcing the Society to economise. The expensive Industrial Authority at Croydon was closed down and the Training Division and the Industrial Administration transferred to the main Headquarters in London. I immediately began preparing to become self-employed, embarking on my third career as a Quality Assurance Consultant. As this was so unexpected I needed every minute of my time to concentrate on the task ahead. Reluctantly, I had to give up the chairmanship of the Parish Scouts and Guides Group. Six months before retirement, at the request of a reputable manufacturer, I started working at home to prepare for my first contract.

SULTAN CLUB

HMS SULTAN
CHRISTMAS VARIETY SHOW
1970

FULL AHEAD TOGETHER

STOP

STOP

BY PERMISSION OF CAPTAIN S.F. BARTON, ROYAL NAVY

Hilarious Sultan play

All male casts in H.M.S. Sultan's "Full Ahead Together" provides a hilarious evening's entertainment. The variety show is performed by 120 ratings, officers and wrens.

At the centre of the comedy are two all-male pantomime acts and the Dance of the Sugar Plum Fairies performed by mechanicians.

"Full Ahead Together" provides variety in the true sense of the word and incorporates calypsos, comedy, song and dance routine, carols and the H.M.S. Sultan Band.

The curtain falls on the play, directed by Danny Marks, for the last time tonight. *(Portsmouth Evening News)*

The Sugar Plum Fairies in 'Full Ahead Together' - "My Girdle is Killing me."

Sultan show goes 'Full Ahead'

A scene from H.M.S. Sultan's variety show, "Full Ahead Together," which is being presented at Gosport from today until Thursday.

272

With a Rear Admiral Lees-Spalding at the Gas Turbine Propulsion Unit Test House.

With the actor Nigel Patrick, Margaret and Mrs Patrick at the Wardroom Summer ball, HMS Sultan.

273

With guests at the RNR Officers annual dinner. Left to Right: Ian Fraser VC, Commander CJ
Arthurs, Rt. Rev. FJ Walmsley, RC Bishop of the Forces, Rear Admiral R Stevens, D Marks,
Commodore PR Sutermeister, Mr AW Waterworth, Lord Lieutenant of Merseyside.

In the Wardroom HMS Plymouth, Historic Warship, presiding at a dinner aged seventy three.

274

CHAPTER 20

MY THIRD CAREER

Retirement at Last

At Lloyds I was responsible for inspecting a number of factories for Van Leer (UK) Limited, the Dutch drum manufacturer. The Company Quality Manager was very complimentary about my standard of inspection and the helpful reports I produced. When he learned that I was to retire and set up my own consultancy, he suggested that I acted as the Company Quality Assurance Consultant to produce Quality Systems leading to certification for each of their factories, to conform to a new British Standard, BS 5750 'Quality Systems Management'. However, I needed to qualify as an assessor. Lloyds had previously sent me on a Quality Assurance Assessor's Course to Portsmouth Polytechnic. Six months later it was decided to send all candidates to sit an examination at Strathclyde University in Glasgow. The examination was to take place in the afternoon. I had previously arranged to have lunch with Desmond Kelly, an old friend living in Glasgow who had served with me in the navy. We celebrated our reunion with a few drinks, the after effects of which I felt as I sat at my desk in the examination hall. With the passage of time I had forgotten much of what I'd been taught. The situation deteriorated further when I discovered that I was to sit a 'Book Reference' examination where I could refer to the 'Standard' to answer the questions, but I didn't have it with me. Obviously I was not well prepared nor sober enough, and I failed the examination. The only consolation was that most candidates also failed due to the lapse of time between the course and examination. When I decided to set up my own business, I had to qualify as an assessor through another channel.

By the time I retired from Lloyds I was ready to introduce the first Quality System at Van Leer followed by another five. As Inspection Authorities from the Oil Industry visited these factories they were impressed with the systems I introduced and I started getting telephone calls and enquiries from several companies. Purely by word of mouth my business took off. I was also asked to take on contracts on behalf of Merseyside Innovation Centre and the Department of Trade and Industry. The demand for my services grew so much that I couldn't cope with the volume of work, and I had to reject enquiries. I was carrying out consultancies in the North West and beyond. I began planning to expand the business by employing three newly qualified assessors. On reviewing their Quality Systems, I found that they were not producing satisfactory results and I was spending my week-ends correcting their work. I paid them off and gave up the idea of enlarging my consultancy, and the dream of sitting back watching others working for me. In total I put through fifty six companies, ranging from a one-man band to one with 600 employees, manufacturing a variety of products from heavy structures for the North Sea Oil Rigs and Rolls Royce Turbine driven equipment, to stationery and clay pigeon traps, to qualify to BS 5750 and its successor ISO 9000.

My third career proved to be a great contrast to my previous experience. I was enjoying every minute of it, acting as my own boss, without anybody ordering me about and without having to look over my shoulder. But the time had arrived when I should begin to think about retiring completely. However much I was enjoying my work there were periods of stress, especially during the few days when companies were undergoing their final inspection by the Assessing Authorities. I was conscious that I was not enjoying enough leisure time and was hardly playing any golf. I decided to start winding down my business activities, cutting down on the number of contracts and spending more time on the Golf Course with a group of friends. I noticed how a few of them were worrying about their business commitments and rushing back to work. In the space of about six weeks two of them died without ever enjoying retirement. Alarm bells were ringing and, at the age of sixty nine, despite the lucrative nature of the business, I decided to pack up work completely. By this time the family had grown in size. The children were settling down nicely and I became a grandfather several times over, now proudly boasting of seven grandchildren. I began to take more interest in the associations to which I belonged, heavily involved in fund-raising. As the President of Rotary I presided over an interesting project when we sold postcards to parents and grandparents to be sent to children by Father Christmas from Rovaniemi in the Arctic Circle in Finland. Three members of the club drove all the way in a 'four-wheel drive' to post hundreds of cards with stamps bearing the image of the 'real' Father Christmas. They took it in turn to drive over snow and frozen hilly roads in what they described as a hair-raising experience. When they returned, I presented them with a modified version of the Blue Nose Certificate which was presented to me on two occasions when I crossed the Arctic Circle. We raised 15,000 pounds which we donated to Alder Hey Children's Hospital in Liverpool and Claire House Children's Hospice in the Wirral.

Having given time to charities and a youth movement, I felt justified in pursuing a more relaxed and leisurely life. I now play golf more often while continuing to give limited support to various charities. Having played golf under floodlight at the Dubai Golf and Racing Club, I can now boast of having played in the snow. At a recent Seniors competition, 'The Yellow Ball', in a team of four, we were scoring well when, on the 16th hole, it started snowing. Since there was a chance that we may win the competition, we decided to carry on until the end. But there is much more to golf. It is a source of meeting people from all spheres of life, associating with friends, old and new. On one occasion, a visitor playing on his own asked me to join him. During our conversation, it transpired that he had served as a Fleet Air Arm pilot on the aircraft-carrier HMS Implacable, at the same time as me, and yet we never met. Just recently while discussing the imminent publication of this book with my golf partner, I made a surprising discovery. While talking to him, I mentioned the convoy, including the famous tanker Ohio, which arrived in Malta just in time to save the island from surrender. He told me that his father had been a member of the crew and gave me a vivid description of the ordeal that his father had gone through as the tanker was hit by bombs over and over again, described earlier in this book. Through golf and playing snooker for the club I have been fortunate to enjoy the company and friendship of some very nice people.

I spend more time in the garden now where there is something to do throughout the year. Although I have a gardener to help me with the heavy work, keeping it in good shape presents a challenge, especially as the garden slopes down to the Dibbin Brook. There are times when I spend hours by the stream in peaceful surroundings, among the trees, as I listen to the birds singing and the water flowing. I still dig the borders and vegetable patches when necessary and I have just finished erecting, with some help, a long handrail along the tortuous pathway of the slope leading down to the brook. I am often asked by clubs and societies to speak about my life and experiences. One particular subject which I'm asked to speak frequently is 'The Siege of Malta during The Second World War'.

As I ponder the past, I feel I owe much to the Royal Navy for the privilege of serving my country while at the same time travelling to the five continents, seeing and admiring the beauty and histories of so many countries and their different cultures. I have visited hundreds of ports and adjoining towns and cities, mountain ranges, rivers, lakes and oceans, and yet the urge to travel has not diminished. Since I left the Navy, Margaret and I have visited the children when they lived in Spain, Qatar, Dubai and Australia as well as holidaying in New Zealand the US and Canada and much of Europe. Further opportunity to travel came when Margaret, with the Royal Liverpool Philarmonic Choir and Orchestra gave concerts all over Europe. I learned to appreciate music from Mahler to McCartney and much in between. There was always time for sightseeing and socialising on these trips as well as the enjoyment of special events such as British Week during Expo 1992, in Spain, with Lloyd Webber and his team in Seville, riding a train up the Eiger in mid-winter, the Proms in the Albert Hall as well as concerts in many great cathedrals and churches at home and abroad. We managed a trip to Venice when the choir sang at the Villach Festival in Austria, but the heat and crowds of tourists meant that we couldn't see very much, so I promised Margaret that I'd take her back one day.

Before I finish writing this book I feel that it would be fitting to say something about the family. As my 80th birthday was approaching I started looking to my wife and daughter for some inspiration for a celebration. I got nowhere. As I persisted, my daughter told me to stop asking questions, assuring me that something would happen and that I should be patient. What I wasn't aware of was that the family were planning something quite unusual, secretly shared with many of our closest friends. On the evening of Sunday the 10th July, 2005, a minibus arrived outside our house. Inside were the children and grandchildren and a couple of young friends. When Margaret and I joined them we set off for what was to me an unknown

278

destination. As we went along I tried guessing where we were heading, until eventually we arrived in Chester alongside the jetty where the Mark Twain Showboat was berthed. I couldn't believe my eyes when I saw the people on board. It was packed with friends, some of whom I hadn't seen for years. As we approached, the bosun's pipe sounded and five of my old friends, including Margaret's brother, with their swords, formed a guard of honour and I was ceremoniously piped on board. The evening was spent wining, dining and cruising down the beautiful River Dee in glorious weather with entertainment by a small jazz group and a version of 'What are we going to do about Grandpa', written and sung by the children and grandchildren. The family did me proud on that day, making it one of the most memorable of my life.

With two children living abroad it is difficult to get everybody together. In August 2007, Simon and Tracey, in Sydney Australia, decided to christen their first child, Charlotte, in Malta where I was born and christened. The whole family, together with the godparents and friends, assembled in the same hotel to celebrate the occasion. On the 12th April, 2009, we were together again to celebrate our 50th Wedding Anniversary and the christening of Simon and Tracey's second child, Isabel. In a marquee in our garden, on a clear and sunny day, to the sound of a string quartet, surrounded by friends and relatives, we celebrated one of the most unforgettable occasions of a lifetime. Led by our Parish Priest, we renewed our marriage vows. Isabel's godfather, who toasted the health of the new baby, was followed by each member of the family recollecting some of the many family milestones. As I rose to speak, to the accompaniment of the musicians, I was greeted with a loud rendering of 'What shall we do with the drunken sailor'! At the end of the year I fulfilled my promise to take Margaret back to Venice. The children treated us to a holiday in Spain and, to complete a memorable year, our best man and his wife invited us to Southern France for their daughter's wedding.

Paul is now working in Mauritius. We see him often as well as his two children, Katie, now at Leeds University and Rachel in Dubai. Ruth lives about eight miles away with her husband Damian, Edward and the twins, George and Alice. Simon has just bought a house in Sydney where he lives with his wife, Tracey and their two children, Charlotte and Isabel.

Listening to accounts of my adventures around the globe, my family urged me to write the story of my 'Life and Exploits'. It has been a fascinating exercise, especially as I browsed through the log books of the ships in which I served, at the National Archives. I owe them my gratitude for the pleasure and enjoyment it has given me in writing this book during the past three years. I thank my wife, Margaret, for her love and devotion, as she copes with her dedication to education and her musical activities, despite a series of illnesses which she faced with patience and fortitude. I am proud of my children and their families, watching them grow and achieve. As for me, there is still life left in the old sea dog, and I intend to continue to make the best of it.

The Family

Danny and Margaret.

Paul with Katie and Rachel in Dubai.

Ruth and Damian with Edward and twins George and Alice.

Simon and Tracey with Charlotte and Isabel in Sydney.

283

APPENDIX A

THE FLIMSIES

(Handed to an Officer by the Captain on leaving or when the Captain leaves the Ship. The first flimsy is shown in its complete form.)

This is to certify that A/Cd Engr Daniel Francis Xavier Marks has served under instruction in HMS Thunderer from the 29th day of February 1956, to the 10th day of August1956 during which period he conducted himself to my entire satisfaction. Full of self-confidence, he has played an active part in all college activities. He has done well during his time here.

J Walsham Captain HMS Thundere
(Royal Naval Engineering College)

Sub Lieutenant D F Marks has served under my command from the 24th April 1957 to 7th October1958..... to my entire satisfaction. A first rate officer who has done extremely well in the ship. He has not spared himself in organising sport and has taken his full share in every activity.

E Dunsterville HMS Gambia

Note: I joined the ship in July 1956 during a refit when there was no Captain. He joined the ship on the 24th of April 1957.

Sub Lieutenant DFX Marks.......27th October 1958 to 1st August 1960...... most satisfactorily. An exceptionally able and industrious officer who has obtained marked success in his dealings with the Naval and Dockyard Officers due to his undoubted efficiency and pleasant manner. An outstandingly popular and respected messmate.

RG Raper HMS Caledonia

Sub Lieutenant DFX Marks.......2nd August 1960 to30th September 1960.... to my entire satisfaction. A most competent and efficient officer who is unsparing in his efforts. Although determined, he is always co-operative and is conspicuously successful in dealing with other departments.

RG Raper Captain HMS Caledonia

Engineer Lieutenant DFX Marks......5th December 1960 to 2nd November 1961... to my satisfaction. An exceptionally keen, energetic and competent officer, who sets, demands and obtains a very high standard in all he does. He has maintained the machinery under his charge in excellent condition and has achieved a very high state of morale, efficiency and cleanliness throughout his department.

PD Jenks Lt Cdr. Captain HMS Pellew

Engineer Lieutenant DFX Marks.......23rd September 1962 to 10th May 1963....entirely to my satisfaction. A hard working and capable Engineer Officer who has carried out a difficult and responsible job with ability, unflagging enthusiasm and much credit to himself.

JAF Lawson Lt Cdr. in Command

......22nd June 1963 to 26th September 1963....to my entire satisfaction. An able officer with plenty of drive and initiative.

RW Mayo Commodore HMS St Angelo

........28th September 1963 to28thMay 1965.....to my entire satisfaction. His efforts have been largely instrumental in improving enormously the condition of the whole range of P.A.S. craft in Malta. He takes great interest in sports and mess activities, and gives much of his spare time to Service interests.

E Palmer Commodore HMS St Angelo

.......26th May 1965 to 2nd December 1966.....very much to my satisfaction. An energetic and loyal Naval Officer, who has led his department well. He leaves an efficient maintenance organisation in the P.A.S and has busied himself in many extra circular activities both in St Angelo and the Naval Base, where he will be missed.

M. Crawford Commodore HMS St Angelo

..........26th April 1967 to 7th August 1967........ to my entire satisfaction. A cheerful and efficient officer of great technical ability. He has settled down quickly and is doing very well as a Head of Department and as a Divisional Officer. Plays a full part in all the ship's activities.

D Reffell Commander Captain HMS Sirius

Engineer Lt Cdr. DFX Marks......7th August 1967 to 9th December 1968.......
to my entire satisfaction. An outstanding officer on whose professional advice
I have leaned heavily. Possessing great charm and sincerity, he earns the respect
and admiration of all who serve with him. He has always had my complete
confidence.

J N Humphrey-Baker Commander Captain HMS Sirius

...10th December 1968 to 5th May 1969......to my entire satisfaction. A first
class officer both technically and in the broader meaning. A sound administrator
who in some difficult times has been a great support to me. A very pleasant
shipmate who I would be honoured to serve with again. Recommended for
early promotion.

J Deleittes Commander Captain HMS Sirius

...28th May 1969 to 11th January 1971.......to my entire satisfaction.
Throughout this appointment he has shown an excellent grasp of the work,
strived tirelessly for the achievement of high standards, and overcome many
obstacles. A cheerful and lively officer with many outside interests that he
devotes unstintingly to the good of the Service.

S Barton Captain HMS Sultan

....12th January 1971 to 5th May 1972......to my entire satisfaction. An officer
of outstanding ability who has performed all his duties with zeal, energy and
panache. Highly competent, he has produced excellent results by firm, tactful
and thorough management. He has played a very successful part in both
Establishment and Wardroom activities. I am sorry to lose him.

R A Harcus Captain HMS Sultan

...8th May 1972 to 31st January 1974.......to my entire satisfaction. Marks is
a high calibre Special Duties officer whose experience, technical knowledge,
adaptability and initiative have been key factors in the successful way he has
performed his Fleet Staff function. By this, together with his capacity for
work and his inherent enthusiasm, he has set a good example and continued to
demonstrate his potential for promotion.

I J Lees-Spalding Rear Admiral C-in-C Fleet

...31st January 1974 to 4th July 1975.......to my entire satisfaction. A loyal and hardworking officer who has given of his best during the last appointment of his naval career as he has done throughout his service. Lieutenant Commander MARKS has proved himself to be a very competent engineer, capable staff officer and good messmate. The Royal Navy will be the poorer for his retirement.

D G Satow Rear Admiral C-C Fleet

APPENDIX B

Standard Letter from the Secretary of State sent to Retiring Officers

MINISTRY OF DEFENCE

MAIN BUILDING WHITEHALL LONDON SW1A 2HB

Telephone 01-218 ...2101.. (Direct Dialling)

01-218 9000 (Switchboard)

Ref: D/NAVSEC 11/1/2/110   *26th* June 1975

Sir,

I am directed to inform you that approval has been given to your being placed on the Retired List on attaining the age limit on 10th July 1975.

2. The Secretary of State for Defence has it in command from Her Majesty The Queen to convey to you, on your leaving the Active List of the Royal Navy, her thanks for your long and valuable service.

I am, Sir,

Your obedient Servant,

I.B.C. McLeod

APPENDIX C

Standard Letter from Second Sea Lord to Retiring Officers

FROM: ADMIRAL SIR DAVID WILLIAMS, K.C.B.

MINISTRY OF DEFENCE
MAIN BUILDING WHITEHALL LONDON SW1A 2HB
Telephone 01-218 ...7679... (Direct Dialling)
01-218 9000 (Switchboard)

CHIEF OF NAVAL PERSONNEL
AND SECOND SEA LORD

285/3B

Lieutenant Commander D F X Marks, Royal Navy
1 Fairthorne Gardens
Alverstoke
Gosport
Hants   2 September 1975

Dear Marks,

You will by now have received notice of your retirement,
and in addition to the formal expression of thanks from
Her Majesty The Queen, I should like to send you my personal
thanks for your service in the Navy, and to wish you every
success and happiness in the future.

Yours

David Williams

BIBLIOGRAPHY

Joseph Bonnici and Michael Cassar. *A Century of the Royal Navy at Malta.* BDL Ltd.

P Elliott. *A Naval History of Malta.* Harper Collins.

James Holland. *Fortress Malta.* Orion Books Ltd.

E B Casaway. *Grey Wolf Grey Sea.* Arthur Barker Limited.

Edwin Camilleri. *John F Marks.* Enterprises Group (PEG) Ltd.

Philip Vella. *Malta: Blitzed But Not Beaten.* Progress Press, Malta.

Michael Galea. *Malta Diary of a War.* BDL Ltd.

George Hogan. *Malta-The Triumphant Years.* Robert Hale London.

Steve Nichols. *Malta Spitfire Aces.* Osprey Publishing.

Eric Newley. *On the Shores of the Mediterranean.* Pan Books.

Peter C Smith. *Pedestal.* Crecy Publishing Limited.

Nicholas Monsarrat. *The Kappillan of Malta.* Pan Books Ltd.

Henry Frendo. *The Origins of Maltese Statehood.* BDL Ltd.

Ernle Bradford. *The Great Siege-Malta 1565.* Hodder and Stoughton.

Commander Geoffrey Penn R. *Up Funnel Down Screw.* Hollis & Carter.

GLOSSARY

ASDIC. (Anti-Submarine Detection Investigating Committee). Name given to equipment and training of submarine warfare.

Blue Label Ale. Sailors' favourite beer, brewed in Malta.

CERA. Chief Engine Room Artificer.

Commission. A ship's period on active duty until the next crew takes over.

ERA. (Engine Room Artificer). A Marine Engineer of non-officer status in the Royal Navy. Name has now been changed to Marine Engineering Artificer.

Flimsy. A short report of an officer's performance, written by the Captain of a ship or an Admiral.

Jack. A sailor.

Jolly Roger. Traditional pirate flag.

Liberty. Shore leave.

Liberty Boat. Ship's boat when used to ferry sailors to and from shore.

Logging an Officer. Recording of disciplinary action taken against an officer in the Ship's Log Book.

Matelot. Slang for sailor.

NAAFI. Navy, Army, Air Force Institute

Wash Up. Discussion and conclusions on the outcome of a ship or fleet exercises.

Work Up. A period of intensive training on commissioning.

INDEX